The Future of Educational Change

Educational change has been high on the international agenda for 25 years.

The Future of Educational Change provides a systematic overview and critique of contemporary approaches to educational change from some of the leading writers and scholars in the field. It offers critical perspectives on its flux and flows, its dominant patterns, its inherent tensions, contradictions and dilemmas. The authors question the extent to which research in the field has become increasingly ideologically driven and controlled rather than informed by more broadly based concerns for equity and social justice. They call for policies that seek genuine educational 'reforms' rather than those that perpetuate increasing inequalities in a globalised world.

The book is divided into four sections which address key questions:

- What has been the impact of educational change?
- How has the impact differed in different circumstances?
- What are the new directions for research on policy and practice?
- How can we link research, policy and practice?

By highlighting critical lessons from the past 25 years, the book aims to set an agenda for policy-related research and the future trajectories of educational reforms, while also taking into account the dominant rhetorics of international 'social movements' and the 'refracted' nature of policy agenda at national and local levels.

This book addresses issues with which many educators around the world are currently grappling. It will appeal to academics and researchers in the field, as well as providing an introduction to key issues and themes in educational change for graduates and practitioners.

Ciaran Sugrue is Reader in Leadership and School Improvement at the Faculty of Education, University of Cambridge.

The Future of Educational Change

International perspectives

Edited by Ciaran Sugrue

Routledge
Taylor & Francis Group

LONDON AND NEW YORK

MT

First published 2008
by Routledge
2 Park Square, Milton Park, Abingdon, Oxon OX14 4RN

Simultaneously published in the USA and Canada
by Routledge
270 Madison Ave, New York, NY 10016

*Routledge is an imprint of the Taylor & Francis Group, an informa
business*

Typeset in Times New Roman by
HWA Text and Data Management, Tunbridge Wells
Printed and bound in Great Britain by
TJ International Ltd, Padstow, Cornwall

British Library Cataloguing in Publication Data
A catalogue record for this book is available from the British Library

Library of Congress Cataloging-in-Publication Data
The future of educational change : international perspectives / Ciaran
Sugrue.
    p. cm.
 Includes bibliographical references.
 1. Educational change. 2. Education–Forecasting. 3. Education–
Philosophy. 4. Education and state. I. Sugrue, Ciaran.
 LB41.5.F82 2008
 370—dc22
                                                        2007032572

ISBN10: 0–415–43107–7 (hbk)
ISBN10: 0–415–43108–5 (pbk)

ISBN13: 978–0–415–43107–1 (hbk)
ISBN13: 978–0–415–43108–8 (pbk)

11/05/08

Contents

Illustrations

Figures

Tables

Notes on contributors

Larry Cuban is Professor Emeritus of Education at Stanford University. His background in the field of education prior to becoming a professor included 14 years of teaching high school social studies in ghetto schools, directing a teacher education programme that prepared returning Peace Corps volunteers to teach in inner-city schools, and serving seven years as a district superintendent. His major research interests focus on the history of curriculum and instruction, educational leadership, school reform and the uses of technology in classrooms. His most recent books are: *Cutting Through The Hype: A Taxpayer's Guide to School Reform* (with Jane David, Education Week Press, 2006); *The Blackboard and the Bottom Line: Why Schools Can't Be Businesses* (Harvard University Press, 2004); *Powerful Reforms with Shallow Roots: Improving Urban Schools* (edited with Michael Usdan, Teachers College Press, 2003); *Why Is It So Hard To Get Good Schools?* (Teachers College Press, 2003).

Ivor Goodson has recently joined the Centre for Educational Research at St Edmund's College, University of Cambridge. He is also Professor of Learning Theory at the University of Brighton and Stint Foundation Visiting Professor at the University of Uppsala. He is directing two large research projects, one funded by the European Commission and the other by the UK Economic and Social Research Council. He is the Founding Editor of *The Journal of Education Policy* and European Editor of the journal *Identity*. One of his most recent books is *Learning, Curriculum and Life Politics: Selected Works* (RoutledgeFalmer, 2005). Further information on his current activities, publications and projects may be accessed at: http://www.ivorgoodson.com.

Andy Hargreaves holds the Thomas More Brennan Chair of Education in the Lynch School of Education at Boston College. Before this he was the founder and co-director of the International Centre for Educational Change at the Ontario Institute for Studies in Education (University of Toronto). He has held visiting professorships and fellowships in England, Australia, Sweden, Spain, the United States, Hong Kong and Japan. He is holder of the Canadian Education Association/Whitworth 2000 Award for outstanding contributions to educational research in Canada. His book, *Changing Teachers, Changing Times*

(Teachers College Press, 1994) received the 1995 Outstanding Writing Award from the American Association of Colleges for Teacher Education. Among his other recent books are *Teaching in the Knowledge Society: Education in the Age of Insecurity* (Teachers College Press, 2003) and *Learning to Change: Teaching Beyond Subjects and Standards* (with Lorna Earl, Shawn Moore and Susan Manning, Jossey-Bass, 2001). His work has been translated extensively into more than a dozen languages. His most recent book (with Dean Fink) is *Sustainable Leadership* (Jossey-Bass, 2005).

Ben Levin holds a Canada Research Chair in Education Leadership and Policy at the Ontario Institute for Studies in Education, University of Toronto. In addition to being a well-known researcher and author, he has served as deputy minister (chief civil servant) for education in two Canadian provinces and has worked extensively internationally.

Ann Lieberman is an Emeritus Professor from Teachers College, Columbia University. She is now a Senior Scholar at The Carnegie Foundation for the Advancement of Teaching. She was president of the American Educational Research Association (AERA) in 1992. She is widely known for her work in the areas of teacher leadership and development, collaborative research, networks and school–university partnerships, and on the problems and prospects for understanding educational change. Her recent books include: *Inside the National Writing Project: Connecting Network Learning and Classroom Teaching* (with Diane Wood, Teachers College Press, 2003) and *Teacher Leadership* (with Lynne Miller, Jossey-Bass, 2004). Her many books and articles have been used by schools and universities alike. She has helped to bring research to the field, popularizing the perspective that learning from the field is another way to build important conceptions of knowledge about teaching and learning. Her unique contribution has been to go between school and university, embracing the dualities that plague our field – theory/practice; process/content; intellectual/social-emotional learning; policy/practice – helping to build a more comprehensive understanding of teachers and schools and what it will take to involve them in deepening their work. To do this she has fashioned a way to be both a scholar and an activist, a practitioner and a theoretician.

Martin Lipton is Communications Analyst at UCLA's Institute for Democracy, Education, and Access. A former public high school teacher, Lipton has had a parallel career as education writer and photographer. He is co-author, with Jeannie Oakes, of *Becoming Good American Schools: The Struggle for Civic Virtue in Education Reform* (Jossey-Bass, 2000), and *Teaching to Change the World* (McGraw-Hill, 3rd edn, 2006). His photographs, appearing in *Teaching to Change the World* and *Learning Power* (Teachers College Press, 2006), portray the disappointments and possibilities for educational justice in urban schools and communities.

Milbrey Wallin McLaughlin is the David Jacks Professor of Education and Public Policy at Stanford University, Co-Director of the Center for Research on the Context of Teaching, and Executive Director of the John W. Gardner Center for Youth and their Communities. She is the author or co-author of books, articles, and chapters on education policy issues, contexts for teaching and learning, productive environments for youth, and community-based organizations, some of the more recent of which are listed here: *Building School-Based Teacher Learning Communities* (with Joan Talbert, Teachers College Press, 2006); *School Districts And Instructional Renewal* (with Amy Hightower, Michael Knapp and Julie Marsh, Teachers College Press, 2002); *Communities of Practice and the Work of High School Teaching* (with Joan Talbert, University of Chicago Press, 2001).

Jeannie Oakes is Presidential Professor in Educational Equity and Director of the University of California's All Campus Consortium on Research for Diversity (ACCORD) and Co-Director of UCLA's Institute for Democracy, Education and Access (IDEA). She studies and writes about schooling inequalities and the struggle for more socially just schools, most recently in *Learning Power: Organizing for Education and Justice* (Teachers College Press, 2006), *Keeping Track: How Schools Structure Inequality* (Yale University Press, 1985/2005), *Becoming Good American Schools: The Struggle for Civic Virtue in Education Reform* (Jossey-Bass, 2000), and *Teaching to Change the World* (McGraw-Hill, 1999/2002/2006). Oakes has received three major awards from the American Educational Research Association. She is also the recipient of Southern Christian Leadership Conference's Ralph David Abernathy Award for Public Service and a member of the National Academy of Education.

John M. Owen is Principal Fellow at the Centre for Program Evaluation, the University of Melbourne. He is interested in the dissemination and use of knowledge created through research and evaluation and other forms of social enquiry. During the past three years, he also has undertaken evaluations for the Commonwealth Emergency Management Institute, the Department of Human Services (in Victoria), and the Asia Education Foundation, and has acted as an evaluation adviser for the Victorian Auditor General, and for NZAID in New Zealand. He has won several awards, is on the editorial boards of a number of international journals, and is a regular contributor to journals and at international evaluation conferences in Australia and overseas. A third edition of his book, *Programme Evaluation Forms and Approaches* (Allen & Unwin, 2006) is available in Australasia and published in the USA by Guilford Press.

Michelle Renée is a post-doctoral fellow at UCLA's Institute for Democracy Education and Access. Dr Renée's scholarship focuses on the role of researchers and low-income communities of colour in improving the equity of California's education system by examining the nexus of equity-focused education research and reform, social movements, and public policy. Prior to entering academe, Dr Renée worked as a legislative assistant in the United States Congress.

Kathryn A. Riley is based at the Institute of Education, London University in the Centre for Leadership in Learning. She is interested in how educational change takes place, particularly in urban contexts, and the contribution of school leaders, parents, communities, teachers and pupils to the change process. Current research focuses on urban leadership through the project 'Leadership on the Front-line' which brings together schools in challenging contexts in Belfast, Birmingham, Cardiff, City of Derry, Dublin, Liverpool, London and Manchester and Salford. Some of her more recent publications include: *Urban Pioneers – Leading the Way Ahead: First Lessons from the Project 'Leadership on the Front-line'* (with T. Hesketh, S. Rafferty *et al.*, London: Institute of Education, Issues in Practice Series, 2005); *Children: Why Students Lose Interest in School and What can be Done about It* (with Elle Rustique-Forrester, Paul Chapman, 2002); *Leadership for Change and School Reform: International Perspectives* (with Karen Seashore Louis, RoutledgeFalmer, 2000), and *Whose School is it Anyway?* (Falmer Press, 1998).

John Rogers is an Assistant Professor in UCLA's Graduate School of Education and Information Studies and the Co-Director of UCLA's Institute for Democracy, Education and Access (IDEA). He studies strategies for engaging urban youth, community members, and educators in equity-focused school reform. He is the co-author (with Jeannie Oakes) of *Learning Power: Organizing for Education and Justice*, published in 2006 by Teachers College Press.

Judyth Sachs is Deputy Vice-Chancellor (Provost), Macquarie University where her position has major responsibility for all academic matters. She was Pro Vice-Chancellor, Learning and Teaching for the University of Sydney, after joining Sydney as Professor of Education in 1996. Her other roles have included Chair of the Academic Board (2001–4) and Pro-Dean of the Faculty of Education (1999–2001). She also currently serves on the editorial boards of a range of educational advisory groups in the UK, US and in Hong Kong. She is best known for her book *The Activist Teaching Profession* (Open University Press, 2003) and the *International Handbook for Continuous Professional Development of Teachers* (edited with Christopher Day, Open University Press, 2004). She is a past president of the Australian Association for Research in Education.

Dennis Shirley is professor at the Lynch School of Education, Boston College. He is one of the foremost authorities on community organizing and educational change in the United States today. Shirley's book, *Community Organizing for Urban School Reform* (University of Texas Press, 1997), described innovative strategies for improving public schools by linking them with community groups and is widely used by parents and community members to inspire and guide their efforts to change. He has published in the *Phi Delta Kappan*, the *Peabody Journal of Education*, and many other journals and magazines, and his research has been translated into German, French, and Spanish.

Ciaran Sugrue is Reader in Leadership and School Improvement in the Faculty of Education, University of Cambridge. Previously, he has been Principal Lecturer and Director of Postgraduate Studies in Education at St Patrick's College, Dublin City University. He is General Editor of the journal, *Irish Educational Studies*, and is on the editorial boards of several international journals. Some of his most recent publications are *Passionate Principalship: Learning from the Life Histories of School Leaders* (Routledge, 2005) and *Curriculum and Ideology: Irish Experiences, International Perspectives* (The Liffey Press, 2004).

Foreword

All changed, changed utterly:
A terrible beauty is born
    (W. B. Yeats, Easter 1916)

Change is a constant in all walks of life: the schoolhouse and the school system in which it is nested are no exceptions. Though scholarship on schools and school systems often dwell on constancy across time, especially in the face of planned change orchestrated by policymakers, change is ubiquitous. And schools and schools systems are not immune, though one might be forgiven for thinking otherwise from reading much of the scholarship on them.

Some change is of the revolutionary sort that Yeats writes of, but change is often, perhaps mostly, evolutionary rather than revolutionary, gradually creeping up on us and on the organizations that are part and parcel of our lives. Nonetheless, change that appears gradual, or indeed goes unnoticed at any point in time, can over the long haul amount to monumental change in schools and education systems. Like the rest of us, teachers and the students they teach age, changing the human composition of a school and indeed entire systems. National and neighbourhood demographics shift often slowly but surely, sometimes even at a glacial pace, but over a decade or two these shifts can result in dramatic changes in the make-up of the student population in those contexts.

Hence, the familiar lament of implementation scholars (myself included) that little changed despite the efforts of school reformers is somewhat at odds with the reality that change is everywhere for schools and their inhabitants. This apparent contradiction in part reflects the focus of policy-implementation scholars with planned change, the sort of change orchestrated by policymakers and other 'experts' – academics, school reformers, philanthropic organizations and so on. But change is not always planned.

Though the distinction is not without problems, we can think about change as planned or unplanned. Unplanned change is typically not purposively conceived and may or may not be a function of a decision by some organizational member or external agent. Moreover, unplanned change often goes unnoticed because it is continuous, and its effects are cumulative rather than immediately apparent.

Of course, unplanned change is sometimes triggered by planned change – the unintended consequences of policymaking.

Planned change involves a conscious decision by someone (federal or national policymakers, local government policymakers, school principals) to change or transform some existing practice in a system or organization. The challenge of figuring out how to implement successfully planned change has been a perennial one for both scholars and practitioners. In organized, rule-governed societies, change is not left to chance. And yet, taking leave of past or present involves a degree of risk, uncertainty and imagination (Giddens, 1991). Planned change, therefore, and the policy-making it implies and necessitates, is an attempt to lend predictability to an uncertain future; it is an attempt to reduce risk and uncertainty. We might also think of planned change as an attempt to harness the unplanned continuous change in the system – to nudge it in particular directions.

When there is disagreement among policymakers and policy experts about how past and present are understood, it is entirely predictable that expert opinion will also differ about the shaping contours of the future of educational change. In education, more than many other policy arenas, the future takes on heightened uncertainty since there is little agreement about the nature of the problems faced by education systems. To borrow from McLaughlin (Chapter 10), 'Education is a problem of ...?' How policy makers, the change agents, respond to this question and how the question is framed, will determine to a significant extent the manner in which they choose to shape the future; how education policy and practice will be conducted into the future.

In an era of rapid and unprecedented change, it is not surprising that education policy making has become a significant activity in jurisdictions across the globe. Within government systems, even levels that previously had a poor appetite for education policy-making have developed a much larger one of late. More education policy has contributed to the growth in education policy research and in some respects contributed to a diversification of those engaged in policy analysis. This volume reflects this diversification bringing together scholars with different research foci from three continents to explore educational change.

The book captures many of the complexities of change in education systems – planned and unplanned. In doing so, the authors put to rest the myth that policy analysis is simply about figuring out if policy gets implemented as designed and if it has its intended effects or not. The volume captures how the critical research questions for education policy have to do with change writ large in the education systems, not just the 'official' planned change as decreed by policymakers. In fact, the chapters reinforce the view that how policy questions are framed is critical to the kinds of answers provided, and their capacity to be generative for both future policymaking and practice. While rigorous empirical studies of whether particular policies have their intended effects or not are important, they are not everything when it comes to education policy analysis. Moreover, the chapters capture how education policy analysis has to go beyond a purely functional analysis of particular policies and examine how these policies are situated socially, culturally, politically, and historically.

Policy makers, policy analysts and policy consultants are bridge builders to the future. However, the ideas, the designs, the plans and their execution actually help shape the future as they evolve. The future then is always a work in progress. While policy makers typically identify a new and desirable horizon, a new goal, getting there involves so many more people (and the various organizations they inhabit) that the target frequently becomes obscured, altered, subverted and replaced along the way. Policy making seeks, among other things, to control risk and uncertainty, but these insecurities cannot be eliminated, only managed more or less effectively. The landscape too is littered with unintended consequences of policy-making and its implementation.

If change is a persistent presence in school systems, so too is constancy. Perhaps the more things change the more they stay the same, *or* perhaps *some* things change, and *other* things stay the same. Change and constancy co-exist and need to be treated accordingly. Many of us who labour in the vineyard of policy implementation research tend to be pre-occupied with the constancy in the wake of the planned changes we investigate. We often lament the absence of change; both change and constancy are critical to understanding planned change. As James March notes, 'Changes in organizations depend on a few stable processes. Theories of change emphasize either the stability of the processes or the changes they produce, but a serious understanding of organizations requires attention to both' (March, 1981: 563). Change and constancy (or stability) are close relatives, not distant cousins, and we need to treat them accordingly.

Planned change – even when successfully implemented – never eradicates the past in its attempts to craft the future. Policymakers' grand designs do not play out on blank slates – rather they get layered on and entangled in current ways of doing things. In this way, the past lives even when things change. In those immortal words of Faulkner, 'The past is never dead. In fact, it's not even past.'

The themes discussed in this book will be familiar to some policy scholars: circuitous implementation highways and byways, the unintended consequences of policy, the inequities at the policymaking table, and so on. But, the treatment of these issues under the umbrella of educational change is fresh and enlightening. This is to be expected given the cast. The tone blends optimism and pessimism with a measure of idealism thrown in from time to time. That balance seems right, suggesting a need for caution and criticism but still holding out the hope for something that might resemble progress. Especially striking is how some of the central education policy issues transcend national boundaries. Indeed, this volume suggests that a program of cross-national research in the area of education policy, that is genuinely comparative rather than research of the travel log sort, could generate new understandings of the educational change processes.

The critical stance that is characteristic of many of the chapters fills a void in education policy analysis. Standing back, reflecting on the bigger picture and surfacing those questions that often go unasked, either intentionally or otherwise, is a critical dimension then in any conversation about education change. Giving voice to those who are not part of the discourse is also important. Still, whether this discourse has an impact will ultimately depend on engaging more mainstream policy analysts and indeed policymakers and politicians, of the left and the right. Failure to do so simply results in more preaching to the choir. Speaking truth to power involves more than monologues or conversations among the likeminded; it necessitates forging a dialogue. Absent that dialogue, and the wisdom in this volume is likely to fall on deaf ears especially where it most needs a hearing.

The major strength of this volume is its authority, and the manner in which it has generated an agenda with potential to lend considerable direction to the future of educational change, but in a manner that respects traditions, trajectories and transitions. Read it, and empower your own agency; recommend it and you will build coalitions of interest with potential to nurture collective educational agendas, locally, nationally and trans-nationally.

James P. Spillane, Northwestern University

References

Faulkner, W. (1959) *Requiem for a Nun*, New York: Random House.
Giddens, A. (1991) *Modernity and Self-Identity: Self and Society in the Late Modern Age*, Stanford: Stanford University Press.
March, J. G. (Dec. 1981) *Administrative Science Quarterly*, Vol. 26, No. 4, pp. 563–77.

Acknowledgements

Accumulated debts are an inevitable consequence of editing a manuscript, particularly when contributors are dispersed across three continents. My first debt therefore is to the authors of the chapters, for their contributions and for their patient editing, as well as patience in waiting for the finished product. I am most grateful also for their presence and contributions to the International Invitational Symposium hosted by St Patrick's College, a college of Dublin City University, as part of its doctoral programme in education. The occasion in July 2006 provided an important opportunity to engage with internationally renowned scholars in the flesh, encounters that are qualitatively different from depersonalised engagement with their published work; for keeping faith with me, a particular personal note of gratitude to each and every one of you.

Organising this international symposium was also a collective enterprise thus incurring local debts that I am happy to acknowledge. Through the good offices of my colleague Dr Mark Morgan (Head of Education), funding from Atlantic Philanthropies was available to underwrite some of the costs. Mark was an enthusiastic supporter of the initiative from the outset. A particular word of thanks to Tom Costello, who is often the more public face of Atlantic Philanthropies here in Ireland, and who took time to be present at several of the paper presentations during the symposium. His presence and the support of his organisation were most welcome and much appreciated. The funding was most expeditiously disbursed through the college Finance office, and for this efficient service, I am most grateful to Martin Ward, Eileen McDevitt and Miriam Rigney. At all times the College President, Dr Pauric Travers, was an enthusiastic supporter of the endeavour, and an active participant. His opening remarks set a positive tone that was maintained throughout.

It is often the case that the most onerous work is invisible, particularly when a conference runs smoothly. Consequently, a significant debt of gratitude is owed to the organising committee – Maeve Fitzpatrick, Maria Thornbury, Dr Catherine Furlong, Dr Marie Flynn and Dr Maeve O'Brien, whose support, advice, expertise and sense of humour kept us all going. A particular word of gratitude goes to Maeve Fitzpatrick for her creation and maintenance of the symposium website. Such expertise is too often taken for granted. Other important contributors to the success of the symposium included Mark Carey, Ray Dempsey, Caoimhe de Búrca, Regina Halpin and Edel Ní Bhroin, a group of masters students who contributed significantly, if silently and efficiently, throughout the week to audience participation by effective management of the 'roving mics'. A similar debt to my colleagues who work in catering is readily acknowledged; they always deliver service with courtesy and care, it does not go unnoticed.

The intention was to provide space and opportunity for dialogue, and while there were participants from all parts of the Island of Ireland, Norway, Poland and the UK, those who held the key to a very positive dynamic and fostered it throughout were the doctoral students themselves, who grew in confidence, expertise and stature as the week progressed. Their contribution and very active participation in both academic and social events ensured that the substantive matters discussed will have resonances in their work for many years to come. They are: Francis Duffy, Marie Dunphy, Deirdre Farrell, Marian Farrelly, Geraldine French, Patricia Higgins, Mags Jordan, Zita Lysaght, Fintan McCutcheon, Rory McDaid, Colman Motherway, Niamh O'Brien, Carmel O'Doherty, Margaret O'Donnell, Michael O'Keeffe, Carol O'Sullivan, Noelle Spring, and Bairbre Boylan (present in spirit).

Although Routledge has gone through various transformations in recent times, Anna Clarkson continues to be a stalwart. She is an outstanding example of someone who embodies continuity and change, and her wise counsel was much appreciated at all stages of the publication process. Amy Crowle's reminders of impending deadlines were important in completing the final version of the manuscript.

Putting the final version of any manuscript together is time consuming, and attention to detail is paramount. Siobhán Nolan has provided invaluable support and expertise throughout. Her calm, patience and perseverance appear to know no bounds, and are certainly much appreciated. Clíona Uí Thuma too came to the rescue on several occasions when the blanks contained in incomplete references had to be filled. Her librarian's eye for detail and accuracy provided timely and much appreciated support.

A particular word of gratitude is extended to Jim Spillane who readily agreed to craft the foreword for the manuscript despite the demands on his time and expertise. I am more than happy to commit to the purchase of at least one pint of Guinness as a token of my gratitude when time and space are opportune!

While readily acknowledging the contributions of the authors, and the wide-ranging supporting cast, I have no hesitation in owning up to the shortcomings of the text that may be laid at my door.

Ciaran Sugrue

Introduction

At a recent book launch[1] I shook hands with a couple, both teachers, who had completed an in-service Bachelor of Education degree as students of mine twenty years earlier. As the usual pleasantries and banter were exchanged, almost in unison they stated: 'You haven't changed a bit', and followed spontaneously, despite my protestations as to the inaccuracy of their assertion, with 'and it's younger looking you're getting'. As we all know, both assertions are commonplace, fanciful inaccuracies, and run counter to common sense understandings of the nature of change. Additionally, taken together, both statements cannot be true as they are contradictory! The first statement expresses an attachment to continuity – 'not changed a bit' – despite the passage of two decades, while the latter suggests that I am regressing to a more youthful state – to some land of youth where the ageing process is postponed indefinitely! Alternatively, both statements are a kind of compliment that, despite the passage of time, I appear to be in reasonable shape , have not changed to the point of being unrecognisable, thus a kind of embodiment of change and continuity. Despite the positive camouflage, on closer inspection both statements are indicative of a cultural ambiguity and difficulty with change, particularly in a media-saturated context where 'youth culture' is pervasive; where size zero or an appropriately rippled six-pack are the archetypal benchmarks against which everyone, regardless of age, lifestyle and inherited genetic make up, is 'measured'. In a tacit unarticulated manner, they indicate that culturally we struggle with time, change and continuity. This is not the exclusive domain of the Irish; such dilemmas are ubiquitous!

In the closing line of O'Casey's *Juno and the Paycock*, Boyle declares: 'I'm telling you Joxer th' whole worl's in a terr … ible state o' … chassis!' (O'Casey, 1925/1957: 73). Similarly, a commonplace of my early childhood was to hear adults, in response to some startling news, remark with feigned seriousness: 'the country isn't half settled'. However, it was Heraclitus, resident philosopher in the city of Ephesus about 500 BC, who first shook the ancients and their world from their complacency regarding permanence, by conjuring up his 'theory of flux' typically illustrated for the benefit of undergraduate philosophy students by the statement: 'It is not possible to step into the same river twice', thus change rather than permanence is identified as the constant. We can only imagine the seismic shock such an intellectual breakthrough represented to more ordinary citizens in pre-modern times. In the post-modern world, flux or continuous change is frequently taken for granted, lauded and celebrated in opposition to a more predictable, stable, orthodox social fabric. Bauman sums up this historical legacy and situates it within contemporary 'liquid modernity' when he states:

> ... throughout human history the work of culture consisted in sifting and sedimenting hard kernels of perpetuity out of transient human lives and fleeting human actions, in conjuring up duration out of transience, continuity out of discontinuity, and in transcending thereby the limits imposed by human mortality by deploying mortal men and women in the service of the immortal human species.
>
> (Bauman, 2006: 126)

He is quick to point out that such relentless pursuit of 'progress' and the confidence that motivates those in its pursuit, is in decline to the point where it is increasingly difficult to create collective projects, to agree on a particular 'future' that is worthy of widespread support. Consequently, he concludes that 'progress' is a declaration of belief that history is of no account and of the resolve to leave it out of account (p. 132). Nevertheless, politicians, commentators and historians too are wont to assert that if we ignore the lessons of history we are condemned to repeat them. Such assertions suggest that those whose mission is the relentless pursuit of progress wish to shed the 'iron cage' of history, to evade the constraints of past and present to construct the future they want, that is advantageous to them. This construction of such a future requires a confidence and self-reliance in the here and now rather than any reference to previous times. When this is allied to the dominance of neo-liberal economic ideology, then the future is almost invariably an individual project only. As Bauman asserts:

> ... the matter of improvement is no longer a collective but an individual enterprise; it is individual men and women on their own who are expected to use, individually, their own wits, resources and industry to lift themselves to a more satisfactory condition and leave behind whatever aspect of their present condition they may resent.
>
> (2006: 135)

Such assertions do much to explain the current fashion of privatising education, whereby those who can afford a private education for their children increasingly abandon public education and its collective mission. This trend is consistent with the views expressed above, where public education is no longer perceived by many adults as a collective enterprise. Instead, it is perceived as a commodity to be purchased in pursuit of private gain, part of an individual project that enhances one's capacity to compete in the market-place of the knowledge economy. As Hargreaves perceptively remarks:

The knowledge economy primarily serves the private good. The knowledge society encompasses the public good. Our schools have to prepare young people for both of them.

(2003: xvi)

Similarly, Stone argues from a policy perspective, that policy-making requires a collective dimension, while readily recognising that there are tensions between pursuit of individual and collective gains. She says:

The major dilemma of policy in the polis is how to get people to give primacy to these broader consequences in their private calculus of choices, especially in an era when the dominant culture celebrates private consumption and personal gain.

(Stone, 2002: 23)

In order to avoid the consequences of liquid modernity, which facilitates the replacing of collective actions with individual missions, where identity politics is an individual rather than a collective pursuit, it is not possible to address the 'future of educational change' without some semblance of a collective project. It is to this collective pursuit that the content of this book is dedicated. The future of educational change, beyond individual identity politics, necessitates paying attention to past and present as a means of identifying the grounds that become the foundation for constructing a future that has collective commitment as the basis of progress, not in a prescriptive manner that seeks to imprison the future; not an imposition of a previous or contemporary iron cage intent on replication. Rather, it seeks to create coalitions of confidence and commitment to a re-shaped and emergent collective enterprise.

While each chapter in this volume speaks for itself, focusing on recent reform endeavours within and between various national borders, the additional intention is that each undertaking contributes towards the identification of some signposts and compass readings that become the rudder of educational change, a tiller that gives direction to its future, beyond the more narcissistic pursuit of individual educational advantage; to create and to persuade others of the necessity to construct an appropriate rapprochement between economy and society. I concur with Soete (2006: 207) when he asserts, concerning the future of European Social Model (ESM), that:

... broadening the knowledge and innovation concept to include education more systematically would also enable member countries to address particular weaknesses of their education systems as an integral part of their investment target.

This is not merely a technical question concerning 'best practice', nor the most sophisticated tests that measure outcomes with scientific validity. Rather, it has a moral and ethical dimension that is much more encompassing and reflexive;

in the words of economist Richard Florida: 'What do we really want? What kind of life – and what kind of society – do we want to bequeath to coming generations?' (2002: 235). Recognising the tensions and dilemmas, consistencies and contradictions, while not being paralysed by them, becomes an important first step in setting an agenda for the future of educational change.

The book is in four parts. Each plays its part in constructing a roadmap that, notwithstanding various contradictions and dis-junctures, points the way as a navigational aid to the future. Each section contains three chapters that variously connect aspects of research and policy and how they articulate with, alter, transform and lend direction to the rolling stock of educational change.

Part I, Educational change: for better or for worse, indicates and illustrates the manner in which the contemporary educational landscape is being re-configured; how the winds of change buffet various features of that topography, sometimes for the better, at other times to the detriment of learners, their families and life chances. Getting to grips with and understanding the positive and negative features of these 'change forces' is the task of this Part.

Andy Hargreaves, Chapter 1. In a challenging and provocative manner, Hargreaves interrogates key recent and contemporary national policy reform initiatives while he positions these within international discourses and simultaneously holds these policy rhetorics up to critical scrutiny. These are construed as positive 'popular cultural' events – three weddings, in three distinct national policy contexts – in Finland, England and Canada. His analysis of recent research and policy reforms in these locations provides some grounds for optimism, some growth buds beyond restriction, reaction and punitive regimes of accountability, beyond preoccupation with driving up test scores at the expense of anything resembling a more balanced holistic education. He argues persuasively that restoration of some autonomy and professional judgement to teachers is already providing evidence of positive benefits. By contrast, he argues that continuing preoccupation with test scores in the US, under-girded with a similar preoccupation with economic concerns and rugged individualism, is increasingly discredited and bankrupt. This is the 'funeral' of the piece, a 'graveyard' for society and any notions of the 'common good'. If this funeral pyre of schooling is to be extinguished, and reconstituted as a 'wedding', then nothing less than a Khunian paradigm shift is urgently required but with significant lessons from abroad to light the way.

Ben Levin, Chapter 2. Levin's experience as academic and policy maker (see notes on contributors) leave him optimistic that more recent developments suggest things are getting better. He identifies several jurisdictions in which there is increasing attention being paid to capacity building, along the lines of Elmore's (2004) principle of reciprocity or Fullan's (2005) promotion of system alignment. He is less sure-footed regarding commitment to equity as he trawls through various educational systems over the past 40 years. He recognises that schools by themselves are limited in what they can do since inequality is not just a school phenomenon. He acknowledges too that equity rhetorics need to move beyond this to practical impact at the level of the school. He is particularly sanguine regarding the impact of international organisations such as the OECD on furthering the equity agenda. What is clear is that much more concerted and sustained effort on behalf of equity is necessary if it is to move beyond occasional attention in the policy arena. From a research perspective, he recognises the need for more systematic accumulation of evidence on practice, particularly if such evidence is to work to maximum advantage for the most vulnerable. Nevertheless, his experience suggests that policy makers and the policy-making process is often poorly understood and unfairly criticised by researchers. He ends on an optimistic if more cautious note – things are getting better, but we must all work harder, and in a more understanding, inclusive manner, if equity and better schools and their maintenance are to gain greater priority and sustained attention.

Ciaran Sugrue, Chapter 3. The focus of this chapter is the changing educational landscape in Ireland, while these shifting plate tectonics are situated within international discourses, debates and disagreements on research 'paradigm wars' and their more recent manifestations. Additionally, Sugrue likens the emergence of several new agencies or advocacy groups to 'think tanks' with the consequence that more traditional boundaries between research, policy-making and politics have been blurred or obliterated. He argues that, as a consequence, research in general is brought into disrepute, while quality, rigour and trustworthiness can often play second fiddle to timing, dissemination, lobbying and advocacy. When there is a proliferation of information by a variety of conventional and technological means, policy makers and politicians can selectively choose those bits of evidence that fit their immediate agenda. This new landscape is confounded further by the identity politics of an increasingly crowded list of 'think tanks' that pursue their own identity projects to the possible detriment of other more worthy educational endeavours. These shifting boundaries and reduced solidarities create a dialogue of the deaf where the necessity to listen, to engage, to create public spaces for debate, dissent and disagreement are sacrificed in favour of market place 'insider trading' to gain advantage, often at the expense of others with fewer resources and less socio-political capital to advance their 'cause'. He argues that a more robust public educational research policy, with appropriate funding, and criteria for assessment of quality and disbursement of funding, has potential to be generative of more reliable research evidence. Additionally, the research community has responsibility to take seriously identifiable shortcoming of its work, while seeking also to move beyond more narcissistic identity politics to collective educational agenda that engage the public imagination and build new forms of capital through recapitulation of trust, credibility and integrity.

Part II, Educational change: lessons from home and away, draws on evidentiary warrants from very different contexts, locations and perspectives to identify further lessons from the landscape of educational change with potential also to lend direction to the future.

Larry Cuban, Chapter 4. Cuban takes on the task of deconstructing the impact of the Bush policy, No Child Left Behind (NCLB), and situates its inspiration, initiation and trajectory within historical perspective, indicating clearly that a version of corporate and private sector interest in, and influence on, educational policies has waxed and waned for more than a century. His previous and more recent research provides convincing evidence that dominant pedagogies have been slow to change, but change they have leading to the creation of teaching hybrids, child-centred approaches melded with more teacher-centred teaching, while there is significantly less evidence of this blending of traditions in the secondary school sector. Although his recent evidence suggests that the advent of NCLB and its consequent preoccupation with testing and accountability do not seem to have impacted adversely on these hybrid and informal traditions, he cites a growing body of research evidence that indicates a reduction in time being spent on subjects that are not being tested. Over time, therefore, current regimes of accountability are likely to have more negative consequences as new teachers enter the arena with little memory of autonomy or experience of hybrid teaching styles. Cuban 'proves' his essential thesis that policy is rarely implemented as intended due to the many agencies and agents whose hands it passes through from Whitehouse to classroom, and this meandering is both a curse and a blessing. There are two major lessons about the nature of educational change that I take from his contribution. One, change, as Yeats suggests, 'comes dropping slow'; it takes time for policy reforms to take hold. Two, as researchers, much greater sophistication in our conceptualisations of the complexities of educational change are necessary if they are to be documented more systematically and rigorously.

Dennis Shirley, Chapter 5. In a searing analysis of NCLB through a case study of Texas, Shirley provides a devastating critique of the impact of a top-down, prescriptive, and ideologically driven reform effort, with seriously negative consequences for civic engagement and democracy, for the achievement of learners, while promulgating a rhetoric of inclusion, simultaneously disenfranchising whole communities as well as exacerbating inequalities and undermining social justice agenda. He begins by drawing on the work of Alinsky in Chicago of the 1930s, indicating how good old-fashioned trade union, grassroots organising has significant potential to build 'relational capital', something often absent in poor communities. Shirley's work is of particular interest in education since it draws lessons from a wider constituency, from communities rather than the immediate worlds of schools and schooling, more familiar to educators, researchers and policy makers. He indicates how the Industrial Areas Foundation (IAF) built community action in Texas in the 1980s using such methods, and positive benefits in health and education resulted. However, all of this changed with the enactment of NCLB. A decade later, the debris of this 'hurricane' is strewn over several states. Shirley's analysis identifies the following lessons. What began as well intended policy was too vague in several respects and because of the manner in which resources were dependent on compliance, resistance or rejection became extremely difficult and conformity, regardless of the educational consequences, became commonplace except where educational traditions and teachers' unions were sufficiently robust to withstand the pressures; what were intended as carrots quickly became sticks with resultant negative consequences. Educational change, therefore, needs to be more consultative, less ideological, more tolerant of diversity rather than preoccupied with 'one best way'. The need for accountability is recognised but criteria are necessary whereby individuals at all levels of the system are appropriately held to account.

John Owen, Chapter 6. Through the lens of evaluation, Owen indicates the potential of evaluation for bringing evaluators, policy-makers and practitioners into more productive relationships to improve practice and more expeditiously facilitate and support curriculum and organisational change at the level of the school. Though contested terrain, the lessons from the field that Owen identifies from evaluation of an Australian curricular initiative (Studies of Asia and Australia in Australian Schools (SOAAA)) sponsored by the Asian Education Foundation (AEF) are significant. His study corroborates previous evidence that it takes approximately three years for new pedagogical routines to become embedded in the regular practices of teachers. However, key to the success of this initiative has been the identification of a 'champion' of the reform working within and between schools; individuals with considerable experience in reforms and professional support, but with the important additional responsibility as a political infighter, someone who becomes an advocate for the reform within the micro-politics of the school. This insight moves the discourse beyond more romantic notions of teacher leadership to one that recognises the necessity for turbulence and some turmoil if such initiatives are to bear fruit. This is an important ingredient to add to the mix of educational change. Insights from this case reinforce the necessity for researchers to pay more attention to the manner in which the message is mediated to various stakeholders if the work of researchers is to become a more integral element of building systemic capacity and more evidence-based reforms. Such alliances necessitate trust and distance that require sustained attention and this can only be developed over time, something that is often absent due to unrealistic deadlines and the rush to publish.

Part III, Educational change: finding new directions?, continues the Odyssey through past and present as a means of plotting the navigational chart to the future. Policy, practice and research are closely sieved in search of nuggets of wisdom that are likely to be generative.

Ivor Goodson, Chapter 7. Goodson's study of the field of curriculum for three decades has led him to be profoundly critical of Curriculum as Prescription (CAP). While drawing on segments of his scholarly work, he illustrates very clearly how CAP has been used consistently as an exclusionary device that protects and sustains social hierarchy, privilege and social elites. Even when New Labour, committed to a project of inclusion, takes up the task of promoting greater opportunities for all, this policy pursuit falters consistently as it is promoted within existing curriculum prescriptions. Consequently, he argues, though the policy is well intentioned, achievement gaps continue to be unacceptably high between the usual social groups. Goodson then goes on to illustrate a possible future that has potential to be more democratic and inclusionary. This conduit to a better future he identifies as learning as 'life narrative' and he conceptualises narrative learning as a means of moving away from primary to tertiary learning, whereby learners at all ages are engaged in constructing their own life narratives, creating narrative capital, rather than disengaging from a prescribed curriculum that is often alienating and disempowering. While acknowledging that the sprouts of narrative capital are barely visible, Goodson argues persuasively that we are likely to hear more about it in the future. Narrative capital may have considerable potential to give direction to the future of educational change.

Jeannie Oakes et al., Chapter 8. Oakes and her colleagues (Renée, Rogers and Lipton) begin from a perspective that is becoming more glaringly obvious even if not accepted by more conservative minds, that educational policies, particularly in the US, are overly influenced by a right-wing elite whose solution to lower achievement levels among the poorest students compared with their wealthy peers is to emphasise performance on standardised tests, urge teachers and students to work harder as the most efficient means of improvement, while simultaneously encouraging parents to move their offspring to a 'better' school. They show very clearly how this policy-privileged position has come about, and how it is consolidated to the disadvantage of the poor. Finding intellectual stimulation in the later writings of John Dewey about community participation, the centre in UCLA (where they work) with a particular brief to assist communities to research and become their own advocates and activists, take the reader on a tour that demonstrates beyond all reasonable doubt the aphorism that knowledge is power, all the more powerful when in the hands of those who actively create it, as a means of influencing policy elites and informing them as to how current policies hurt the poor by discriminating against them in various obvious and more subtle ways. These authors provide powerful testament that the future of educational change would be healthier and more progressive by being democratised, put into the hands of communities to enable them to be authors of their own educational scripts rather than the victims of elite's perceptions for them.

Kathryn Riley, Chapter 9. Riley distinguishes between city and urban schools to reflect positive features of the dynamic, racy, unpredictable and often volatile nature of the mosaic of cultures and ethnicities of city schools and their communities. She reminds the reader that such schools have presented persistent dilemmas for decades, while the policy and socio-cultural and economic contexts in which these challenges are played out have altered differently and dramatically in the more globalised world we now inhabit. Beneath this tapestry of changing languages, cultures, religions and life chances lurk more enduring concerns about equity and social justice. Her evidence and argument suggest that the teachers who commit to working in these schools need to engage with the out of school lives of their students, to build on their social capital, while not seeking to romanticise or minimise the challenges involved. Due to the volatile, fragile and rapidly changing nature of these schools and their communities, there is a need for policy-makers to be less bureaucratic, and more responsive to changing needs and circumstances. Delays and short-cuts are no substitute for empathetic and supportive policies and resource provision that enable highly committed professionals to continue to make a difference. There is an ongoing need to build connection and collaborative learning among the professionals who simultaneously need the resources to reach out and connect with parents and the social capital that exists in such communities as well as the educational resources that enhance the individual and collective capital of all concerned.

Part IV, Educational change: linking research, policy and practice. Through a different set of lenses, and working with different data sets, the authors in this section deploy the metal detectors of their respective minds to isolate evidence from earlier and more recent research that contribute further to various arguments they hone with incisive precision to the emergent contours and the re-shaping of educational change.

Milbrey McLaughlin, Chapter 10. McLaughlin identifies key lessons from previous implementation or 'misery research'. First, there is a lack of under-standing of implementation. There are no magic bullet solutions and 'problems' themselves metamorphose over time, thus altering the problem that now requires a different solution. Such solutions are effectively theories of change, thus how we understand and practise implementation is absolutely critical. Second, at system level, from 'top' to 'bottom' policies are interpreted, adapted, so that it becomes necessary to understand policy implementation as a holistic enterprise, including 'street level bureaucrats'. Local actors' capacity to understand and act on a policy initiative determines in a major way the extent to which a policy 'takes hold' or remains surface and superficial, only to be side-swiped into obscurity by the next policy initiative arriving at the schoolhouse door. Third, power relations are critical. The distribution of power determines whether or not policies become coercive, requiring acquiescence and compliance or negotiation, dialogue and capacity building, with ownership of the process at the 'bottom' being much more likely also. Frequently, what counts as successful implementation is superficial, and occurs at the expense of some other programme. Such outcomes raise fundamental questions about the sustainability of policy implementation. These and other lessons become the raw material for setting an agenda for educational change. Additional key considerations include 'timeframe', and the false picture frequently provided by 'early adoption' evidence. Her own research indicates that there is no 'slam bam' superhighway to some imagined end point. Rather, adopting a 'societal sector framework' has strong possibilities as it recognises complexity, multiple actors and the interdependence between the formal and informal policy arena. Sustainability of change depends on taking these lessons seriously from a research, policy and practice perspective.

Judyth Sachs, Chapter 11. Sachs contextualises the knowledge society, its problems and possibilities from an educational change perspective. She recognises its potency, indicates its dark side while simultaneously signalling its generative potential. She acknowledges and recognises that the darker, more negative potential of the knowledge economy in particular with its attendant emphasis on control and surveillance, on standardisation and testing, has led to a serious and sustained erosion of trust in the classroom, playground and beyond. Consequently, there is increasing evidence of litigation-conscious practice, of defensive teaching that restricts and constrains teachers and limits their engagement with learners and their pedagogical repertoires. This results in what she terms 'trained incapacity', a kind of re-enactment of Holt's (1971) 'learned helplessness' for teachers, when never before has there been such a need for professional competence, confidence and commitment. Nevertheless, she recognises too that this does not have to be characteristic of the future of teachers and teaching. Rather, even if the more optimistic picture she paints is a road less travelled, it is nevertheless very attainable. She indicates clearly that there will need to be a shift towards a 'critical professionalism' whereby teachers will have technical competence to access information, while they will also need to hone their critical and analytical faculties, to decipher ideologically driven research and policy from more considered perspectives. Additionally, this future requires teachers to be committed to collective action, to collaboration through networks and learning communities, to equity, social justice and democratic values. They will become the architects of their individual and collective futures. This future is not guaranteed. It will require enormous individual and collective commitment and action to create and sustain it. She concludes that such effort is the only game in town if teacher professionalism is to survive and thrive.

Ann Lieberman, Chapter 12. Lieberman's long and distinguished career has continually focused on teacher learning, teacher professional development and in recent years she has added teacher leadership to this general portfolio. Through the work of the Carnegie Foundation in particular, she has been a catalyst for harnessing new technologies to begin to document teacher's practice, to systematically provide accounts of practice, accumulate evidence and thus build the knowledge base of teaching, while also putting this accumulated 'wisdom of practice' into the public domain. In a context of narrow regimes of external accountability through testing, this work is counter hegemonic, and the evidence she provides in this chapter from a number of research projects indicates clearly that it is empowering for teachers, that their learning and leadership is enhanced in community. However, this evidence also charts a future pathway whereby teachers, in communities of learning, and using some more established research methods as well as new technologies, build the knowledge-base of teaching from the ground up, and in a manner that is sustaining and sustainable. This kind of epistemic evidence has the potential also to refocus energies on professional growth and renewal rather than the more negative and energy sapping accountability regimes currently dominating teachers' lives and work in too many settings. Investing in teachers' professional learning is yet another corner stone of the future of educational change that, due to 'liquid modernity' is less stable, more fragile, and more than ever in need of multi-faceted support to bring adequate stability to the teaching, learning and educational enterprise.

Epilogue: The future of educational change?. In this concluding piece, I argue for an open agenda that includes items that emerge from the foregoing chapters. The epilogue is intended to be both an end and a beginning. From the foregoing analyses, it accumulates the 'bricolage' from which the future of educational change is likely to be constructed; readers and other actors will bring other items to the table of change. As the bricoleur of the piece, I have identified five broad themes with generative potential. These are discussed in an open ended manner since it remains the responsibility of the reader to configure them appropriately depending on local contexts. While bringing the curtain down on this particular text, it also provides the reader with the building blocks from which to construct a future for education, to change it in ways that render it more just and equitable.

Note

1 The book to which I refer is Kelly, J. (ed.) (2006) *St Patrick's College Drumcondra, 1875–2000: A History*, Dublin: Four Courts Press.

References

Bauman, Z. (2006) *Liquid Modernity*, Cambridge: Polity Press.

Elmore, R. (2004) *School Reform from the Inside Out: Policy, Practice and Performance*, Cambridge, MA: Harvard University Press.

Florida, R. (2002) *The Rise of the Creative Class*, New York: Basic Books.

Fullan, M. (2005) *Leadership Sustainability*, Thousand Oaks, CA: Corwin Books.

Hargreaves, A. (2003) *Teaching in the Knowledge Society*, Buckingham: Open University Press.

Holt, M. (1971) *How Children Fail*, London: Penguin.

O'Casey, S. (1957) *Three Plays: 'Juno and the Paycock', 'The Shadow of a Gunman', 'The Plough and the Stars'*, London: Pan Books.

Soete, L. (2006) 'A knowledge economy paradigm and its consequences', in A. Giddens, P. Diamond, and and R. Liddle (eds) *Global Europe Social Europe*, Cambridge: Polity Press, pp. 193–214.

Stone, D. (2002) *Policy Paradox: The Art of Political Decision Making* (rev. edn), New York and London: W. W. Norton and Company.

Part I

Educational change

For better or for worse?

1 The coming of post-standardization

Three weddings and a funeral

Andy Hargreaves

I

We are entering an age of post-standardization. Having reached a plateau of improvement in tested achievement, and a crisis of demographic renewal in teaching and leadership, most Anglo-Saxon and other developed countries are leaving behind policies that force up standards and results at any price. England's National Literacy Strategy and Primary School Targets, the US's gruelling process of Adequate Yearly Progress, Ontario's strategy to reach provincial tested targets within one electoral term that vary only by one year and 5 per cent from the English benchmark from which they were borrowed, as well as Australia's Federal literacy test that takes the achievement and education agenda away from politically more left of centre states – these are the dying embers of a reform fire that is burning itself to a cinder.

In UNICEF's 2007 survey of child well-being in some of the world's richest countries, the English-speaking countries of the UK and the US perform particularly badly, ranking dead last and next to last out of more than 20 countries in total (UNICEF 2007). Prevalence of high-risk health behaviours is especially disturbing in these countries. Canada performs better overall – ranking twelfth on the list – but its results are paradoxical. Children do very well in educational wellbeing as measured by achievement tests and also in terms of excessive material well-being; but in health, family and peer relationships, and self-perceived well-being, Canadians too perform very badly. The lights are on in Canada, but nobody's home.

So it is curious why educational reformers and strategists should, in the last 15 years, have been so enamoured of the policies of standardization, intrusive intervention and market competition propagated by the Disunited Kingdom and Disunited States, whose people spend more hours in the workplace than almost all their international peers (McKibben, 2007; Reich, 1999; Rifkin, 2004), who live and work in countries of rapidly growing gaps between rich and poor, and who seemingly contribute so little to the well-being of their children.

Unwilling to take responsibility for dampening the acquisitive and competitive ethic that drives the Anglo-Saxon economies, the Disunited States and the Disunited Kingdom shift the burden of blame and the remit for redemption on to schools and educators (Berliner, 2006). This occurs, first, through an intensified emphasis on increased attainment and higher standards that only adds to the ethos of anxious competitiveness that already exists, and second, through a multitude of initiatives to mop up the social consequences through earlier and earlier childhood intervention and increasing provision for extra tuition and after-school care. The insatiable economy eats up more and more family time, and through its teachers and child-workers, the state intervenes and intrudes earlier and more often into the lives of the children that are left behind. The result is like prescribing drugs to treat the side effects of previous ones – an untoward emphasis on competitive measured achievement, leading to an excess of initiatives designed to cope with the consequences of excessive material and educational competitiveness.

The result of the age of high-stakes and high-pressure standardization where short-term gains in measurable results are demanded at any price, is that many schools in Anglo-Saxon countries have begun to turn into ethical Enrons of educational change (Batstone, 2003). In *Sustainable Leadership*, Dean Fink and I pointed to the relevant evidence (Hargreaves and Fink, 2006):

- England's National Literacy Strategy and national target setting strategy repeatedly failed to reach their goals, reached a plateau after quick-fix strategies had been exhausted, and produced increments in achievement that were criticized for being largely illusory – a consequence of test items becoming progressively easier.
- The so-called miracle of improvement in Texas schools demonstrated outstanding gains in achievement only on the state tests for which students were prepared, not on national tests for which they had not.
- Early gains in test scores were often secured by concentrating largely on 'bubble kids' who fell just below the passing mark, so that disproportionate attention to increases of just a few per cent among them created appearances of widespread systems gains for schools as a whole – with a concomitant neglect of more seriously underperforming students who fell far below the zone.
- Narrowing the curriculum to focus predominantly on literacy and maths in prescribed and tested programs closed the achievement gap in basic, tested skills, but not in the medium and higher levels of proficiency that give access to knowledge economy opportunities.
- In the UK and US, there has been an inverse relationship between improvements in tested literacy achievement and rates of reading for pleasure.
- The tunnel vision of curriculum that concentrates too much on separately taught literacy and numeracy has been eliminating arts, social studies and health education from the curriculum, making cultural philistines, geographic xenophobes and obese desk potatoes of the next generation. In California, this is now nicknamed the 3-2-1 curriculum: a daily dose of 3 periods of English, 2 of maths, and one of physical education.
- Denied their powers of discretionary professional judgement, diverted from their core mission of deep and broad learning for all students, depleted by the

overwhelming workloads required to achieve dramatic test gains in the time periods required, and demoralized by cultures of administrative culpability and political fear if results fail to materialize, the education profession has faced a crisis of recruitment and retention. These shortages also extend into leadership where large numbers of highly qualified administrators have not wanted to take on the 'big job' once they get as far as the assistant principal's office.

All systems and strategies eventually reach their limit. Leaders become overconfident. Bullies get bored. Statistical improvement curves start to taper off. Evidence surfaces that results were misleading, announcements of victory were premature, promising experiments have not spread and early momentum cannot be sustained. New problems emerge, some a result of the strategies themselves, and existing solutions do not work for them. In the face of a fast-moving global economy, the demand for basic skills gives way to calls for more innovation and creativity (New Commission on the Skills of the American Workforce, 2007). In organizations and in politics, generations turn over, and change agendas turn over with them. Today's gurus become yesterday's news. Governments change and the focus shifts elsewhere. This is when Kuhnian paradigm shifts begin to occur.

II

The first signs of a paradigm shift are when we start to use the word 'post': postindustrial, postcapitalist, postmodern. These epithets point to a world we are leaving behind with only clues and indications, but not yet clear patterns, of what is to come. What are these clues and patterns in an age of post-standardization?

First, there is erosion and eradication of existing patterns – the abolition of all educational testing up to and including age 14, in Wales (Welsh Assembly Government, 2006); the introduction of more flexible testing regimes for primary school pupils in the UK (Gilbert, 2006); the easing of regulations regarding what counts as Adequate Yearly Progress in the US; the formal agreement of a period of peace and stability between teacher unions and the Government of Ontario (Fullan, 2007).

Then, as the existing order shrinks, its remnants are reasserted with grim tenacity: the government's and inspectorate's (expanded) redefinition of failure in the UK to legitimize continuing political intervention; or the imported and imposed emphasis on tested literacy in already high performing Ontario, notwithstanding the province's countervailing increases in professional support and networks.

At the same time, organizations and nations that lagged behind or resisted the reform agenda in the previous era, like Scotland, Ireland or the Nordic countries, are still pulled towards it, but in a more modest and circumspect way, as global change agents seek a reconciliation of old and new strategies for change.

Next, new initiatives as well as recycled innovations from former eras that re-energize those who bear the memory of them, begin to emerge and then proliferate in political cultures of increased experimentation. England establishes a government Innovations Unit; networks for interconnected school-based innovation abound in Australia, the UK, Germany, Alberta and British Columbia; self evaluation gains credence alongside external inspection; professionally shared targets start to replace government-imposed ones; interdisciplinarity is reinvented, creativity makes a comeback and evidence-based improvement emerges almost everywhere.

Internationally, high-level advisors and officials exchange promising ideas and sometimes carry them personally from one jurisdiction to another. Ontario's Premier visits Britain's Prime Minister; South Australia's leading educational bureaucrat goes to work for the Minister of Education in Wales. Change gurus also circulate ideas about strategy around the world. Michael Barber leaves Tony Blair's office to advise reformers and Foundations in the United States; Michael Fullan develops a model of tri-level reform with five jurisdictions across the world; David Hopkins promotes initiatives to develop cross-school systemic leadership with OECD after advising the UK Secretary of State for Education on these matters in his former post; and New York hires dozens of literacy coaches and strategists from Australia and inspection/self-evaluation experts from Britain to raise standards in the city. International organizations then adopt and advocate for the strategies and directions that show greatest promise, as in the OECD's (2004) emphasis on redesigning the teaching profession to be able to teach in and prepare young people for high performing knowledge economies, the World Bank's shift from increasing access and accountability to improving quality (Hargreaves and Shaw, 2006), and UNESCO's (2005) world-leading emphasis on Education For Sustainable Development.

Meanwhile, a retiring Boomer generation of teachers and leaders precipitates a demographic shortfall of replacements (OECD 2004). In order to entice new candidates, and in line with the evidence of history, power and control begin to move back from the bureaucracy to the profession. The emergent generation who will be the demographic drivers of the profession over the next three decades bring new missions and dispositions to it in terms of assertiveness, change management and work–life balance (Goodson *et al.*, 2006).

Eventually, from an initial period of chaos and cacophony in innovation, with its attendant feelings of overload, emerging directions become clear, new orthodoxies evolve, and fresh professional language and discourse begin to justify and activate them. Britain's John Dunsford, Executive Director of the country's largest association of secondary school leaders, takes intelligent accountability from the world of philosophy (O'Neill, 2002) and moves it into educational change; Michael Barber heralds a new era of informed professional judgement (Barber, 2001); and Michael Fullan promotes an ethos of positive pressure where targets are clear, professional support is strong, most improvement efforts are directed at building capacity, and excuses are then taken off the table (Fullan, 2007).

Confronted by data on the failure of existing strategies; challenged by new economic and social directions that embrace innovation and creativity and that are increasingly concerned about child well-being, social cohesion and national security; and driven by a demographic crisis of generational succession in teaching and leading, a paradigm shift in educational reform is already upon us. The remainder of this chapter sets out four specific scenarios that send signals of how this paradigm shift might ultimately evolve. These scenarios are embedded in the United States, Canada, the United Kingdom and Finland.

III

All attempts to bring about change are driven by an implicit or explicit theory-of-action: a set of tacit assumptions or explicit theoretical guidelines concerning the need for change, the solutions required, and the means for achieving them in terms of knowledge, attitudes, skills, learning processes, incentives, rewards, sanctions, human motivation, leadership, resources, timescales, structures, participation and stakeholder investment – to name just a few (Hatch, 2002). Theories of action are driven not only by assumptions and ideas about which of these elements are most important, but also about how they are interconnected and the causal relationships among them. Each of the reform examples that follow either parallel or supersede the strategy of standardization – where change has been driven by political and bureaucratic specification of standards in learning and teaching, then enforced by mechanisms of tight regulation, oversight, reward and punishment to ensure compliance with the systemic effort to raise measured educational standards (Hargreaves, 2003; McNeil, 2000; Achinstein and Ogawa, 2006). Beside and beyond standardization, each of the alternatives outlined below contains different theories of action, and carries different consequences – though all, to some degree, wed proposals for change with traces and legacies from the past.

First wedding

In January of 2007, with team colleagues Gabor Halasz and Beatriz Pont, I undertook an investigative inquiry for OECD into the relationship between leadership and school improvement in one of the world's highest performing educational systems and economies: Finland. After visiting and interviewing students, teachers, headteachers, system administrators, university researchers and senior ministry officials, a remarkably unified narrative began to surface about the country, its schools and their sense of aspiration, struggle and destiny.

Finland is a nation that has endured almost seven centuries of domination and oppression – achieving true independence only within the last three generations. In the context of this historical legacy, and in the face of a harsh and demanding climate and northern geography, it is not surprising that one of the most popular Finnish sayings translates as 'It was long, and it was hard, but we did it!'

Yet it is not simply stoic perseverance, fed by a Lutheran religious ethic of hard work and resilience that explains Finland's success as a high performing educational system and economy. At the core of this country's success and sustainability is its capacity to reconcile, harmonize and integrate those elements that have divided other developed economies and societies – a prosperous, high performing economy and a decent, socially just society. While the knowledge economy has weakened the welfare state in many other societies, in Finland, a strong welfare state is a central part of the national narrative that supports and sustains a successful economy.

In *The Information Society and the Welfare State* Castells and Himanen (2002: 166) describe how

> Finland shows that a fully fledged welfare state is not incompatible with technological innovation, with the development of the information society, and with a dynamic, competitive new economy. Indeed, it appears to be a decisive contributing factor to the growth of this new economy on a stable basis.

The contrast with Anglo Saxon countries where material wealth has been gained at the expense of increasing social division, and also at the cost of children's wellbeing (UNICEF, 2007) could not be more striking.

> Finland stands in sharp contrast to the Silicon Valley model that is entirely driven by market mechanisms, individual entrepreneurialism, and the culture of risk – with considerable social costs, acute social inequality and a deteriorating basis for both locally generated human capital and economic infrastructure.
>
> (Castells and Himanen, 2002: 167)

At the centre of this successful integration that, in less than half a century, has transformed Finland from a rural backwater into a high-tech economic powerhouse, is its educational system (World Bank, 2006). As the respondents interviewed by the OECD team indicated at all levels, Finns are driven by a common and articulately expressed social vision that connects a creative and prosperous future – as epitomized by the Nokia telecommunications company whose operation and suppliers account for about 40 per cent of the country's GDP (Haikio, 2002) – to the people's sense of themselves as having a creative history and social identity. One of the schools we visited was just two miles from the home of Finland's iconic composer Sibelius. And the visual, creative and performing arts are an integral part of children's education and lifelong learning all through and even beyond their secondary school experience.

Technological creativity and competitiveness, therefore, do not break Finns from their past but connect them to it in a unitary narrative of lifelong learning and societal development. All this occurs within a strong welfare state that supports and steers (a favourite Finnish word) the educational system and the economy. A strong public education system provides education free of charge as a universal right all the way through school and higher education – including all necessary resources, equipment, musical instruments and free school meals for everyone. Science and technology are high priorities, though not at the expense of artistic creativity. Almost 3 per cent of GDP is allocated to scientific and technological development and a national committee that includes leading corporate executives and university vice chancellors, and that is chaired by the Prime Minister, steers and integrates economic and educational strategy.

As Finnish commentators and analysts have also remarked, all this educational and economic integration occurs within a society that values children, education and social welfare, that has high regard for education and educators as servants of the public good, that ranks teaching as the most desired occupation of high school graduates, and that is therefore able to make entry into teaching demanding and highly competitive, drawing on the top tenth percentile of the ability range (Salhberg, 2006; Aho *et al.*, 2006).

Within a generally understood social vision, the state steers but does not prescribe in detail the national curriculum – with trusted teams of highly qualified teachers writing much of the curriculum together at the level of the municipality, in ways that adjust to the students they know best. In schools characterized by an uncanny calmness, teachers exercise their palpable sense of professional and social responsibility in their efforts to care especially for children at the bottom, so as to lift them to the level of the rest. This is achieved not by endless initiatives or targeted interventions but by quiet, professional cooperation (another favourite word) among all the teachers involved.

Headteachers in Finland are required by law to have been teachers themselves and most continue to be engaged in classroom teaching for at least 2–3 hours per week – which lends them credibility among their teachers, enables them to remain connected to their children, and ensures that pedagogical leadership is not merely high-flown rhetoric but a living, day-to-day reality.

How is it, my OECD colleagues and I in Finland asked, that headteachers could still teach as well as lead in their high performing educational system on the leading edge of the global economy? 'Because', one said, 'unlike the Anglo-Saxon countries, we do not have to spend our time responding to long, long lists of government initiatives that come from the top'.

It is important to acknowledge that Finland's integration of the information economy and the welfare state as a continuous narrative of legacy and progress that defines the national identity, is not without its blind spots. Having been an embattled and oppressed historical minority, Finland, in comparison to many other nations, remains a somewhat xenophobic society, suspicious of immigrants and outsiders, and threatened by those who challenge or diverge from the Finnish way of life (Castells and Himanen, 2002). Without a willingness to accommodate higher rates of immigration, the impending retirement of large proportions of Boomer employees (as many municipal administrators described it to us) will also increase the financial burden on the welfare state, and jeopardize the basic sustainability of Finland's economy and society that depends on it. Despite its resistance to educational testing, the eventual demographic and economic necessity for increased immigration will mean that teachers and schools will require some degree of objective data to help them understand and track the progress of a more diverse group of children who are not as easily or automatically included because they do not look (and sometimes act) like existing Finns, themselves.

Despite these difficulties, Finland contains essential lessons for societies that aspire, educationally and economically, to be successful and also sustainable knowledge societies – beyond an age of low-skill standardization. Building a future by wedding it to the past; supporting not only pedagogical change but also continuity; fostering strong connections between education and economic development without sacrifice to culture and creativity; raising standards by lifting the many rather than pushing a privileged few; connecting private prosperity to the public good; developing a highly qualified profession that brings about improvement through commitment, trust, cooperation and responsibility; embedding and embodying pedagogical leadership into almost every headteacher's weekly activity; and then emphasizing principles of professional and community-based rather than merely managerial accountability – these are just some of the signs about possible reform pathways to be taken from Finland's exceptional educational and economic theory of action as well as in action that has preceded and pre-empted Anglo-Saxon strategies of standardization.

Second wedding

In a project that my colleague Dennis Shirley and I evaluated in England that was initiated by the Specialist Schools and Academies Trust, more than 300 secondary schools that had experienced a dip in measured performance over one or two years, were networked with each other, provided with technical assistance in interpreting achievement results, given access to support from mentor schools, and offered a modest discretionary budget to spend in any way they chose provided it addressed the goals of the project (Hargreaves *et al.*, 2006). Participating schools were also provided with a practitioner-generated menu of proven strategies that bring about short, medium and long-term improvement. The initial results of the project are remarkable. More than two-thirds of these exceptionally energized schools improved at double the rate of the national average over 1–2 years through peer-networks which share experientially proven strategies and without the characteristic mandates and prescriptions that had typified English educational reforms before this point.

In this high-trust culture of schools-helping-schools, teachers and administrators praised the availability of flexible budgeting that was focused on improvement, gave plaudits to the network's conferences for their inspirational input and practical assistance, and greatly appreciated the availability (rather than forced imposition) of mentor schools and heads who would share practical strategies and advice with them in professionally respectful and reciprocal relationships.

Schools were especially successful in improving in the short term, stimulated by the menu of short-term strategies provided by experienced colleagues. Teachers and schools excitedly implemented and exchanged short-term change strategies such as providing students with test-taking strategies, paying past students to mentor existing ones, feeding students with lettuce, water and bananas before examination events, bringing in examiners and university teachers to share their marking schemes with students, collecting mobile phone numbers to contact students who were not showing up on examination days, introducing motivational speakers for vulnerable groups such as Year 11 boys, providing web-based support for home learning, and so on.

While these short-term strategies do not bring about deeper transformations of teaching and learning, they do give instant lifts in measured attainment – and in ways that largely avoid the unethical manipulation of test-score improvement within regimes of standardization (e.g. selecting only higher performing students, narrowing the curriculum, or teaching only to the test). Useful in their own right, these strategies have even greater value when they serve as confidence-building levers to further more challenging improvement in the longer term.

In the past era of standardization, imposed short-term targets and strategies have been experienced by many teachers as an unwanted professional intrusion – not so much in terms of their inhibiting effect on long-term transformation, but in terms of challenging the autonomy of teachers and distracting them from their own present-time preoccupations with the ways they prefer to teach (Goodson *et al.*, 2006). In other words, it is not so much the short-term nature of imposed targets, but the imposed as well as hurried nature of targets that do not belong to them, and threaten their autonomy, that have been the source of teachers' objections. The Raising Achievement/Transforming Learning project of the Specialist Schools and Academies Trust has conquered teachers' aversion to short-term measurable improvement through peer-supported, professionally validating and emotionally uplifting strategies that make real differences to the measured attainment of the students that teachers teach in the here-and-now.

Of course, this strategy too has its limitations. These are embedded in the very success and attractiveness of the short-term strategies that put teachers and schools at risk of being not merely attracted but almost addicted to them. The strategies are 'so gimmicky and great', as one headteacher put it, they can be used right away, and do not challenge or encourage teachers to question and revise their existing approaches to teaching and learning. The rush to raise achievement injects teachers with a repeated 'high' of short-term success. The result is a somewhat hyperactive culture of change that can be exhilarating but also draining and distracting.

> It's been the hardest year I've ever had, this year, because I've just been pulled in so many directions. I've really enjoyed doing the job, but you get a little bit of overload, because you go to conferences and you hear all of this stuff that's being done. And you think 'oh, we're not doing that! And how do we do? We need to go back and perhaps need to do some things.' So you get that pressure, that you think 'Oh, wow – are we as good as we really are? Should we really be here?' … The other schools are really, really high-flying schools. And then I have the dreadful pressures from the head of department. And guilt … And so I feel I've been very torn this year … And I'm rushing – just rushing from place to place.
>
> (Goodson *et al.*, 2006: 101)

In one of the conferences we observed, the majority of the strategies shared by heads and assistant heads at their tables were short-term. Not only are these strategies quick and easy to implement but they are quick and easy to explain – especially in a setting that has limited opportunity for extended conversations. In these 'speed dating' activities, as they were termed, in which heads were asked to engage, those of them who shared common interests frequently and excitedly exchanged ideas and then business cards just before they left.

The project's successful short-term strategies therefore currently seem to serve less like levers to longer term transformation than lids upon it. Part of the reason for this is that the project – successful as it is – remains embedded within a wider English national policy culture of short-term funding and proposal cycles, pressure for quick turnarounds and instant results, proliferation of multiple initiatives (initiativitis) and a performance-saturated language of standard-raising where teachers and headteachers refer not to engagement with learning but to the movement of students into the right achievement cells by 'targeting' the right groups, 'pushing' students harder, 'moving' them up, 'raising aspirations', 'holding people down' and 'getting a grip' on where youngsters are.

The power of professional collaboration is therefore harnessed to an intensifying short-term orientation that perpetuates 'a culture of presentism' (Hargreaves and Shirley, forthcoming) in which deeper, more creative learning and longer-term more sustainable goals are harder to discuss or develop. By embedding the energizing power of high-trust networks, within unchanged structures of high-stakes accountability, sustainable improvement is threatened by the short-term orientation – all the more so for it being immensely addictive and immediately effective. Yet the success of high-trust networks, school-to-school collaboration, discretionary budgeting, and a combination of proven insider experience with powerful outside-in evidence, points to a potential for an even greater transformation that has still to be unleashed. This alternative theory of action holds great promise if it can be separated from its overly-standardized antecedents of bureaucratic accountability and wedded instead to higher-level principles of accountability that can now be realized through professional and peer-driven forms of it.

Third wedding

In the latter half of the 1990s and beyond, the Canadian province of Ontario was the epitome of standardization. Its conservative agenda of diminished resources and reductions in teachers' preparation time, along with accelerating reform requirements that saw more legislation passed on educational change in eight years than in all the province's preceding history, exacted high costs on teaching and learning (Gidney, 1999). Research I conducted in the province with Ivor Goodson and other team members, exposed the pernicious impact of its policies (Hargreaves, 2003; Hargreaves and Goodson, 2006). Teachers complained of there being 'too many changes, too fast', 'too much, too quickly', 'just so much, so soon', to an extent that was 'too vast and just overwhelming.' They could never implement anything properly before other multiple demands surfaced, there was less time to plan and engage in professional development; they had no time to collaborate or learn, or even to return their students' assessed work on time. There was no 'time to reflect and plan', 'to understand the curriculum', 'learn how to implement' or 'catch up with professional reading'. Having to 'take shortcuts' meant that teachers did not 'always feel (they) could do (their) best work.' 'What a waste of my intelligence, creativity and leadership potential?' one teacher concluded.

In 2003, the Progressive Conservative Government was succeeded by Liberals and a Premier whose wife is a kindergarten teacher, with an agenda in which education took pride of place. Appointing a well-published educational policy scholar, Ben Levin, in the education ministry's most senior position, and being formally advised by international change consultant and former Dean of Education at the University of Toronto, Michael Fullan, the province set out a post-standardization strategy that wedded a continuing commitment to educational accountability with a range of initiatives that built capacity for improvement and provided professional support (Fullan, 2007).

A guiding coalition of regularly meeting politicians and advisors defined targets for improvement in tested literacy largely by the end of the sitting government's term of office, then set about mobilizing schools and districts to be able to deliver the targets. The climate for improvement was assisted significantly by increased financial investment and by bringing to an end a period of union-government conflict and signing an agreement for peace and stability which included commitment to reduced class sizes, restored preparation time and investment in early childhood education.

A Literacy and Numeracy Secretariat has driven the improvement of instruction with large teams of consultants and coaches working in schools with the support of quality materials to assist improvement while avoiding the worst excesses of overly-prescribed models that have characterized literacy strategies in the UK and US. Though the provincial targets are fixed, schools and districts are also encouraged to commit to and set their own.

Within this 'aspirational' framework, considerable emphasis is placed on capacity-building – the assumption or theory-in-action being that failure to improve is due to lack of capacity until there is overwhelming evidence to the contrary. The teacher unions have been allocated $5m to spend on professional development, successful practices are networked across schools, high quality support and intervention is provided for vulnerable groups, positive exemplars are identified so other schools can see what successful changes look like in action, and underperforming schools are encouraged (not compelled) to seek assistance from government support teams and higher performing peers.

As with the Specialist Schools and Academies Trust initiatives in the UK, lateral support across schools is also wedded to positive peer pressure as schools push each other to higher and higher standards of performance. Increasing transparency of evidence about school performance, that includes contextualized and value-added achievement measures, and that, in agreement with newspaper editors, is not published in hierarchical league tables of performance, adds to the impetus for this culture of positive pressure and increased support.

As with the other examples, this reform strategy has imperfections. The measurement-driven emphasis on literacy and numeracy seems to be a politically expedient import from England and Australia more than an educationally necessary improvement strategy given Ontario's already strikingly high performance in literacy on international tests (Hargreaves and Fink, 2006). This orientation can easily divert energy and attention from other important teaching and learning outcomes in creativity, arts, citizenship and education for sustainable development, for example. Despite the complementary emphasis on locally negotiated achievement targets, the continuing insistence on imposing politically arbitrary literacy targets also retains the likelihood that Enron-like responses will intrude into the system, not least in the form of accelerating, intensifying and increasingly frenetic interventions directed only at literacy and numeracy as the final target date approaches. Indeed, the New Democratic Party has criticized the province's test-creating body – the Educational Quality and Accountability office – for increasing scores by making test items progressively easier. Last, the system remains rather micromanaged and top-down, and, by its advocates' own admission, classroom teachers as well as community members therefore end up being the last to get engaged with the reform effort (Fullan, 2007). Ordinary classroom teachers remain the ultimate target of change rather than its integral partners and participants.

Notwithstanding these limitations – which can be easily remedied by widening the reform focus, developing professionally shared rather than politically imposed targets, and testing sample populations rather than administering a complete census for accountability purposes – the lessons to be learned from Ontario's theory of action about wedding intelligent accountability to increased investment, heightened trust and strengthened professional networking and support remain compelling.

And the funeral ...

Early in 2007, the US National Center for Education and the Economy released a report by its New Commission on the Skills of the American Workforce (2007). In its sequel to its 1990 Commission Report that drove much of the educational standards movement in the United States, this august body, that comprised two former Secretaries of State, several state and metropolitan Superintendents and Chancellors of Schools, along with an assortment of CEOs and union leaders, launched a blistering critique of the inability of the nation's underperforming and inflexible public education system to meet the opportunities and seize the challenges of the contemporary global economy.

Belatedly following (though scarcely acknowledging) the lead of international policy-steering organizations like OECD (2001b), finally heeding the long-standing prognostications of the late management guru and futurist Peter Drucker (1993), and eventually coming into congruence with the educational diagnoses of knowledge society analysts such as Phillip Schlechty (1990) and myself (Hargreaves, 2003), the Commission pointed to America's declining educational performance compared to other advanced industrial nations. The reasons for the decline, the Commission argued, were rooted in the relatively poor quality of the nation's teaching force, in a system that had become skewed by the excesses of narrowly tested standardization that was ill-equipped to produce the creativity and innovation necessary for a high-skill, high-wage workforce in a rapidly changing global economy.

In the words of the Commission, establishing economic advantage and leadership in the global economy

> depends on a deep vein of creativity that is constantly renewing itself, and on a myriad of people who can imagine how people can use things that have never been available before, create ingenious marketing and sales campaigns, write books, build furniture, make movies and imagine new kinds of software that will capture people's imaginations and become indispensable to millions.
> (New Commission of the Skills of the American Workforce, 2007: xviii)

Educationally, the Commission argued, these economic demands require much more than a conventionally and unimaginatively tested curriculum focusing on basic skills and factual memorization that prepare most people only for the routine work of low-skill economies which other nations or mere machines can now perform more cheaply than the US workforce. Success in a broader, deeper, more imaginative curriculum for all is called for instead:

> Strong skills in English, mathematics, technology and science as well as literature, history and the arts will be essential for many; beyond this, candidates will have to be comfortable with ideas and abstractions, good at both analysis and synthesis, creative and innovative, self-disciplined and well-organized, able to learn very quickly and work well as a member of a team and have the flexibility to adapt quickly to frequent changes in the labour market as the shifts in the economy become ever faster and more dramatic.
> (pp. xviii–xix)

The barriers to achieving these goals, which these American policy makers and advisers are eventually embracing later than almost every other developed nation, are, the Commission argues, considerable. They include poorly qualified teachers drawn from the middle to low ranks of college graduates; delayed starts and interventions for children who actually need the strongest support; the educational consequences of widening income and wealth disparities between rich and poor; a levelling off in recent gains in tested achievement; a predominance of easy courses and mediocre expectations that reinforce an under-charged adolescent work ethic; inflexible and ineffective systems of teacher compensation, bureaucratic regulation and educational testing; and insufficient attention to adult literacy and continuing education for those already in the workforce.

This ultimate acknowledgement of and even enthusiasm for an agenda of apparent post-standardization in education as an essential pre-requisite to increased competitiveness in the global economy is extremely welcome – as is the nation's essential engagement more generally with the economic and educational realities of the world around it.

It is hard not to concur with much of the Commission's educational and economic diagnosis, in this respect, given my own stance of analysis and advocacy on these very issues in my book *Teaching In The Knowledge Society* in 2003. Here, I pointed out that contemporary knowledge economies were 'stimulated and driven by creativity and ingenuity' (p. 1), with profound and pervasive consequences for public education:

> In the knowledge economy, wealth and prosperity depend on people's capacity to out-invent and outwit their competitors, to tune in to the desires and demands of the consumer market, and to change jobs or develop new skills as economic fluctuations and downturns require. In the knowledge economy, these capacities are the property not just of individuals but also of organizations. They depend on collective as well as individual intelligence. Knowledge-society organizations develop these capacities by providing their members with extensive opportunities for upskilling and re-training; by breaking down barriers to learning and communication and getting people to work in overlapping, flexible teams; (and) … by developing the 'social capital' of networks and relationships that provide people with extra support and further learning.
>
> Teaching for the knowledge society … involves cultivating these capacities in young people – developing deep cognitive learning, creativity and ingenuity among students; drawing on research, working in networks and teams, and pursuing continuous professional learning as teachers; and promoting problem-solving, risk taking, trust in the collaborative process, ability to cope with change and commitment to continuous improvement as organizations. (p. 3)

The diagnosis, in *Tough Choices or Tough Times*, of the need for new educational solutions in an innovative and accelerating economic environment apparently aligns with these of four years earlier. But actually, the Commission's case for educational reform addresses only half the educationally pressing issues posed by a climate of competitive globalization. Moreover, its proposed solutions and the theory-of-action on which they are based are diametrically opposed to not only my own preceding proposals, but also to those being adopted by almost all the developed world.

The push for post-standardized educational reform certainly comes from the demands of a creative and globally competitive economy, but for the New Commission, it is *only* about the economy. Yet *Teaching In The Knowledge Society* also argued that the knowledge economy is what Joseph Schumpeter called a force of creative distinction – its relentless pursuit of profit and self-interest leading to strain and fragmentation in the social order, as well as widening divisions between rich and poor countries and communities across the world. It was therefore also essential, I argued, that post-standardized reforms served the public social good as well as the private economic good – pulling back together what economic competitiveness sometimes tore apart by emphasizing the compassion, community, citizenship, democracy and cosmopolitan identity that would include, support and sustain people while everything changed around them. In this context, teaching has to be viewed not just as a skilled profession but also as a sacred vocation that, in Emile Durkheim's (1977) words, creates the generations of the future. Yet, apart from making references to child well-being and advocating integration of education with social and health services in vulnerable communities, the social and public goals of community and democracy are almost completely absent in the New Commission's report. In effect, the report proposes to develop only half the child and half the teacher – the half that suits the economy.

The effects of these omissions are equally evident in the Commission's proposals and in its underpinning theory-of-action for strategic reform. Its team visited and/or collected data about reform strategy from many countries (listed in the rear of the report). Yet, in the strategic recommendations section, of the 13 exemplars listed as side-bars, eight are from the United States, two (outdated ones) are from the UK and three are from Andres Schleicher, Head of OECD's Education Indicators and Analysis Division.

These narrowly selective citations are used to support the New Commission's questionable theory-of-action. This begins uncontroversially by proposing more and better educational access and provision for all before formal schooling begins, and in adult education after it ends, along with parallel support for the health and social service needs of children that are integrated into the school setting. Within school itself, a more challenging and broader curriculum is called for with agreed commitments to demanding exit exams in high school (allowing them to be taken when ready and as necessary until passed). This, it is proposed, will cultivate the harder work among students that is presumed to be lacking in schools' expectations and student culture. Higher calibre teachers whose job it is to deliver the more challenging curriculum will be attracted by higher starting salaries and more flexible pay and pension structures linked to performance rather than seniority. Competitiveness (though not overt selectiveness) among schools will be encouraged by detaching them from all but skeletal school district control, creating opportunities to innovate as well as network with other schools within and outside the immediate vicinity – with procedures for intervention and takeover being retained in cases of serious underperformance or crisis. In the New Commission's theory of action, all this will be achieved by reallocating rather than increasing financial resources.

Andreas Schleicher is cited in support of the argument for administrative decentralization and Britain bolsters the Commission's strategy on pay-structure-driven teacher supply. But otherwise, the way forward into the age of post-standardization is an intrinsically, inimically and individually American one that returns to and reinvents the very solutions of ruthless and rugged competitive individualism that in combination with the strictures of soulless standardization, have brought the US to its educational knees in the first place.

The striking and dangerous distortions in *Tough Choices or Tough Times?* are to be found not in its inclusions, but in its omissions. For instance, OECD's Schleicher (2004) has been quoted in the *Economist* as being a supporter not merely of administrative flexibility but also (within broader national frameworks) of greater curriculum flexibility that allows for increased creativity in the classroom. He has been vocally critical of Anglo-Saxon strategies of top-down interference, intervention and bureaucratic control – such as those centralized curriculum control demands perpetuated in the New Commission's report – that restrict this flexibility. Internationally, despite all the Commission's contacts and visits, there is no reference to the Netherlands (at the top of UNICEF's child well-being survey) and its massive moves towards curriculum decentralization in recent years. Nor is there any discussion of OECD's highest economic and educational performer, Finland, and its commitment to developing considerable portions of the curriculum at the level of the municipality. Omitted is any inclusion of China's commitment to more school-developed curriculum, or even to England's considerable easing up of its National Curriculum requirements over the past five years. Unlike most other countries, therefore, the US National Commission wants to retain its inflexible grip on curriculum content and standards, and devolve only the administrative means (or blame!) for delivering it.

Then there is the question of attracting higher calibre teachers. The New Commission revives the business sector's long-pursued strategies of restructured, performance-related pay along with defined contribution (rather than defined benefit) pension schemes, but it pays no heed to the high performing Canadians on the US's 'soft' northern border, who, apart from a brief neo-conservative interlude in the late 1990s, have simply paid their quality teachers well through higher redistributive taxation without the necessity of complex and 'competitive' restructurings. England can attract more teachers through front-loaded salary incentives but still has great difficulty retaining them and their leaders, especially in urban areas, where it is poor working conditions and excessive intervention that pulls teachers away, not a lack of extrinsic benefits. In teaching, research repeatedly shows that, beyond a basic point, teacher recruitment, retention and effectiveness are driven by status and quality of work–life factors, not strictly economic ones – with teachers valuing the freedom and support to develop and share their own strategies to meet the needs of their diverse students within smaller classes that will help them teach more effectively (Lortie, 1975; Nias, 1989). In a recent statewide survey, when California teachers were asked what factors would most attract them to teaching in challenging urban schools, the top priorities were not connected to increased pay or other extrinsic incentives, but to small class sizes and outstanding school principals that would enhance the conditions for teaching and learning in ways that supported their work. And the reason that Finland accords such high status to its high calibre teachers is because they are part of a great social and public mission that merits strong state investment and enhanced social esteem not because they are treated as competitive, performance-driven individuals who prepare their students only for the economy (Salhberg, 2006).

Reassuringly for taxpayers and the business community, *Tough Choices or Tough Times* proposes to allocate no further resources to educational renewal even given the severity of the crisis. Unlike the high performing Nordic countries, or its own northern neighbour, Canada, the United States does not advance a case and a cause for a strengthened welfare state in the spirit of the Johnsonian Great Society or the post-war New Deal, in which higher taxes among the wealthy channel increased resources for children and the public good into health, communities and social welfare (rather than merely integrating the entrails of what is currently provided on the school site). No imagination is applied to the demographic dividend that will return considerable resources to public education as the retiring Boomer generation at the end of the pay scale gives way to their younger and cheaper replacements at the other end. There is no plan like the UK's Building Schools for the Future Program, for a one-time investment that would remove the depressing legacy of dilapidated school buildings that plague many US urban school systems, to replace them with facilities that are at least equal to their suburban neighbours in ways that have proven impact on student success. And, shamefully, amid caustic criticisms of low expectations and young people's lack of commitment to hard work, there are no suggestions for eliminating or restructuring the part-time labour among teenagers that draws them away from their schoolwork to supply a cheap and flexible workforce for the service economy.

Tough Choices or Tough Times is really about no choice and not enough time. It is about business's and government's restriction and regulation of professional and community choice in what will become even tougher times. As the Commissioners make their final surge into more school choice and competition, into resurgent efforts to restructure teachers' pay, and into unabated emphases on centralized curriculum control – all of which fly in the face of contemporary international experience and opinion – they express and exude the fatal obstinacy of American exceptionalism in a nation whose business community's ideological obsession with economic and educational competition excludes any sense of social vision, any commitment to public good, any grasp of where, in human terms, the nation should and could be headed beyond what is strictly and restrictingly economic. In the end, *Tough Choices or Tough Times* requires change from everyone involved in education, apart from the business community that is behind it.

IV

This chapter has set out three ways to take the best from the standards and accountability movement, and wed it to the future agenda for economic and social change in a context of fast and fluid global activity. These three weddings of accountability to innovation, and social values to system coherence and future prosperity, provide good grounds for optimism about the possibilities for educational reform and social change in an age of post-standardization. But the US's most prominent options beyond the age of standardization promise only another surge of over-regulated curriculum and assessment, of increased appeals to competitive individualism in the ways in which these are delivered, and of bankrupt efforts to introduce more strategies of performance-related pay. This dangerous relationship between continued standardization and resurgent individualism is scarcely a wedding at all but more of a sordid, protracted and doomed affair that will only plunge America deeper into the educational abyss that it already occupies among developed nations. Is it too late for Americans to see it's not *just* the economy, stupid? Is it unreasonable to expect United States education not to improve alone, but to learn from other nations about the most productive ways forward? And is there any good argument why the wealthiest nation in the world should be coy or ashamed about investing more and better in all the nation's children and their future both within and outside the school system? Is there still time for there to be four weddings, and no funeral? That is the true challenge of innovation and creativity, of hope and destiny, that all Americans who care about their nation's future generation must now face.

References

Achinstein, B. and Ogawa, R. (2006) '(In)Fidelity: what the resistance of new teachers reveals about professional principles and prescriptive educational policies', *Harvard Educational Review*, Vol. 76, No. 1, pp. 30–63.

Aho, E., Pitkanen, K. and Sahlberg, P. (2006) *Policy Development and Reform Principles of Basic and Secondary Education in Finland since 1968*, Washington, DC: World Bank.

Barber, M. (2001) 'High expectations and standards for all, no matter what: creating a world class education service in England, in M. Fielding (ed.) *Taking Education Really Seriously: Four Years Hard Labour*, New York: Routledge/Falmer Press.

Batstone, D. (2003) *Saving the Corporate Soul and (Who Knows?) Maybe Your Own*, San Francisco, CA: Jossey-Bass.

Berliner, D. (2006) 'Our impoverished view of educational reform', *Teachers College Record*, Vol. 108, No. 6, pp. 949–95.

Castells, M. and Himanen, P. (2002) *The Information Society and the Welfare State: The Finnish Model*, Oxford: Oxford University Press.

Drucker, P. (1993) *Post-Capitalist Society*, New York, NY: HarperCollins.

Durkheim, E. (1977) *The Evolution of Educational Thought: Lectures on the Formation and Development of Secondary Education in France*, London: Routledge & Kegan Paul.

Durkheim, E. (2005) *The Evolution of Educational Thought: Lectures on the Formation and Development of Secondary Education in France*, New York, NY: Routledge Press.

Fullan, M. (2007) *Turnaround Leadership*, San Francisco, CA: Jossey-Bass.

Gidney, R. D. (1999) *From Hope to Harris: The Reshaping of Ontario's Schools*, Toronto: University of Toronto Press.

Gilbert, C. (2006) *2020 Vision: Report of the Teaching and Learning in 2020 Review Group*, London: Department for Education and Skills.

Goodson, I., Moore, S. and Hargreaves, A. (2006) 'Teacher nostalgia and the sustainability of reform: the generation and degeneration of teachers' missions, memory, and meaning', *Educational Administration Quarterly*, Vol. 42, pp. 42–61.

Haikio, M. (2002) *Nokia: The Inside Story*, Helsinki: Edita.

Hargreaves, A. (2003) *Teaching in the Knowledge Society: Education in the Age of Insecurity*, New York, NY: Teachers College Press.

Hargreaves, A. and Fink, D. (2006) *Sustainable Leadership*, San Francisco, CA: Jossey-Bass.

Hargreaves, A. and Goodson, I. (2004) *Change over Time? A Report of Educational Change over 30 Years in Eight U.S. and Canadian Schools*, Chicago, IL: Spencer Foundation.

Hargreaves, A. and Shaw, P. (2006) 'Knowledge and skills development in developing and transitional economies: an analysis of World Bank/DfID Knowledge and Skills for the Modern Economy Project', World Bank.

Hargreaves, A. and Shirley, D. (forthcoming) 'The persistence of presentism', *Teachers College Record*.

Hargreaves, A., Shirley, D., Evans, M., Johnson, C. and Riseman, D. (2006) *The Long and the Short of Raising Achievement: Final Report of the Evaluation of the 'Raising Achievement, Transforming Learning' Project of the UK Specialist Schools and Academies Trust*, Chestnut Hill: Boston College.

Hatch, T. (2002) 'When improvement programs collide', *Phi Delta Kappan*, Vol. 83, No. 8, pp. 626–39.

Lortie, D. C. (1975) *Schoolteacher: A Sociological Study*, Chicago, IL: University of Chicago Press.

McKibben, B. (2007) *Deep Economy: The Wealth of Communities and the Durable Future*, New York, NY: Times Books.

McNeil, L. (2000) *Contradictions of School Reform: Educational Costs of Standardization*, New York, NY: Routledge Press.

New Commission on the Skills of the American Workforce (2007) *Tough Choices or Tough Times*, San Francisco, CA: Wiley.

Nias, J. (1989) *Primary Teachers Talking*, London: Routledge.

OECD (2001a) *Knowledge and Skills for Life: First Results from the Program for International Student Assessment*, Paris: OOECD.

OECD (2001b) *Schooling for Tomorrow: What Schools for the Future?* Paris: OECD.

OECD (2004) *Innovation in the Knowledge Economy: Implications for Education and Learning*, Paris: OECD.

OECD (2005) *Teaching Matters*, Paris: OECD.

O'Neill, O. (2002) *A Question of Trust: The BBC Reith Lectures 2002*, Cambridge: Cambridge University Press.

Reich, R. (1999) *The Work of Nations: Preparing Ourselves for the 21st Century Capitalism*, New York, NY: Alfred A. Knopf.

Rifkin, J. (2004) *The European Dream: How Europe's Vision of the Future is Quietly Eclipsing the American Dream*, New York, NY: Jeremy P. Tarcher/Penguin.

Sahlberg, P. (2006) 'Education reform for raising economic competitiveness', *Journal of Educational Change*, Vol. 7, No. 4, pp. 221–65.

Schlechty, P. (1990) *Schools for the Twenty-first Century: Leadership Imperatives for Educational Reform*, San Francisco, CA: Jossey-Bass.

UNESCO (2005) *Asia-Pacific Regional Strategy for Education for Sustainable Development/ UN Decade of Education for Sustainable Development (2005–2014)*, Working Paper, Bangkok: UNESCO.

UNICEF (2007) *An Overview of Child Well-being in Rich Countries*, Florence: United Nations Children's Fund.

World Bank (2006) *World Development Report 2007: Development and the Next Generation*, Washington, DC: The World Bank; and New York, NY: Oxford University Press.

2 These may be good times

An argument that things are getting better

Ben Levin

Introduction

This chapter is an inquiry into the state of education policy at the present moment. Asking this question at an international level is an act of hubris; a judgement about even one country requires a large dollop of generalization so judgement at an international level is necessarily a highly uncertain undertaking. In particular, the United States seems to be an outlier to much of the argument in this paper, so US colleagues may have a different perspective than expressed here.

The title of this chapter is deliberately provocative. Academic work by its nature tends to have a critical focus, paying attention often to what is not going well. I intend, on the other hand, to suggest that we have seen some positive developments in education policy in many jurisdictions, and that when one takes into account the inevitable limitations of political processes many things in education, contrary to much current opinion, are going well. Schools are, within the limits of their capacity and institutional structures, working hard to improve performance, and governments are, within the limits of their capacity and constraints – which, I argue, are generally poorly understood – trying to improve that performance in ways that are often quite positive. In particular, equity issues have resurfaced as important education policy concerns, with significant attention to reducing achievement gaps among social groups. The chapter concludes with a discussion of some of the implications of a more positive view for the work of researchers and theorists.

To say that things are improving does not imply a Panglossian view that all is for the best in this best of all possible worlds of education. Education policy will continue to be an area of conflict. The forces that favour status quo approaches remain strong. Large numbers of students do not yet receive sufficient benefit from their education. Schools can be agents of inequity as well as equity. Governments do not always pay attention to what is most important nor do they always adopt policies that serve the real interests of students. Some features of the political process that tend to push policy in some undesirable directions are discussed a little later. Yet, despite these very real limitations, there are some grounds for optimism that were not in place a few years ago, and I call for a balanced assessment of what is going well and not so well.

This inquiry does not start from a neutral perspective. My job when this chapter was written as a senior civil servant involves working hard to implement what I consider to be a very positive government agenda for education. The Ontario government has an ambitious education agenda that is focused on improving a broad range of student outcomes while simultaneously reducing inequities in those outcomes and building public confidence in public education. Indeed, it was the chance to be part of this positive agenda that drew me back to government a couple of years ago. The task of managing and implementing that agenda certainly tends to focus me on the positives.

This is the third time I have been involved in managing education policy for Canadian provincial governments, experiences that have greatly shaped my understanding of the dynamics of education politics and policy. My other career as an academic and researcher has given me the opportunity to study education policy in quite a few other settings, and to examine closely much of the scholarly policy literature not just in education but in political studies generally. (As an aside, the separation of research and writing in education politics and economics from the larger disciplines of politics and economics has not served either education or its sister fields well. Important concepts and insights do not move back and forth in the way that they should.)

The contention that we are seeing an improvement in education policy focuses on three important areas in which recent developments seem to give promise of a more fruitful approach, drawing examples from several countries. These developments are:

- an increased emphasis on capacity-building as central to school and system improvement;
- greater attention to more equitable outcomes;
- a stronger role for research and evidence in shaping education policy and practice.

Each of these is now discussed more fully.

Capacity-building

In 2000, Fullan wrote about 'The Return of Large-Scale Reform'. Many people in schools were probably unaware that it had ever left the scene. The changes in New Zealand in the late 1980s and early 1990s, or in England from 1988 onwards, or in various Australian and US states throughout these decades, were large-scale by just about any definition. Some US states have gone through a major policy shift every few years since the early 1980s and only a few have had a consistent policy approach over a decade or longer. Many European countries also went through dramatic policy changes in education, and most of the states of the former Soviet Bloc faced colossal upheavals after 1989. Many of these changes were draconian in nature – beginning with the idea that school systems would have to be forced into change against the wishes of those working in them. The rhetoric, as well as the practice, in many places was highly critical of school systems and existing practice, and much of the change focused on new forms of governance (Levin, 2001).

Large-scale education change continues unabated – perhaps even intensified. However the policy climate in many countries since the start of the millennium or a little before is different because of the emphasis on helping the system improve to meet changing demands rather than simply demanding improvement and threatening dire results if it did not occur. No Child Left Behind (NCLB) in the United States is now an exception to larger trends in its apparent assumptions that improvement can be generated solely by changing information and related incentives. Most other education reform programmes embody a more sophisticated understanding of what is required.

The idea behind capacity building has grown out of gradual recognition that it is hard to change school practices even when there is broad agreement on what the new practices should be. Since the beginning of serious study of the implementation of new policies and programmes, literally hundreds of studies have shown how difficult it has been to get widespread use of new teaching methods or curricula. The idea behind capacity building is well expressed by Elmore:

> For each unit of performance I demand of you, I have an equal and reciprocal responsibility to provide you with a unit of capacity to produce that performance ... [schools] should not be expected to do those things for which [they] do not have capacity unless you [government] accept joint responsibility ... to create that capacity.
>
> (Elmore, 2004: 244–5)

What Elmore means by capacity here is the sustained work of changing daily systems and practices – instruction, curriculum, assessment, parent engagement, student engagement, leadership, and so on – to be more effective.

Fullan, another strong advocate for capacity-building as a key element in education policy, defines capacity building as

> ... the development and use of policies, strategies, and actions that increase the collective power or efficacy of whole groups, organizations, or systems to engage in continuous improvement for ongoing student learning. Typically, capacity-building synergizes three powerful collective phenomena:
> * New skills and dispositions
> * More focused and enhanced resources
> * Greater shared commitment, cohesion, and motivation.
>
> (Fullan, 2005b: 213)

Capacity-building is something much more extensive than training; it implies a developmental process that changes settings as well as the people working in them. So, for example, teachers may be asked to learn new ways of teaching reading but at the same time school processes, leadership, reporting and accountability processes also need to change so that the system as a whole takes on tasks in a new way.

These ideas are not just being expressed by academics in scholarly and professional journals. They are showing up increasingly in policy directions, albeit in different ways and to different extents.

Consider some examples. The Labour government elected in the UK did not reduce the amount of policy change from that of the previous Conservative government. Indeed, Labour introduced many more changes (Fielding, 2001). However, an important difference is that the changes under Labour were supported by increased funding and by an emphasis on helping schools do better, rather than just insisting that they do so (Hopkins, 2005). A prime example would be the development of the National Literacy and Numeracy Strategies (NLS and NNS) beginning in 1998, an initiative evaluated between 1998 and 2002 by a Canadian team of which I was a part (Earl *et al.*, 2003). The government created a substantial infrastructure to help teachers, schools and local authorities improve their literacy practices.

To be sure, not all of these steps were seen by teachers and schools as helpful. It is certainly possible to be critical of aspects of the NLS and NNS, and our team was. But even those who do not particularly like the Strategy would accept that the Department for Education and Skills (DfES) put considerable energy into supporting its implementation, including acting on many of the suggestions made by our evaluation team during our work. Indeed, the very act of commissioning an independent external evaluation of the initiative, with public reporting of its results, reflects a commitment by government to learn and adjust as the strategy developed. A variety of other later initiatives in Britain have also included substantial emphasis on elements of capacity and it would be fair to say that several initiatives, such as those around leadership development (see www.ncsl. org.uk) or networked learning communities (www.ncsl.org.uk/nlc), are primarily about capacity building.

The same increased attention to capacity building can be seen in other examples as well. In Canada, the Alberta Initiative on School Improvement (AISI) (McEwen *et al.*, 2005; www.education.gov.ab.ca/k_12/special/aisi/) puts substantial emphasis and money into helping school districts develop the will and capacity to support sustained improvement in student outcomes. Quebec has spent several years developing school success plans that require school-determined changes in roles and practices. The Manitoba K-S4 Agenda (Levin and Wiens, 2003; www.edu.gov.mb.ca/k12/agenda/index.html) sets out a six priority strategy that emphasizes professional learning for educators, research-based practice and sustained community involvement as key elements. Two major initiatives in Ontario also give capacity-building a central place. Our Literacy and Numeracy Strategy, launched in 2004, focuses on elementary school literacy and numeracy using an agenda that gives substantial emphasis to capacity building (www.edu. gov.on.ca/eng/literacynumeracy/moreinfo.html). The Strategy has put together target-setting, leadership development, professional development and community engagement in an integrated way, accompanied by a substantial investment in more teachers and improved on-the-job training. More recently we have adopted a similar approach to secondary school reform, with very substantial investments in staffing and training to accompany ambitious goals and requisite policy changes (www.edu.gov.on.ca/eng/parents/studentsuccess.html).

Several Australian states are also developing education programmes that take account of capacity, looking at approaches that push schools to plan for improvement and providing the supports needed to do so effectively. In Ireland Michael Fullan has also been involved in helping to generate support for capacity-building (2006). Governments in Scotland and Wales are also adopting approaches that focus on positive capacity. Sahlberg (2006), discussing Finland's highly successful system, also points to ongoing work to ensure teachers and school leaders are well trained and supported.

In the United States the arguments around the No Child Left Behind legislation are to a large extent around capacity-building. Many critics of the legislation (e.g. Elmore, 2004) contend that while its intentions are reasonable, it lacks the supports for schools that would allow the mandates to be met. In other words, there is insufficient capacity-building.

Talking about capacity building, and even committing to it, is not the same as knowing how to do it effectively and on a large scale but as noted in the later section of this paper on research, we are at least seeing some commitment to doing the necessary learning. Even among firm advocates of capacity building there is debate about how prescriptive the approach ought to be in regard to particular practices. The 'train the trainer' model that was widely used a few years ago is being replaced by an approach that relies more on school and district leadership teams. Indeed, the research on capacity building (Straw, 2004) is itself an exciting area of work.

A systematic approach to capacity-building also creates a requirement in federal or decentralized education systems to what Fullan in his latest book (2005a) calls system alignment – the need to have state or provincial, district and school approaches that are mutually reinforcing. It is clear from education policy history that where alignment does not exist between the various levels of the system, efforts at one level will be constantly thwarted or undone by contradictory pressures coming from another level. Many are the stories of exciting developments in schools that disappeared due to externally imposed changes in programmes or leadership, just as exciting developments in districts can be brought to nothing by requirements from the state or national government. In Ontario we are also learning that even the best provincial policies do not go far without effective support and leadership at the district and school level. So system alignment becomes a crucial part of a capacity-building strategy.

Here, too, there is increasing awareness by governments. Whereas a number of jurisdictions, including Canada, the UK and New Zealand, all moved power away in the 1980s from intermediate bodies such as school districts, each jurisdiction is now, in its own way, trying to create a more aligned system with intermediate structures of various kinds playing a more important role. These intermediate structures may include local authorities or other kinds of vehicles such as third party organizations with particular mandates in areas such as leadership development. Although there has been some recent empirical and conceptual work around the role of third parties (e.g. Honig, 2004), in general this area of creating system alignment as well as capacity remains underexplored both conceptually and empirically.

Attention to equity

Forty years ago the education policy world was rocked by the finding that the context around schools had more impact on student learning than did anything within schools. A fuller examination of the evidence to date suggests that while schools do not compensate for all the inequities in society, they do have some independent impact, though the size of that impact is hotly debated (see discussion in Levin, 2004b). It is also reasonably clear that with the right policies and practices the impact of schooling could be increased. However, an abundance of research demonstrates that socio-economic status (measured in various forms) remains the single most powerful predictor of all educational and other life outcomes.

In the 1960s a great deal of education reform was driven by a desire to improve the situation of those worst-off in society – the poor and marginalized minority groups. A decade or so later, dissatisfaction with the results of various policies and changes in the global context (such as increasing public sector deficits and higher oil prices) were part of a general move away from government intervention (Levin, 2001). For twenty years in many countries concerns about equity largely disappeared from policy agendas. Objectively, in countries including the United States, Canada, and England income inequality increased and child poverty worsened, with consequent bad results for schools as well as for society generally (Micklewright, 2003). The very word 'equity' was struck from the policy vocabulary in some jurisdictions.

In the last few years equity has returned to the policy agenda. To be sure, the arguments around equity are different from what they were forty years ago. They are less rooted in concerns about fundamental justice and more connected to the requirements of successful modern economies and societies. Equity is often seen as necessary to allow prosperity, as societies realize that they cannot be successful if large numbers of young people are not achieving satisfactory educational results. Still, there is once again recognition that large inequalities in outcomes based on socio-economic status, language, gender, ethnicity or immigration status are undesirable and need attention.

As a result, many governments have refocused attention on measures aimed at reducing what is called in the US 'the achievement gap'. The measures being used may be contentious – for example the extensive use of testing as a main accountability vehicle has many critics – but the intent of reducing disparities in outcomes is hard to criticize. Reading the US education literature one can be overwhelmed by the studies and reports looking at the achievement gap and assessing the many different strategies being attempted to reduce it; a query to Yahoo Search while writing this chapter turned up more than 5 million hits on the term 'achievement gap'. The debate in the United States over testing as having both positive and negative potential impacts on equity is well illustrated in Skrla and Scheurich (2004), an unusual venture in that the editors have deliberately sought to include critics of their own argument that large-scale testing can be central to greater equity.

The issues taken up for study by the OECD often serve as a barometer of changing interests in the international education policy world. In 1996 the OECD produced *Lifelong Learning for All* (OECD, 1996), a sophisticated statement about the importance of improved educational outcomes and of greater equity in those outcomes. Over the last 10 years the OECD has given substantial attention to equity in its education policy work, including in early childhood (OECD, 2001b), adult education (OECD, 2003), and school to work transitions (OECD, 2000). The analysis of the results of PISA has also given great prominence to equity, with countries being assessed as much on the size of their achievement gap as on their overall standing (OECD, 2001a; Sahlberg, 2006). In several countries, such as Germany and Hungary, the equity gaps identified in PISA have led to a fundamental rethinking of education policies. The OECD is currently conducting a project looking specifically at equity issues across the lifespan, a project for which I wrote a background paper (Levin, 2003).

One can readily point to policy attention to equity in many jurisdictions around the world. The Statement of Strategy for the Irish Department of Education and Science, 2003–2005 (which was still current as of May 2006 on the Department's website) lists equity and inclusion as a priority goal. New Zealand has produced some important analyses of the power of socio-economic status (Mayer, 2002), and the country's attention to greater success for the Maori people is one of the strongest efforts anywhere in the world to respond to the educational needs of indigenous peoples, who are in most places much less successful in the mainstream education system than are majority populations. The European Union and the Soros Foundation have been advocates of better education for Roma children, who have been badly treated by education systems across Europe (see www.errc.org and www.soros.org). In Canada many provinces have increased the policy attention to those populations performing less well, notably recent immigrants, Aboriginal people and people with disabilities (Levin, 2004b).

A further important international development concerns the growing recognition of respect for diversity and of finding new ways to reach minority and immigrant populations. Countries such as Ireland are now coping for the first time with the challenge of significant populations who do not speak the national language, while other countries that have long had immigrant populations are showing much greater interest in enhancing their educational success (Joshee, 2004).

As is the case with capacity building, just paying attention to an issue does not necessarily lead to success. Talking about an achievement gap is not the same as actually doing something to reduce that gap. Inequities have remained stubbornly resistant to previous educational efforts, in large part because inequity is produced in society as a whole, not only in schools (Anyon, 1997; Mortimore and Whitty, 2000). The ability of the school alone to change these entrenched patterns is clearly limited (Levin, 2003; Thrupp, 1999). At the same time, it would be fair to say that efforts to address inequities have been sporadic and limited in the range of strategies used. If one considers the possible options – ranging from support services in schools to early childhood development to changed instructional practice to community outreach to community economic and political development – the history of the last 35 years or so shows only quite limited efforts in many domains, with limited evaluation of impact (Levin, 2003; Gaskell and Levin, 2006). For example, Levin and Riffel (2000) found that schools were much more likely to focus on compensatory services for needy children than they were to examine overall instructional practices. An interesting body of US research has illustrated the poverty (ironically!) of instructional practice for high need children (e.g. Knapp *et al.*, 1995, Kozol, 2005). Although there is a long history of community development efforts in high poverty communities in many countries, these approaches are still not fundamental to equity efforts in schools.

It is too soon to claim any success from these latest efforts to improve equity of outcomes from education. The pressures in the other direction, such as those for greater privatization or increased differentiation of schools, remain powerful and are deeply rooted in broader structural and political inequalities in all societies. In many countries these broader social inequities are larger than they were twenty or thirty years ago, making the work of the schools even more difficult. At the same time, growing attention in education policy and discourse to equity as a vital goal is a step in a good direction. Not least, the many efforts being made in schools and with communities to improve the situation of the least well-off could help us learn more about what strategies may be most effective and how these approaches can be used more widely.

The role of research and evidence

A third heartening development in education policy has been the increasing interest in making more use of data and research to shape policy and practice. This interest is shared by governments, professionals and the public. The reasons for this shift in attention are multiple, including a more educated profession, more educated citizens, more reliable guidance as a result of more and better research, better tools for analysis, and others (Levin, 2004a). Even at the most basic political level, citizens and voters are clearly more interested than ever before in evidence about 'what works' – witness the massive use of the internet to disseminate and to locate policy alternatives in areas such as environment or health care. When voters want more evidence about policies, governments will feel themselves under pressure to provide it.

The OECD concluded a few years ago that the expenditure on research in education in all countries was typically well under 1% of education expenditures – a low investment relative to other knowledge-intensive sectors, especially health (OECD, 2002). Moreover, education research tends to be small scale and fragmented, generally lacking the programmatic approach – many studies looking at aspects of an issue of interest – that is most likely to yield significant cumulative evidence. Yet research is providing increasing guidance to policy and practice in a range of areas, from the importance of early childhood development to effective instruction in early reading to knowledge about the factors that shape the likelihood that students will graduate from high school.

One can therefore find much more evidence than was the case a decade or so ago of governments paying attention to research as they formulate policy positions. The OECD (2002) has identified effective use of research as a priority area for study and policy development, and the organization's own research is widely read in many countries, including its recent work on evidence-based policy. The policy results of PISA, mentioned earlier, have had powerful effects in many participating countries. To take a national example of attention to research, the UK Department for Education and Skills has commissioned public external evaluations of many of its most important policy initiatives and has used the results of these evaluations to reshape policies (Earl *et al.*, 2003). The British government has also funded the EPPI (Evidence-Informed Policy and Practice) Centre (eppi.ioe.ac.uk) to do syntheses of research in selected areas. Their work has a strong focus on implications for practice including involvement of users in choosing topics for synthesis, participating in the reviews, and preparing reports aimed at particular audiences such as teachers or school governors. The National Education Research Forum (NERF – www.nerf-uk.org) is a vehicle for broad discussion of research issues and is linked to some other creations, such as the Teacher Research Panel and the Teaching and Learning Research Program (www.tlrp.org) funded to promote quality research on teachers and teaching while also increasing the capacity of educators to find and use relevant research.

Canada substantially increased funding to research on education and learning in 2000, but more importantly, the Social Sciences and Humanities Research Council (www.sshrc.ca) put in place a substantial effort around what it called 'knowledge mobilization', or better efforts to link research to policy. Canada has also created and funded the Canadian Council on Learning (www.ccl-cca.ca) as an independent organization with a specific mandate to bring research and evidence to bear more strongly on all areas of education policy and practice.

In the United States the role of research remains highly controversial as there is concern about whether the current administration's initiatives in this area are too narrow (Shavelson and Towne, 2002) but the debate in the US is itself a sign that many people, including powerful political actors, see research as playing an important role in shaping education policy. The US also has some longstanding practices and organizations devoted to research impact, such as the ERIC system and a number of large, publicly-funded research centres that have research impact as an important part of their mandate. National agencies such as the Council of Chief State School Officers, the ASCD, the National Governors Association and the American Educational Research Association (AERA) have been involved with efforts to strengthen the impact of research in education.

The increased role of research is not only important for governments, but also for schools. Quite a few recent books (e.g. Holcomb, 1999; Bernhardt, 2003) and other learning materials, as well as many workshops and other projects show a growing interest by schools in using data to support school improvement. There has been a sea change in the extent to which schools now generate and use information on student outcomes as part of their planning and assessment. School leaders – principals and superintendents – are also more interested in research, as shown by sales of books that draw implications from research (e.g. Marzano, 2003), participation in workshops, and membership in research-oriented organizations such as ASCD or Phi Delta Kappan. Surveys of educators show that research plays an important role in shaping their ideas about their work (Biddle and Saha, 2002; Figgis *et al.*, 2000).

Still, there are challenges. While educators' interest in research has increased, very few schools or districts have much capacity to find, disseminate and use relevant research no matter what their level of interest. Thus one of the main research initiatives in Ontario – as in a number of other jurisdictions – is to increase the capacity of districts and schools to make use of available evidence, both in terms of data on students and in access to research findings more broadly.

Research is not suddenly – or even gradually – going to become the main determinant of education policy and practice. Political processes will continue to dominate policy-making, as they should in a democracy. Moreover, research often reaches educators and governments through results as reported by the media or by third parties of various kinds, and a great deal of third party research or interpretation is driven by partisan agendas of various kinds. The interplay of ideas through political processes is an important part of democratic governance (Lindblom, 1990; Stone, 1997). However, one result of multiple voices is that neither user organizations nor the public know what sources to turn to, what sources to trust, or how to identify high quality work, leading to the view that 'you can prove anything with research'. Still, it would be hard to argue that greater attention to research and evidence is other than a positive development.

The role of critique and the limitations of government

I take the view that all of these developments are positive for education and deserve support. Nor are they the only positive developments in education policy one might mention. To cite a few others, many jurisdictions have increased their investment in education, efforts are being made to create stronger links with families and communities, and working conditions and wages for teachers have improved in a number of countries in recognition of the critical role that teachers play (Santiago, 2005).

I believe we are at a positive moment in education, where the potential exists to make significant progress towards an effective education for all students. In this light it is important to examine the responsibility of researchers and theorists. Critique is and must remain an important part of what academics do. It is a responsibility that goes with the privilege of academic freedom, and constructive, independent critique of social policy is a necessity for a democratic society. Academic work plays an essential role in this regard.

At the same time, academic work cannot be only about critique. As researchers we have a responsibility to acknowledge what is positive and useful as well as what is negative and harmful. Many academics in education see themselves unabashedly as professional educators or advocates for educators. The concerns and views of educators are important; they deserve real attention from all parties to the educational enterprise. As already noted, many countries have found that it is impossible to build educational improvement without paying careful attention to support for teachers. The views of teachers are not, however, the only views that matter. The educational profession has much to be proud of yet we must also acknowledge that schools have not always been instruments of liberation or equity, and that professional educators have sometimes stood in the way of positive developments.

An important consideration is that theorists are often ignorant about the realities and limitations facing governments. Thus we often hear calls for political will, as if the failure of governments to do what we thought best was a kind of cowardice. One might come to the conclusion that political will means asking governments to do what we like even though it is unpopular. Of course when governments do what they think best and we dislike it, we call it 'ideology', not 'political will'.

I have described the limitations on governments in more detail elsewhere (Hopkins and Levin, 2000; Levin, 2005). Here I will only say that governments can only do what citizens and voters are willing to support. Governments are not suddenly going to turn into organizations that are only concerned about empirical evidence and long-term consequences, because that would not be consistent with the realities of our political processes (Stone, 1997). Politics will remain a difficult, contentious, sometimes ugly enterprise. Governments are, and have to be, concerned with what voters think even if the voters are wrong; as my former Premier, Gary Doer, said to me when I was deputy minister in Manitoba, 'What you're arguing may be true, Ben, but it's not what people believe'. A government that ignores what people believe will find itself out of office and unable to make any advances in policy – what was described in the *Yes, Minister* television series as 'courage'.

It is not the job of researchers to be apologists for any government or any political programmatic. Every policy direction can be improved, and someone needs to be pointing out what those improvements could be. Part of the responsibility of academics is to try to shape the public debate and to deepen public understanding. For those commenting on public policy there is also an obligation, I would argue, to take into account (which does not mean accepting uncritically) political realities, public views of what is acceptable, and institutional capacity to change.

Conclusion

As indicated at the outset of this chapter, despite the significant improvements discussed here, nobody should think we are about to enter some kind of paradise of education policy in which harmony and clear, widely shared direction will prevail. Education will continue to be subject to considerable and sometimes very heated debate because people want many different things from our schools. Even when we agree on goals, we may disagree on how they can best be achieved. Because education is so important – because our children are so important – educational issues will engage people's feelings and commitments strongly, whether in individual schools or in regard to national policy. Some developments will be positive, and others negative (and which are seen as which will depend on people's beliefs and interests). Researchers play an important role in illuminating these issues and fostering informed debate. My plea is that our efforts give due consideration to the positive elements of the present situation, and to the real limitations on what can be done at any given moment.

References

Anyon, J. (1997) *Ghetto Schooling*, New York: Teachers College Press.

Bernhardt, V. (2003) *Data Analysis for Continuous School Improvement*, Larchmont, NY: Eye on Education.

Biddle, B. and Saha, L. (2002) *The Untested Accusation: Principals, Research Knowledge, and Policy Making in Schools*, Westport, CT: Ablex.

Earl, L., Watson, N., Levin, B., Leithwood, K., Fullan, M. and Torrance, N. (2003) 'Watching and learning 3: final report of the OISE/UT evaluation of the implementation of the National Literacy and Numeracy Strategies', prepared for the Department for Education and Skills, England, available online at http://www.standards.dfes.gov.uk/literacy/publications/.

Elmore, R. (2004) *School Reform from the Inside Out*, Cambridge, MA: Harvard University Press.

Fielding, M. (ed.) (2001) *Taking Education Really Seriously: Four Years Hard Labour*, London: RoutledgeFalmer.

Figgis, J., Zubrick, A., Butorac, A. and Alderson, A. (2000) 'Backtracking practices and policies to research', in *The Impact of Educational Research*, Canberra, Department of Education, Training and Youth Affairs, pp. 279–374.

Fullan, M. (2000) 'The return of large-scale reform', *Journal of Educational Change*, Vol. 1, No. 1, pp. 5–28.

Fullan, M. (2005a) *Leadership and Sustainability*, Thousand Oaks, CA: Corwin Press; Toronto: Ontario Principals' Council.

Fullan, M. (2005b) 'Professional learning communities writ large', in R. DuFour, R. Eaker and R. Dufour (eds) *On Common Ground: The Power of Professional Learning Communities*, Bloomington, IN: National Educational Services, pp. 209–23.

Fullan, M. (2006) 'Quality leadership=quality learning', paper prepared for the Irish Primary Principals' Network.

Gaskell, J. and Levin, B. (2006) 'What shapes inner-city education policy?', paper presented to the Canadian Society for the Study of Education, Toronto, May.

Holcomb, E. (1999) *Getting Excited About Data*, Thousand Oaks, CA: Corwin.

Honig, M. (2004) 'The new middle management: intermediary organizations in education policy implementation', *Educational Evaluation and Policy Analysis*, Spring, Vol 26, No. 1, pp. 65–87.

Hopkins, D. (2005) 'Every school a great school: meeting the challenge of large scale, long term educational reform', paper for The London Centre for Leadership in Learning,

London Institute of Education, June 2005, published by the Specialist Schools Trust in the iNet series.

Hopkins, D. and Levin, B. (2000) 'Government policy and school improvement', *School Leadership and Management*, Vol. 20, No. 1, pp. 15–30.

Joshee, R. (2004) 'Citizenship and multicultural education in Canada: from assimilation to social cohesion', in J.A. Banks (ed.) *Diversity and Citizenship Education: Global Perspectives*, San Francisco, CA: Jossey-Bass, pp. 127–56

Knapp, M., Shields, P. and Turnbull, B. (1995) 'Academic challenge in high-poverty classrooms', *Phi Delta Kappan*, Vol. 76, No. 10, pp. 770–6.

Kozol, J. (2005) *The Shame of the Nation*, New York: Crown.

Levin, B. (2001) *Reforming Education: From Origins to Outcomes*, London: Routlege Falmer.

Levin, B. (2003) 'Approaches to equity in policy for lifelong learning', paper prepared for the OECD, Paris, available online at http://www.home.oise.utoronto.ca/~blevin.

Levin, B. (2004a) 'Making research in education matter more', *Education Policy Analysis Archives*, Epaa.asu.edu/epaa, Vol. 12, No. 56.

Levin, B. (2004b) 'Students at risk: a review of research', report to The Learning Partnership, available online at http://www.thelearningpartnership.ca.

Levin, B. (2005) *Governing Eeducation,* Toronto: University of Toronto Press.

Levin, B. and Riffel, J. (2000) 'Current and potential school system responses to poverty', *Canadian Public Policy*, Vol. 26, No. 2, pp. 183–96.

Levin, B. and Wiens, J. (2003) 'There is another way', *Phi Delta Kappan*, Vol. 84, No. 9, May, pp. 658–64.

Lindblom, C. (1990) *Inquiry and Change*, New Haven, CT: Yale University Press.

McEwen, N., Sakyi, A. and Millard, D. (2005) 'Improving student learning through diversity and accountability: Lessons from the Alberta Initiative for School Improvement', paper presented to the American Educational Research Association, Montreal, April.

Marzano, R. (2003) *What Works in Schools: Translating Research into Action*, Alexandria, VA: ASCD.

Mayer, S. (2002) *The Impact of Parental Income on Children's Outcomes*, Wellington: New Zealand Ministry of Social Development, available online at http://www.msd.govt.nz.

Micklewright, J. (2003) 'Child poverty in English-speaking countries', Innocenti working paper #94, Florence: UNICEF Innocenti Research Centre.

Mortimore, P. and Whitty, G. (2000) 'Can school improvement overcome the effects of disadvantage?', in T. Cox (ed.) *Combating Educational Disadvantage*, London: Falmer, pp. 156–76.

OECD (1996) *Lifelong Learning for All*, Paris: OECD.

OECD (2000) *From Initial Education to Working Life: Making Transitions Work*, Paris: OECD.

OECD (2001a) *Knowledge and Skills for Life: First Results from PISA 2000*, Paris: OECD.

OECD (2001b) *Starting Strong: Early Childhood Education and Care*, Paris: OECD.

OECD (2002) 'Knowledge management in education and learning', report prepared for the *Oxford Forum*, March.

OECD (2003) *Beyond Rhetoric: Adult Learning Policies and Practices*, Paris: OECD.

Sahlberg, P. (2006) 'Education policies for raising student learning: the Finnish approach', paper presented to the American Educational Research Association, San Francisco, April.

Santiago, P. (2005) 'The teaching workforce: meeting aspirations and enhancing motivation', in S. Field (ed.) *Educational Policy Analysis*, Paris: OECD.

Shavelson, R. and Towne, L. (eds) (2002) *Scientific Research in Education*, Washington, DC: National Academy Press.

Skrla, L. and Scheurich, J. (eds) (2004) *Educational Equity and Accountability*, New York: RoutledgeFalmer.

Stone, D. (1997) *Policy Paradox*, New York: Norton.

Straw, E. (2004) *The Dead Generalist: Reforming the Civil Service and Public Services*, London: Demos.

Thrupp, M. (1999) *Schools Making a Difference: Let's be Realistic*, Buckingham: Open University Press.

3 The plate tectonics of educational change in Ireland

Consequences for research quality, policy and practice?

Ciaran Sugrue

Introduction

It has become commonplace to assert that we are living in a time of unprecedented change both in terms of extent and pace. Several Irish titles attest to this reality (Peillon and Slater, 1998; Corcoran and Peillon, 2002; Peillon and Corcoran, 2004; Keohane and Kuhling, 2004). Perhaps the one that captures this most dramatically, *Changed Utterly*, a title borrowed from W. B. Yeats' poem (Easter 1916), asserts:

> Two social processes have partly overlapped in Ireland in the last two decades: one is a general modernisation, with its greater individualism and secularism; and the other is a tremendous surge in economic growth, with its spiralling materialism, consumerism and increased choice.
>
> (O'Connell, 2001: 7)

The 'terrible beauty' that has been spawned by the 'Celtic Tiger' economy elicits the following warning:

> For real change to occur in people's values, economic growth is important but just as important is the context and manner in which the growth occurs. Without the guarantee of security and fairness, our values will be overshadowed by fear and materialist obsession. Under those circumstances, the Irish psyche will experience change, but not transformation.
>
> (O'Connell, 2001: 188)

Both statements recognise implicitly that in times of social and economic upheaval, individuals' value systems, cherished beliefs and taken-for-granted mores are challenged and held up to critical scrutiny. In an educational reform context, the kind of radical transformations identified by O'Connell rarely work; evolution rather than revolution is strongly recommended (Fullan, 1991, 2005, 2003; Sarason, 1990, 1996). Conservative forces frequently seek to imprison the future in the past, while more radical voices sometimes invoke a kind of historical amnesia in an attempt to set the future adrift from past and present. Set adrift from the anchoring effects of cultural glue, what many describe as the 'essential self' or 'authentic' self (Taylor, 1991, 1992), potentially we become the 'empty self' only to be endlessly exploited and exploitable by rampant consumerism, victims of the individualism so trumpeted by the market. International echoes of this discourse are readily detectable in the work of Sennett (2006: 115) when he suggests that:

> Cutting-edge firms and flexible organisations need people who can learn new skills rather than cling to old competencies. The dynamic organisation emphasises the ability to processs and interpret changing bodies of information and practice.

When amnesia becomes a valued asset, fear and insecurity become prevalent (Furedi, 2002; Bauman, 2000). However, in the context of the present chapter, it is more significant to recognise the shaping influence of context, national history and international 'social movements' and how these are melded within national reform rhetorics; how they become significant in shaping and reshaping institutional as well as policy trajectories. It is the interstices of ongoing and emergent systemic plate tectonics that largely determine the nature and quality of educational research, and its capacity to influence and lend direction to educational reforms. An important purpose of this chapter is to connect recent surface change to underlying structures, to provide more perspective while seeking also to indicate some of the more enduring as well as ephemeral aspects of the field of education, while also seeking to harvest some insights that may provide shaping influences on future research agendas, as well as lend some generative thinking to policy and practice.

Another frequently asserted contemporary commonplace, articulated by our policy-making masters, experts and think tanks, is that we are already in the process of building a new kind of society – the knowledge society. In order to further this agenda we have to invest as never before in the knowledge economy. Consequently, the education system is immediately harnessed as a major resource in building such a future, but often in such circumstances economy takes precedence over society. For, as Hargreaves (2003: xvi) succinctly puts it:

> The knowledge economy primarily serves the private good. The knowledge society also encompasses the public good. Our schools have to prepare people for both of them.

Consequently, teachers are faced with an enormous challenge; underfunded they are likely to become 'the drones and clones of policy makers' anemic ambitions for what underfunded systems can achieve' (p. xvii), but with appropriate resourcing and professional support the teaching profession has the potential to 'reach far beyond the technical tasks of producing acceptable tests results, to pursuing teaching as a life-shaping, world-changing social mission ...'.

As teacher educators, researchers, policy analysts, postgraduate students, teachers and citizens with a social conscience, we have become increasingly aware over the past decade in particular of the extent of this major fault line of economy v. society. While I am against this bifurcation, educational research has become increasingly polarised in an ideological manner around the shaping of the future. In short, the 'paradigm wars'[1] have taken on a more virulent adversarial language in the battle for the future of education, whereby the hearts and minds of the public are fodder to be accumulated. This polarisation is frequently reduced to a war about test scores as sole criterion of a sound education. In these circumstances, as the battle lines are drawn in relation to the shape of the future, the nature and quality of educational research has become another frontier on which to skirmish.

The paradigm wars that have been waged on both sides of the Atlantic have largely passed us by here in Ireland in the sense that there has been little if any public discourse on research quality. Nevertheless, we have not been insulated from the ideological struggles that are a very definite subterranean influence on more public pronouncements, and information flows. The case of Ireland therefore becomes instructive in gaining additional understanding on how international discourses are 'refracted' within national arenas, while simultaneously illustrating the manner in which the language of reform insinuates itself into policy documents, thus altering the educational landscape in identifiable ways (Goodson, 2004).

The chapter is in four parts. First, the contours of the paradigm wars and their more recent manifestations are identified as a means of framing subsequent analysis of selected published research in the Irish context. Contemporary debates are briefly situated within the field of educational research at the turn of the twentieth century, a legacy that continues to cast lengthy shadows on current discourses. Second, an additional element of the framing includes attention to changing educational structures in the Irish context since the 1990s. This is described as the plate tectonics of the educational landscape, its deep structures as well as its more recent surface changes, and the importance of such changes for the nature and conduct of research. Third, against this general international and national backdrop, selected recently published reports are critically analysed through the dual lens articulated in the previous sections. The purpose of this analysis is to comment on the nature and quality of research in the Irish setting, to situate it within international discourses and to illuminate the state of educational research, while indicating simultaneously how changing educational structures, in the absence of a clearly articulated educational research policy and attendant ethics, has potential to undermine rather than enhance public policy-making and, in the process, traditions of democratic schooling. This account is partial and not exhaustive, but sufficient to illustrate and illuminate the surface and deep structures of education and their consequences for the quality or research, and, by implication, the quality of education. Fourth, discussion focuses on 'lessons learnt' and their possible shaping influences on the future of educational research in Ireland both from a policy and practice perspective, mindful of educational change internationally, and the role of researchers in this 'glocal' setting (Beck, 2000).

Theoretical perspectives – mapping the contours of paradigm wars

During the past decade in particular, and on both sides of the Atlantic, there has been virulent and often polarised debates about the quality of educational research, the necessity to improve it, and, in the process, determine the kinds of research that will be given the seal of approval, especially by governments and funding agencies. Given current globalisation, new technologies and market forces, turbulence in the field of education is hardly surprising. However, at such critical junctures, or dis-junctures, there is a strong tendency and temptation to allow ideology to triumph over evidence, to determine that the prejudices of yesteryear hold sway in preference to the warrants of contemporary research. Conservative voices seek to shape the future in the mould of the past, to envelop it in what Giddens (1991) describes as a 'protective cocoon', when it is preferable and necessary to recognise that taking leave of the past requires both risk-taking and imagination. He argues that we need to recognise the reality of globalisation, since 'it is not incidental to our lives today. It is a shift in our very life circumstances. It is the way we live now' (Giddens, 2002: 19).

By late nineteenth and early twentieth century, educational research was still very much an emergent field; initially 'quite shapeless circa 1890 and quite well shaped by roughly 1920. By then educational research had become more technical than liberal' (Condliffe Lagemann, 2000: 236). At the turn of the twentieth century, as the titans Thorndike and Dewey 'squared off' it is generally accepted that the former 'won', thus progressive education was consigned to the 'outside', a minority pursuit. More importantly, in the context of this chapter, Thorndike's prolific writing and his captive audience in Teachers College enabled him to dominate the market. His psychology was narrowly behaviouristic, decidedly quantitative in orientation and he was committed to 'deep-seated genetic determinism' (Condliffe Lageman, 2000: 234–5; Labaree, 2004: 193). Similarly, Labaree asserts that 'educational traditionalists have already won ... and the tests drive the classroom process'.

While this sweeping generalisation hides considerable variation, and not every reader would concur with the polarisation of 'lost' and 'won', his analysis does contribute to an either/or, them and us confrontational approach not conducive to more sustained and reflective dialogue. From the perspective of the present analysis, however, both Labaree and Condliffe Lagemann share the view that the lowly position of educational research, the educational professoriate[2] and its marginalisation within the academy can be attributed, in part at least, to the social-class origins of teachers, its domination by females and consequent lack of status, and the relative marginalisation of education from other disciplines within the academy as well as the particular trajectory of colleges of education in this country (see Sugrue, 2006). In the Irish context, consistent with other jurisdictions, the vast majority of those in teacher education and educational research are former classroom teachers. Such realities have led to more contemporary criticisms of educational research as lacking in appropriate training, lack of rigour and too subject to fashion.

The 1960s and 1970s, in the postwar optimistic period of economic expansion and growth of welfare state in Western Europe in particular (Esping-Andersen, 2000; Esping-Andersen *et al.*, 2002) bore witness to a period of significant ferment in education and educational research. As 'new' sociology emerged (see Young, 1971), as critique of the modernist agenda gave way to more poststructuralist and postmodernist perspectives, the field of educational research became more fractured as a reflection of this more expansionist, less conformist world. This fresh ferment was extended and enriched by an emergent feminist critique of positivistic dominance of the field (see, for example, hooks, 1994; Casey, 1993). Thus, the early twentieth-century shake down between the empiricist instrumentalists and the liberal progressives became transmogrified into a new battleground that was generally categorised as the 'paradigm wars' in educational research. While this was conceptualised by Lincoln and Guba (1985) as two competing world views – positivist and postpositivist or naturalistic – in more recent times this 'war' has been replaced by a more pragmatic rapprochement between these competing traditions and generally referred to as mixed methods (Creswell, 2003). However, this gloss on matters has tended to paper over the cracks, disputes, disagreements and ideological differences. Consequently, it is necessary and appropriate briefly to delve into the more recent debates that have raged on both sides of the Atlantic and recorded in the pages of *Educational Researcher* (*ER*) and *British Educational Research Journal* (*BERJ*) in particular.

In his celebrated address to the AERA annual conference in San Francisco in 1988, and consistent with the argument advanced above, Gage suggested that 'the attempt to lay a scientific basis for the art of teaching had failed ... the search for scientifically grounded ways to understand and improve teaching had led nowhere' (Gage, 1989: 135–6). Gage's imaginatively constructed paper projected forward twenty years to 2009, a year that is now almost upon us. He begins with the critiques provided in the late 1980s of the dominant positivistic paradigm, and on this basis ventures to speculate three alternative possibilities for the future of educational research. Table 3.1 briefly summarises the critique, and the subsequent discussion paints the scenarios that he imagined as alternative futures for educational research.

From a contemporary vantage point it is easy to understand the legitimacy of these critiques, to engage with them, and to locate and position ourselves within the general field of educational research. In effect, the critiques are premised on differing assumptions about the nature and purpose of research, and are underpinned also by differing sets of beliefs and values that are also impossible to separate from the research endeavour. What Gage could not have predicted in 1988–1989 was how dramatically the world would change in the intervening two decades. In fact one such seismic shift was to occur before the end of 1989 – the fall of the Berlin Wall; thus, rather like the walls of Jericho all those centuries earlier, the Cold War ended dramatically, and the titanic struggle between Communism and Capitalism was allegedly over – in this instance, Capitalism rather than Thorndike

Table 3.1 Paradigm wars: critique of the field of educational research – 1989

Anti-naturalist critique	Interpretivist critique	Critical theorists critique
• Human affairs cannot be studied with the scientific methods used to study the natural world.	• ... the standard researchers had grievously neglected meaning-perspectives because they tried to observe behaviour (not action, defined as behaviour plus meaning) objectively.	• ... what is needed is a reconsideration of the whole structure of society in which education, including teaching, goes on.
• There are no such 'billard-ball' causal connections between teacher behaviour and student learning.	• [alternatively] interpretative research on teaching ... would examine the conditions of meaning created by students and teachers as a basis for explaining differences among students in their achievement and morale. (pp. 136–7)	• ... human beings can change social structure; they need not be dominated by it.
• ... we should search for the kind of insight that historians, moral philosophers, novelists, artists and literary critics can provide. (p. 136)		• Schools ... must be the scenes of the necessary struggles for power. Educational research ought at least to be aware of the possibility of such struggles ... to enter into them on the side of the oppressed so as to reconstruct education and society at large for the achievement of greater social justice. (pp. 138–9)

Source: Adapted from Gage (1989)

had won! However, his ghost was lurking in the rubble, to be given new life by an unfettered neo-liberal agenda, aided and facilitated by emergent new technologies – what Castells (2000: 339) calls 'the globalisation of economy, technology and communication'. However, in the first instance, it is worth paying some attention to the possible futures that Gage imagined in 1989.

Paradigm wars and their aftermath – possible futures (1989–2009)

In the first instance, Gage suggested that 'scientific research' 'ground to a halt' (p. 139) and, as a consequence, graduate programmes in testing and measurement all but disappeared, funding became impossible to secure, publications of this genre of research virtually ceased, and instead teachers became researchers, ethnographic work contributed incremental changes that made considerable differences. He concludes: 'some of the fondest hopes of the interpretative students of classroom phenomena were realised' (1989: 140). Similarly, critical theorists had their day in the sun to the extent that:

> ... pupils were sensitised to the ways in which their previous history courses had neglected almost everything done by people who were not white men, political leaders, military heroes, or industrialists ... . The hard cruel facts about what had been done to slaves, striking coal miners, union organizers, radical journalists and left-wing political parties began to get equal time in the social studies classes of the nation. (p. 140)

While some might suggest that there are glimpses of this rather utopian vision being enacted within Social Environmental and Scientific Education (SESE) in Irish primary schools, or in Civic, Social and Political Education (CSPE) in the secondary sector, there may be a more general realisation, at least in part contributed by the critical tradition, that education is fundamentally a political engagement, even if we choose to behave as if this were not the case.

The third scenario he painted, and probably the more realistic of the three, was that there would be a rapprochement between competing paradigms, and some acceptance from a pragmatic perspective that different approaches had some legitimacy, depending how research questions are actually framed. Such pragmatism was manifest in the following conclusions that:

> ... it was finally understood that nothing about objective-quantitative research precluded the description and analysis of classroom processes within interpretative-qualitative methods. (p. 142)

or, alternatively that:

> ... scientific methods could be used for purposes other than building a science – a network of laws that would hold forever everywhere ... [but] could be used for 'piecemeal social engineering' as envisioned by Karl Popper ... for making 'small adjustments and readjustments which can be continually improved upon'. (p. 143)

I concur with the more recent conclusion by Erican and Roth (2006: 14–15) that a focus on 'certain types of data collection', determined on ideological grounds is much more likely to result in 'inappropriate inferences' being drawn from such efforts, when it is potentially more fruitful to focus 'on the construction of good research questions and conducting good research'.

However, as several lessons in the intervening years have suggested, cessation of hostilities *per se* do not resolve conflicts or guarantee a peace. Rather, depending on external conditions and policy contexts, conditions are created that enable the resurgence and dominance of particular paradigms, and their particular ways of viewing the world. In the context of the analysis presented here, it is as important to identify these external influences as it is to indicate the contours of internal disagreements and disputes within the field of educational research.

Paradigm wars – most recent outbreak – 1996 and after

David Hargreaves sparked the most recent outbreak of a bush war in educational research in his 1996 annual lecture to the Teacher Training Agency ('Teaching as a research-based profession: possibilities and prospects'). Borrowing from the emergent model of evidence-based medicine, whatever his intention, his comments and critique of the field provided the fuse to ignite a debate that continues unabated (see Hammersley, 2007). Similarly, if somewhat more recently in the US, the legislation in 2001 on No Child Left Behind (NCLB), dictated that 'scientifically-based research' become the only basis on which federal funding could be secured for educational research. As Feuer *et al.* (2002) indicate: 'Congress … codified into … elementary and secondary education legislation a set of requirements for SBR as a condition for receipt of federal funds' (p. 5). Overnight, randomised controlled experiments became the only game in town worthy of federal funding. This is espousal of the 'scientific' model in a rather narrow instrumentalist manner. While Hargreaves in his 1996 lecture did not advocate similarly, he did appropriate evidence-based medicine as a model worth emulating. His major criticisms of educational research were that:

- Educational research fails to provide a sound evidence base for teaching.
- It does not generate a cumulative body of knowledge.
- It is not geared towards enabling teachers to resolve classroom problems (see Hargreaves, 1996).

Although it is possible to argue that educational research does not meet these criteria sufficiently, this does not mean that these are the sole criteria for judging educational research or that it does not influence practice in all kinds of indirect ways that would be extremely difficult to link in a neat rational causal, 'billard-ball' manner. Oancea (2005) subjected subsequent debates in *BERJ* and beyond to detailed textual analysis. Her conclusions are that depending on the critic's disposition, the following were advocated instead of research 'orthodoxy':

- *Philosophically reflective approach* as part of the perennial conversation about aims, values or processes'
- *… a new model of the research-practice relation,* or
- … the *acceptance* of ambiguity, interpretation, emotionality, irrationality, plurality, disagreement, unexpected, discontinuity and reflexivity for 'telling better stories'.

(Oancea, 2005: 177, italics in original)

Her analysis clearly points to the necessity to pay particular attention to the language of these 'wars' lest we become seduced by the dominance of particular language, and allow language to do our thinking for us. She concludes (2005: 164–5) that as the decade of the 1990s advanced, neo-liberal ideology became more dominant, and new technologies began to have more impact on globalising tendencies, educational research came under critical scrutiny internationally. Although contexts continued to have a shaping influence, key concerns were similar, thus indicating also a general homogenising tendency. Yet, one of the consequent criticisms of the debate as it evolved was of increasing 'fragmentation' into different (ideological) camps. Being aware of the changing external environment in which this debate was situated is key to understanding internal struggles within the field. Two elements are critical: there is the increasing dominance globally of neo-liberal ideology with its attendant managerial discourse; what Oancea describes as the 'rhetoric of a new orthodoxy' characterised by an emphasis on '*diagnosis* (what is good and what is wrong about existing educational research); *explanatory* and mitigating circumstances (why did the 'wrong' part go wrong); and *prescriptive* statements of possible solutions (what to do about it) (2005: 169). One of the major reasons why it has been possible to insist on this agenda has been the emergence of new agencies with significant power over teacher education, and, increasingly also, on the nature and conduct of educational research. As an additional element of the scene-setting in the Irish context, it is necessary to indicate the changing nature of the educational landscape over the past two decades as a means of situating subsequent analysis.

Changing educational landscape: agencies as 'think tanks'?

One of the more notable features of the Irish education system is the creation of new agencies, many on a statutory basis, as a very definite re-shaping of the educational landscape during the past two decades. As a means of framing this changing topography, I turn briefly to the work of Rich (2004). He points out that in the US the number of 'think tanks' has 'quadrupled from fewer than seventy to more than 300 between 1970 and the turn of the century' (p. 4). He indicates that when think tanks were initially established at the beginning of the twentieth century the kinds of experts who were hired were generally 'thought of as neutral, credible, and above the fray of the rough and tumble of policy making' (p. 2). The accepted orthodoxy was that 'experts remained ostensibly neutral and detached … offered ideas and policy prescriptions that were rigorously crafted, rational and, in the long run, helpful to the work of decision makers' (p. 3). I agree that the proliferation of think tanks in the last two decades in particular has eroded the 'distance' traditionally maintained by researchers and policy-makers and several such agencies have been established to be entirely partisan, to pursue particular missions. Consequently, 'many of these most aggressive experts are based at think tanks; think tanks have become an infrastructure and an engine for their efforts' (p. 6).

My argument is that while there are some distinctions between the kinds of 'think tanks' that have been created in a US context, there are sufficient similarities also between them and the kinds of agencies established here, that we take the changes evidenced by these seriously, and inscribe them into a multi-focal lens for considering the quality and future of educational research in the Irish context. I concur with the conclusion that:

> An appreciation of think tanks is helpful not just for understanding the political role of expertise and ideas in ... policy making but for accounting for how ideology informs policy making.
>
> (Rich, 2004: 10)

Similarly, I extend this argument to suggest that the emergence of several agencies in the Irish educational landscape is fundamentally altering the research agenda; it is likely to render it more partisan, unless there is a very strong public policy agenda that is above and beyond more partisan research pursuits. However, it is possible that agency interests and the public interest are not mutually exclusive, but in the absence of research policy and priority, as well as transparency around funding, criteria for evaluation of research, as well as its publication and dissemination, then the context becomes more fertile ground for partisan pursuits rather than promotion of the common good.

However, the concept of think tank is contested. As Rich points out, 'in some accounts, they are undifferentiated from government research organisations' (p. 11). If his view that 'drawing irrefutable distinctions between think tanks and other types of organisations is neither entirely possible nor desirable' and that this is due to the fact that 'institutional boundaries are frequently amorphous and overlapping', then it is possible to argue that several of the new agencies listed below, may be regarded as 'think tanks', Irish style. He defines then as:

> ... *independent, non-interest-based, nonprofit, organizations that produce and principally rely on expertise and ideas to obtain support and to influence the policymaking process.* (p. 11, italics in original)

There is growing recognition in the postmodern world that it is not necessarily the quality of research that ensures favour with policy-makers and politicians. Rather, there is a time and place when pushing a particular agenda has much greater possibility of success, thus emphasis has shifted to issues about dissemination, of writing research findings for different audiences, that increasingly it is the responsibility of the researcher to be political as well as expert. Rich argues that this kind of 'advocacy' work by researchers actually erodes rather than enhances credibility of the research community, and undermines the work of such agencies or think tanks, as they are all ultimately understood as partisan; when experts become politically partisan, they effectively sacrifice their professional autonomy, and can be dismissed like any other politician.

Proliferation of think tanks has consequences also for claims to expertise and the autonomy of researchers. He observes that:

> By responding to a political environment in which ideology and marketing often override basic credibility as the criteria by which experts are judged, some think tanks contribute to lowering the standards of expertise.
>
> (Rich, 2004: 217)

Within this emergent landscape, he argues, 'experts at many think tanks frequently have MAs or BAs rather than PhDs' but to assert this openly in any context, but particularly in the Irish setting, is likely to evoke accusations of snobbery or elitism, or both. However, I concur with Sennett (2006: 190) that 'status' is a 'most elusive word' often used as a 'synonym for snobbery' when 'its deeper value has to do with legitimacy'.

It is legitimate to ask in the Irish context, what these new agencies or think tanks are and in what ways their roles and presence are re-shaping the educational landscape and research agenda.

Regime change – emergent structures, new 'think tanks'?

I am in agreement with Esping-Andersen (2000: 4) that we live in a postindustrial society, while accepting also that 'postindustrial transformation is institutionally path-dependent'. Hence, 'existing institutional arrangements heavily determine, maybe even over-determine, national trajectories'. This is an important point of departure for this chapter, and what I say about the extent and quality of educational research – present and future. The challenge, in the first instance, is to gain greater understanding of the dynamics of the changed and changing system – the interaction between established and emerging elements – its more sedimented deep structures and its more recently emerged and emergent agencies, both permanent and statutory as well as more temporary 'dwellings'. Table 3.2 lists these various types of 'think tanks'.

These lists are not exhaustive while they are illustrative of recent proliferation of both statutory and less permanent bodies. I have borrowed the notion of building in canvas from Sergiovanni when he says that form should follow function. Consequently, in a time of rapid change, he declares: 'building in canvas is not a bad idea' (2001: 9). It is worth noting therefore, from a policy and systemic perspective, what is deemed permanent and temporary. Despite their temporary nature, recently emerged canvas categories or more 'temporary arrangements' are sufficiently significant and 'semi-permanent' to change the systemic dynamic. Furthermore, it is primarily support for teachers across the lifespan that constitutes the mainstay of the canvas category – insecure, temporary with the threat of 'elimination' in response to a sudden policy tremor or economic reversal. Additionally, some if not all of these canvas creations have become a career path into more established professional groves, particularly the inspectorate and principalship (see Hogan, 2005).

Table 3.2 Established and recent agencies – 'think tanks'

Established	Recently emerged	Canvas	Externals
Department of Education & Science (DES)	Educate Together (umbrella body for multi-denominational schooling)	Primary Curriculum Support Programme (PCSP)	Equality Authority
Education schools/faculties in universities & colleges of education	Gaelscoileanna (umbrella body for Irish immersion schools)	School Development Planning Service (SDPS)	HIQA (Health Information & Quality Authority)
(Teacher)/Education Centres	National Council for Curriculum and Assessment (NCCA)	Leadership Development for Schools (LDS)	Irish Research Council for Humanities and Social Sciences (IRCHSS)
Educational Research Centre (ERC)	National Parents' Council (NPC)	Cuiditheoireacht (Support service to individual schools)	European Network of Policy Makers for the Evaluation of Education Systems
Economic & Social Research Institute (ESRI)	Welfare Board	Second Level Support Service (SLSS)	EU
Catholic Primary School Managers' Association (CPSMA)	National Council for Special Needs		OECD
Joint Managerial Body (JMB)	Teaching Council		
Teachers' Unions	Association of Community and Comprehensive Schools (ACCS)		
Leargas	Irish Primary Principals' Network (IPPN)		
Curriculum Development Unit (CDVEC)	National Association of Principals and Deputies (NAPD)		
	National Council for Technology in Education (NCTE)		

In this context, IPPN serves as a particularly good example, where it has sponsored and published a considerable amount of 'research' with the express intention of furthering educational reforms from principals' and deputy principals' perspectives (IPPN, 2007). This is precisely the kind of approach that Rich has identified among think tanks in the US whereby they have become more ideological, more partisan, and more self-serving. As argued above, and elaborated further in the next section, information overload has a number of negative consequences. One more general consequence is that considerations regarding the ethics, quality and integrity of such research are ignored by media in general. In such circumstances, it is legitimate to ask: 'what is the role of the research community?' Further, in what sense can it be asserted that there is a recognisable 'research community' beyond these think tanks, and is there a research policy of a more general nature, focused on systemic interests and the quality of teaching and learning, beyond sectoral, partisan interest?

At another level, it gives rise to questions about these different 'think tanks' and their respective agenda, since increasingly they have been assigned a 'research' role, one that they are delighted to embrace as it is perceived as enhancing their status and claim to expertise, while it also confers considerable responsibility that is less talked about. Suffice to say that there has been a marked proliferation of 'think tanks' in the Irish context, sufficient to alter the nature of power relations in a more competitive environment. Consequently, with regard to the future of educational research and its quality, it is necessary to recognise the manner in which there are more and more bodies competing for the attention of policy-makers. This brings the researchers, and their sponsoring bodies, into closer connection with policy-making and politicians, thus blurring the boundaries between research production, its publication and dissemination through media and other means. From a political and more partisan perspective, the more launches organised, the more publicity garnered, while also succeeding in keeping other messages, particularly more difficult contentious and negative issues and concerns, off the radar of the media, PR spin, and publicity have potential to become ends in themselves rather than a genuine contribution to public discourse on education policy and future directions. Against this manifold backdrop, the next section turns attention to two recently published reports, one by the long-established inspectorate, the other by the much more recently emerged IPPN. These are selected to illustrate how the plate tectonics of educational change have enormous consequences for research in general, the research community and the politics of policy making.

'Research' in the 'new' educational landscape

It would be foolhardy to pretend that the changing landscape, nationally and internationally, has not impacted on educational research within national borders. However, indicating how precisely these international 'social movements' (Castells, 2000, 2004) have been 'refracted' (Goodson, 2004) within policy and practice is a much more difficult challenge. Nevertheless, a partial means of holding some of these changes up to critical scrutiny is through analysis of selected recently published research reports. It is not the whole story, but provides the ground on which to make some observations about the 'health' of educational research in the Irish context, and to derive some tentative signposts for possible future directions.

Giorraíonn Beirt Bóthar Distributed Leadership – Deputy Principals (IPPN, 2007) is the most recent publication by IPPN. This 'think tank' emerged from the policy churn of the 1990s where the intensity of reforms left primary principals, without their own union or body, feeling neglected and put upon. After a number of annual national primary principals conferences, IPPN was established on a more 'permanent' footing, and is currently registered as a company with charitable status.[3] It very quickly began to advocate for principals on a range of issues. Having included deputy principals in the network, it became necessary to advocate on their behalf, having similarly highlighted the challenges to principals of incessant policy churn.[4]

The title of the report (Giorraíonn Beirt Bóthar) makes use of a well known Irish language saw – 'two shorten the road'; perhaps its closest equivalent in the English vernacular is – 'two heads are better than one'. 'Distributed leadership' has been added to this catchy 'slogan', a concept that has gained significant international currency in educational research literature due to recent work by Spillane in particular (Spillane, 2006; Spillane and Orlina, 2005), and to this potent linguistic cocktail, the voices of deputy principals have been mixed – an elixir with evident 'sound bite' quality and immediate 'marketability'.

Despite the prominence afforded 'distributed leadership' in the title, what is meant by this term is not indicated in the text. Neither is there any reference to 'teacher' leadership, a concept that has gained in prominence in international literature in recent times (Lieberman and Miller, 2004; Harris and Muijs, 2005). Rather, the term is used interchangeably with 'shared' leadership, while terminology generally is not defined. Chapter 3 (though the text uses the term 'paper' repeatedly), 'Deputy Principal Reviewed: Current Research Findings' is based almost exclusively on the content of a masters thesis. The subsequent chapter purports to document 'best practice' (used in the title) as reported by deputies themselves, but apart from indicating that up to 150 of them were consulted in 'focus groups', there is no indication as to how systematically or otherwise these data were generated and analysed. The report simply states: 'IPPN has also had the opportunity to conduct some action research ... the main aspect of this research work being some focus-group interviews with Deputy Principals' (2007: 16). Exclusive use of focus groups is not normally construed as action research. The term 'best practice' itself is contested and problematic, while an exclusive focus on 'what works' currently may not be the most secure basis for 'practice' in the future, particularly if one of the substantive criticisms the report offers is lack of clarity regarding the role. While it offers some valuable insights, and argues for additional resources for professional support for Deputies, this is premised on the assumption that this will 'translate' into better leadership, and, one assumes, better quality teaching and learning. From the evidence provided, this work, and the background of its chief architects strongly suggests that Rich's comments are apposite – the endeavour reflects the 'tendency to value marketing commentary over doing original research' while this too is a more indirect comment on levels of expertise – 'producing commentary rather than their own original contributions of research' (2004: 117). With the resources to publish and disseminate widely, both in hard copy and electronically, such work gains credibility as 'legitimate' research, and takes its place in the increasing pantheon of information on educational restructuring. Finally, by having the report endorsed with pithy sentences by prominent national and international researchers, principals, and teacher educators (myself included!), the work is given a certain 'seal of approval'.

In contrast to IPPN's very recent arrival on the educational landscape, the Schools Inspectorate is probably one of the oldest. A national system of primary education was established in Ireland in 1831, and, as O'Donovan indicates:

> In many ways, inspectors were the hub around which the national system revolved. Their position was pivotal because they had vital links with the schools at the local level and with the centralised authority in Dublin. Thus, inspectors were at the heart of the national school system and their role was a significant and crucial one in the evolution of primary education in Ireland.
>
> (O'Donovan, 1992: iii)

A significant element of that role for much of the nineteenth and twentieth centuries was as 'extern' examiners for initial primary teacher education. This role came to an end in the 1970s when the Colleges of Education became 'affiliated'[5] to universities and awarded a degree (BEd) rather than a Department of Education diploma, and the period of preservice preparation was extended from two to three years (a fourth year for honours in a minority of cases). Effectively, the universities became the quality assurance authority through its system of extern examiners. Much more recently, the OECD (1991: 43) commented that 'the primary inspectors are charged, mainly and unequivocally, with the task of evaluating the performance of schools and the competence of teachers …'. Significantly, the report does not indicate that inspectors' responsibilities include pre-service teacher education. Subsequent reforms have given effect to the OECD's recommendation of 'concentration on auditing school performance and reporting to and advising the Minister and the Department' (p. 44). In a climate of greater 'performativity' from teachers, and internal and external accountability regimes, in recent years the inspectorate has published several reports as the base of its professional identity has narrowed (www.irlgov.ie).

Against this general backdrop, one of its most recent publications is critically analysed (*Learning to Teach Students on Teaching Practice in Irish Primary Schools*, DES, 2006). It is not possible here to deal with every element of the report in detail. Consequently, a number of key concerns are highlighted and foregrounded for particular attention given the focus of analysis in this chapter.

Ethics

Despite claims in the foreword to the report that it has been completed 'in accordance with its quality assurance remit' (2006: v), the Education Act (1998) does not support this claim.[6] Since this is not within their legal remit, the students who participated in the study were not accorded their ethical entitlements, the right to decide on participation. This presumption of power and authority, according to my institutional ethics committee and codes of conduct is a violation of the rights of individuals, particularly those vulnerable due to others having 'power over' them. Additionally, to presume such power signals a mindset that is outmoded and displays a lack of regard for others, while this might be more benignly interpreted as a lack of awareness of the requirements and standards that have become integral to the research process. While research ethics must always be taken seriously, this is particularly the case in a policy context where 'partnership' is frequently articulated as accepted orthodoxy.

Sampling

The report states that: 'in some respects the sample selected for the survey was a convenience sample' (DES, 2006: 8), but neither was it a 'random sample'. Consequently, the report acknowledges: 'the confidence levels for the statistical estimates obtained are unknown, and caution is therefore urged in generalising findings to the full cohort of final-year student teachers'. More accurately, since the sample is not random, it is not possible to generalise to the entire population. However, the next sentence seeks to lend legitimacy, objectivity and integrity to the work by appealing to the size of the sample. It states:

> ... the size of the sample (10%) was relatively large, and the survey was carried out in a variety of schools throughout the country; the findings, therefore, are likely to be an accurate reflection of trends in relation to student teachers' performance ... . (p. 8)

While it is generally accepted that 'size matters', since the sample in the study was not random, statistically the size of the sample does not enhance reliability and validity. Consequently, claims to generalisability are seriously flawed. Despite the veneer that seeks to camouflage the design flaws in this evaluation, circumspection regarding 'findings' has entirely evaporated by the time the 'main findings' are stated in chapter 8, where it states categorically:

> The evaluation found that the majority of student teachers were excellent, very good or good in their general work in the classroom. However, more than a third were found to be fair or weak, and one in twenty was judged to be an ineffective practitioner. (p. 35)

Further doubt is cast on the rigour of the research when the 'instruments' used, and the manner in which they were deployed are scrutinised.

Research instruments

The work of the student teachers was observed and evaluated under four headings – planning and preparation, teaching (classroom management and organisation, methodology, and use of resources), learning and assessment, and in each case a number of criteria were identified under these four broad categories, ranging from as few as three in the case of resources, to as many as twelve for classroom management and organisation. In general, the criteria used are remarkably similar to those used in other recent studies on the work of beginning teachers (DES, 2005a), and on the implementation of three subjects in the revised curriculum (DES, 2005b). Collectively, these reports suggest that the same criteria are applied to student teachers, NQTs and experienced practitioners. Despite a policy commitment to continuing professional development that recognises 'the teaching continuum' (GoI, 1995),[7] all three reports suggest that they are, in effect, implementation studies, designed to determine the extent to which all three categories are putting into practice the revised curriculum – as intended, or as interpreted by the inspectorate in this instance. The reports do not acknowledge that such a linear theory to practise understanding of the complexity of teaching and learning is highly problematic and contested, and leaves no room for an understanding of curriculum reform as 'continuous adaptation' (Cuban, 1992, 1993; Cuban and Usdan, 2003). Is it appropriate to evaluate student teachers by the same or very similar criteria to those deployed in the evaluation of qualified teachers? This question is not addressed. However, by far the more fundamental concern in terms of the reliability of the instruments used is inter-rater consistency. All observations were conducted as 'one-off' encounters, while no conversations with students were conducted. Consequently, student intentions are not part of the evaluative process, thus lending a behaviouristic quality to 'findings' that has a Thorndike-esque dimension as well as serious limitation. The report does not acknowledge the impact of a lack of consistency. Instead, each evaluation is idiosyncratic; and notwithstanding the use of a common set of criteria, in the absence of systematic training, consistency and replicability of 'findings' – one of the hallmarks of such research endeavours – cannot be assumed. As Posavac and Carey (1988: 55) assert, 'subjective ratings are usually less reliable since they are influenced not only by the behaviour of the person being rated but also by the person doing the ratings'. The fact that the classes being observed are those of qualified teachers, with the students as guests only for a short period of time, is not acknowledged as a major source of data contamination, with major consequences for validity.

In all cases, provisional grades for the observed students were supplied to the inspectorate by the respective colleges. It would have been possible therefore to compare the (composite) 'grades' assigned by three college supervisors with those assigned by inspectors on the basis of one-off visits. This would certainly be one means of seeking to address the issue of 'quality assurance'. However, it would intrude into the work of the university thus exposing the blurring of boundaries.

However, when reports such as this are put into the public domain, either in hard copy and increasingly also by electronic means, publicity-grabbing headlines become more of a reality than research rigour. The proliferation of such 'information' in the public domain at a time when politicians too conduct their own 'research' creates the general climate and mindset which suggests that all research is self-serving, thus enabling politicians and policy-makers to be highly selective, to pick those bits of evidence on the over-loaded smorgasbord that suit existing or opportunist policy-rhetorics. Perversely also, with the proliferation of recent and recently emerged 'think tanks', the necessity for a national educational research policy has been obscured. Instead, each think tank competes in the market place to gain access to decision-makers, thus increasingly research of whatever hue and quality becomes politicised and the boundaries between research, policy-making and politics become more permeable and invisible. Specifically, in the case of the Irish inspectorate, is there a flexing of muscles regarding control of initial teacher education, as evidenced in other jurisdictions, where competencies are increasingly prescribed (OECD, 2005); and is there concern also that with the advent of the Teaching Council, a body effectively controlled by the teacher unions, more traditional state 'control' of the teaching profession is being eroded or reasserted?

What are the consequences of these 'market forces' for the future of educational research? What lessons may be learnt that have applicability in post-Celtic Tiger Ireland and possibly elsewhere?

Situating the 'glocal' within the global: some compass readings

The foregoing analysis strongly suggests that the deep structures of education are being rapidly over-laid with a plethora of 'think tanks' and, over time, these are likely to alter irrevocably the very plate tectonics of the educational landscape; and the outcomes, as seismologists frequently suggest, are not entirely predictable. Even when it is argued that established and emergent agencies seek to create new and emergent identities, consistent with identity politics generally, in the absence of a more robust public sphere and an attendant public discourse around issues of quality in educational research, shaped by some sense of the 'common good', politics rather than policy-making and rigorous research are likely to be to the fore. For example, education systems have been smothered by a veritable avalanche of information in the form of reported research that is disseminated by a variety of means which frequently bypass more traditional peer review procedures within the academic research community, thus blurring boundaries between research, advocacy and politics. Bauman gives shape to this global phenomenon when he states:

> The melting of solids led to the progressive untying of economy from its traditional political, ethical and cultural entanglements. It sedimented a new order, defined primarily in economic terms.
>
> (Bauman, 2000: 4)

The reports discussed in the previous section, and by extension the proliferation of think tanks and agencies, may be understood as the private anxieties of like-minded individuals being articulated publicly. When this becomes pervasive, 'thereby denuding the public sphere of all substance except as the site where private worries are confessed and put on public display', the grounds for collective action are minimised (Bauman, 2000: 52). Think tanks become another form of 'talk show' where existential insecurities are aired. As Hobsbawm asserts:

> Never was the word 'community' used more indiscriminately and emptily than in the decades when communities in a sociological sense became hard to find in real life. Men and women look for groups to which they can belong, certainly and forever, in a world in which all else is moving and shifting, in which nothing else is certain.
>
> (Hobsbawm, 1998: 40)

Proliferation of such bodies has created a cacophonous flood of information, but this general attention seeking is not conducive to listening, responding and sustained engagement. Rather, advocacy and access to policy makers becomes the only game in town, and supplants 'real politic'. But, when politics and policy making is also effected by the absence of communication and debate rather than information management, disengagement, apathy and passivity hallmarks of behaviour; 'slogans', 'being on message', 'getting the message out' become ends in themselves, and international gurus such as Schoen and Luntz spread their message of 'spin' across several countries.[8] This is not the place to detail the machinations of these 'experts' and their generally pernicious influence on politics and the public sphere. Suffice to quote Luntz by way of summary and illustration:

> Bill Clinton made Frank Luntz because Bill Clinton discovered the power and the influence of words. Now, I'd like to think that I apply them to clients, to philosophies, to products and services and corporations that I believe in, that are good. I don't argue with you that words can sometimes be used to confuse, but it's up to the practitioners of the study of language to apply them for good and not for evil. It is just like fire; fire can heat your house or burn it down.
>
> (www.pbs.org/wgbh/pages/frontline/shows/persuaders/interviews/luntz.html)

Using focus groups and dial technology, these 'consultants' document the public's views on various issues, and then repackage them in simple language, in sound-bites and slogans for politicians to 'replay' to their respective publics what they want to hear. What hope has the more traditional research community in such circumstances, and what responses and actions seem appropriate to re-create dialogue and debate and policy-making beyond safe slogans and no risk policy-making that are characterised by lack of courage and political leadership?

In stable and more predictable times in the Irish context, that were also frequently static and stagnant in the educational sphere, the educational research community was arguably more active, visible and participative in educational debate, frequently and most audibly through the all-Ireland Educational

Research Association of Ireland (www.easi.ie). However, it may be argued that postmodern identity politics, intensification of workloads, perpetuation of publish or perish, restructuring of universities on marketplace competitiveness, have combined to contribute to a much more rugged individualism that is the antithesis of, antipathetic and antagonistic to, a sense of public service. Amidst this much more polyphonic maelstrom of information, it appears that the research community, if it exists in any meaningful sense, has been rendered impotent. Part of its own identity politics therefore is to re-engage with established and emergent agencies as a means of establishing a more secure research community, policy and practice, while recognising also that the research community is multi-vocal.

A significant iatrogenic consequence of agency proliferation is the absence of a coherent national research policy and priority. All pursue particular lines of research that may be more self-serving than pursuit of collective endeavours – a tower of Babel babble of streamlined slogans promulgated as a self-serving substitute for dialogue, debate and dissent. In such circumstances, think tanks begin to resemble ethnic enclaves that are exclusive and inward looking, thus building internal solidarities, often around grievances that subsequently translate into pursuit of particular policy agenda, and the marshalling of 'evidence' in support of the 'case' being made. In the face of the demise of community, powerfully articulated by Putnam (2000) in particular, the work of think tanks takes on the following hue:

> ... to keep the 'other', the different, the strange and the foreign at a distance, the decision to preclude the need for communication, negotiation and mutual commitment ... [becomes] the expectable response to the existential uncertainty rooted in the new fragility or fluidity of social bonds.
>
> (Bauman, 2006: 108)

The provision of a coherent educational research policy that includes rather than excludes becomes an important basis for re-creating public dialogue about what matters in education, beyond self-serving enclaves. This is a particular challenge to the research community in the first instance. Pursuit of a clearly articulated policy and transparency regarding the awarding of funding and contracts has potential also to engage with concerns about research quality.

It is incumbent upon the research community and researchers more generally to take seriously and engage with criticisms of research, its rigour and lack of cumulativeness being two major inadequacies cited earlier. However, a headlong rush to perpetuate and disseminate 'best practice' by accumulating 'evidence' of what works, typically labelled 'evidence-based practice', is to tie the future to the present to an unacceptable degree. Rather, I am at one with Sennett (2006: 158) when he asserts: 'nor should the test of utility and practicality rule: this test emphasises what is rather than what might be'. By contrast, he espouses 'craftsmanship' which he describes as 'doing something well for its own sake' (2006: 104). He continues:

Self-discipline and self-criticism adhere in all domains of craftsmanship; standards matter, and the pursuit of quality ideally becomes an end in itself. (p. 104)

My comments in the previous section suggest that such craftsmanship and reflexivity is increasingly absent from disseminated reports where 'getting the message out' becomes a self-serving activity, privileged over engagement and rigour. Perversely, proliferation of information 'prompts disengagement' (p. 172) while enabling policy-makers and politicians to concentrate decision-making at the centre; the inevitable consequence of the size of the smorgasbord of 'evidence' is a greater emphasis on what is safe, 'what works' rather than providing leadership with potential to create a better future. This almost inevitably leads to the kind of policy churn that has become commonplace, when 'spewing out policy ... in education' in the English context resulted in 'the same disenchanted effect' (p. 174). Craftsmanship, pursued tenaciously has potential to re-create real engagement, extended debate and communication, while also creating the necessary conditions for rigour to flourish. There is a concomitant responsibility however on the research community to conduct research that serves the common good rather than being self-indulgent. Nevertheless, an exclusive focus on what works has a tendency to kill more imaginative endeavours that are a necessity for creating an alternative future rather than replicating past and present. In order to achieve this, research cannot be tied to economic agenda exclusively; there is need for a more sophisticated and sensitive balance between emotional space that provides security and continuity necessary for craftsmanship to flourish, beyond the iron cage of market efficiency or the economic imperative.

I am in agreement with Yates when she asserts:

I too think that good research needs to be technically good (to have methodological integrity or logic), to be making a contribution to knowledge (to be doing something distinct from public relations or propaganda), and to be doing something that matters (to be framing questions that contribute to better and fairer education experiences, outcomes, social arrangements rather than punitive, deficit-oriented, anachronistic ones).

(2004: 212)

To achieve this, it is necessary also to become more adroit and sophisticated in our individual and collective readings of the fields in which educational research is situated. The purpose of this analysis has been to facilitate such readings, both at home and abroad, and to provide the building blocks for individual and collective fresh ferment.

Acknowledgements

I would like to acknowledge helpful comments and suggestions made on earlier drafts of this chapter by colleagues Maeve O'Brien, Jimmy Kelly and Mark Morgan (St Patrick's College) and Jim Gleeson (University of Limerick).

Notes

1 I am borrowing the phrase 'paradigm wars' from Gage's seminal paper 'The Paradigm Wars and Their Aftermath: A "Historical" Sketch of Research on Teaching since 1989' (pp. 135–49), and this will be commented on later in the chapter.

2 It is worth noting that in colleges of education in the Irish context, despite being constituent colleges of various universities, they are denied a professoriate; a significant element of their historical legacy and perspectives on education, that continue to have contemporary implications for the status of the field and those who labour within it.

3 I was an active participant and member of the organising committees that planned these annual conferences. I was also present at the meeting that more formally gave 'birth' to IPPN. My comments are not intended as a criticism of key members of the network, nor of the work they have undertaken. Rather, my intention is to illustrate what a proliferation of think tanks does in changing the dynamics of the educational landscape and its consequences for educational research, its interactions with and contributions to the policy-making process.

4 The secondary sector in some respects led the way in terms of this Janus-faced approach. The National Association of Principals and Deputies (NAPD) has included deputies as members and in its title from the outset, perhaps reflecting the fact that in many large secondary schools, deputies have little or no teaching responsibilities, unlike the vast majority of their primary counterparts. Members of both NAPD and IPPN continue to be members of their respective unions – Association of Secondary Teachers of Ireland (ASTI) and Irish National Teachers Organisation (INTO).

5 The report published by the DES (2006) uses the word 'affiliated' when describing the relationship of colleges of education to the universities, but this is inaccurate. In the case of St. Patrick's College, for example, it is 'a college of Dublin City University' since a linkage agreement was signed in 1993, at the insistence of the DES!

6 It is important to distinguish here between historical precedent and practice and legal responsibility. The claim being made by the inspectorate, in my view, seeks to blur the boundaries. While indicating that it 'has worked closely with the colleges over many years' this does not amount to a legal responsibility. Rather, this close working relationship is a legacy of pre-degree working patterns.

7 The government's White Paper on Education, *Charting Our Education Future*, describes the 'teaching career' 'as a continuum involving initial teacher education, induction processes and in-career development opportunities …' while it also states: 'initial teacher education cannot be regarded as the final preparation for a life-time of teaching' (GoI, 1995: 121).

8 These extremely influential and wealthy 'consultants' have advised Democrats and Republicans as well as political leaders in approximately thirty countries world wide during the past twenty years.

References

Bauman, Z. (2000) *Liquid Modernity*, Cambridge: Polity Press.
Beck, U. (2000) *What Is Globalization?* Cambridge: Polity Press.

Casey, K. (1993) *I Answer With My Life: Life Histories of Women Teachers Working For Social Change*, New York and London: Routledge.

Castells, M. (2000) *The Information Age: Economy, Society and Culture. Volume III: End of Millennium*, second edition, Oxford: Blackwell Publishers.

Castells, M. (2004) *The Information Age Economy, Society and Culture. Volume II: The Power of Identity*, second edition, Oxford: Blackwell Publishing.

Condliffe Langemann, E. (2000) *An Elusive Science: The Troubling History of Educational Research*, Chicago: University of Chicago Press.

Corcoran, M. P. and Peillon, M. (eds) (2002) *Ireland Unbound: A Turn of the Century Chronicle*, Dublin: Institute of Public Administration.

Creswell, J. W. (2003) *Research Design Qualitative, Quantitative, and Mixed Methods Approaches*, second edition, London, Thousand Oaks and New Delhi: Sage.

Cuban, L. (1992) 'Curriculum stability and change', in P. Jackson (ed.) *Handbook of Research on Curriculum*, New York: Macmillan.

Cuban, L. (1993) *How Teachers Taught: Constancy and Change in American Classrooms 1890–1990*, London and New York: Teachers College Press.

Cuban, L. and Usdan, M. (ed.) (2003) *Powerful Reforms with Shallow Roots Improving America's Urban Schools*, New York and London: Teachers College Press.

DES (2005a) *Beginning to Teach Newly Qualified Teachers in Irish Primary Schools*, Inspectorate of the Department of Education and Science, Dublin: Stationery Office/Government Publications.

DES (2005b) *An Evaluation of Curriculum Implementation in Primary Schools English, Mathematics and Visual Arts*, Dublin: Government Publications.

DES (2006) *Learning to Teach Students on Teaching Practice in Irish Primary Schools*, Dublin: Government Publications.

Erican, K. and Roth, W. M. (2006) 'What good is polarizing research into qualitative and Quantitative?' *Educational Researcher*, Vol. 35, No. 5, June/July: 14–23.

Esping-Andersen, G. (2000) *Social Foundations of Postindustrial Economies*, Oxford: Oxford University Press.

Esping-Andersen, G., with Gallie, D., Hemerijk, A. and Myles, J. (2002) *Why We Need a New Welfare State*, Oxford: Oxford University Press.

Feuer, M. J., Towne, L. and Shavelson, R. J. (2002) 'Scientific culture and educational research', *Educational Researcher*, Vol. 31, No. 8: 4–14.

Fullan, M. (1991) *The New Meaning of Educational Change*, London: Cassell.

Fullan, M. (2003) *The Moral Imperative of School Leadership*, Toronto and Thousand Oaks: Ontario Principals' Council and Corwin Press.

Fullan, M. (2005) *Leadership Sustainability*, Thousand Oaks: Corwin Books.

Furedi, F. (2002) *Culture of Fear*, London and New York: Continuum.

Gage, N. L. (1989) 'The paradigm wars and their aftermath: a "historical" sketch of research on teaching since 1989', *Teachers College Record*, Vol. 91, No. 2, Winter: 135–47.

Giddens, A. (1991) *Modernity and Self-Identity: Self and Society in the Late Modern Age*, Stanford: Stanford University Press.

Giddens, A. (2002) *Runaway World: How Globalization is Reshaping Our Lives*, London: Profile Books.

Goodson, I. F. (2004) 'Change processes and historical periods: an international perspective', in C. Sugrue (ed.) *Curriculum and Ideology: Irish Experiences, International Perspectives*, Dublin: The Liffey Press.

Government of Ireland (GoI) (1998) *Education Act*, Dublin: Government Publications.

Hammersley, M. (ed.) (2007*) Educational Research and Evidence-based Practice*, published in Association with the Open University.

Hargreaves, A. (2003) *Teaching in the Knowledge Society*, Buckingham: Open University Press.

Hargreaves, D. (1996) 'Teaching as a research-based profession: possibilities and prospects', Annual lecture of the Teacher Training Agency, London.

Harris, A. and Muijs, D. (2005) *Improving Schools Through Teacher Leadership*, Maidenhead: Open University Press.

Hobsbawm, E. (1998) 'The cult of identity politics', *New Left Review*, May–June: 36–47.

Hogan, M. (2005) 'Home, school, community coordinator: a route into principalship?', Unpublished Med. thesis, St. Patrick's College, Dublin.

hooks, b. (1994) *Teaching to Transgress*, New York and London: Routledge.

IPPN (2007) 'Giorraíonn Beirt Bóthar distributed leadership – deputy principals', Cork: IPPN.

Ireland, Government of (1995) *Charting our Education Future. White Paper on Education*, Dublin: The Stationery Office.

Keohane, K. and Kuhling, C. (2004) *Collision Culture: Transformatons in Everyday Life in Ireland*, Dublin: The Liffey Press.

Labaree, D. F. (2004) *The Trouble With Ed Schools*, New Haven and London: Yale University Press.

Lieberman, A. and Miller, L. (2004) *Teacher Leadership*, San Francisco: Jossey-Bass.

Lincoln, Y. and Guba, E. (1985) *Naturalistic Inquiry*, New York: Sage Publications.

O'Connell, M. (2001) *Changed Utterly: Ireland and the New Irish Psyche*, Dublin: The Liffey Press.

O'Donovan, P. F. (1992) 'The national school inspectorate and its administrative context, in Ireland 1870–1962' *Education Department*, Dublin: University College Dublin.

Oancea, A. (2005) 'Criticisms of educational research: key topics and levels of analysis', *British Educational Research Journal*, Vol. 31, No. 2: 157–84.

OECD (1991) 'Reviews of national education policies for education: Ireland', Paris: OECD.

OECD (2005) *Teachers Matter: Attracting, Developing and Retaining Effective Teachers*, Paris: OECD.

Peillon, M. and Corcoran, M. P. (eds) (2004) *Place and Non-Place The Reconfiguration of Ireland*, Dublin: IPA.

Peillon, M. and Slater, E. (eds) (1998) *Encounters with Modern Ireland: A Sociological Chronicle 1995–1996*, Dublin: IPA.

Posavac, E. J. and Carey, R. G. (1989) *Programme Evaluation Methods and Case Studies*, Englewood Cliffs, NJ: Prentice Hall.

Putnam, R. (2000) *Bowling Alone: The Collapse and Revival of American Community*, New York and London: Simon and Schuster.

Rich, A. (2004) *Think Tanks, Public Policy, and the Politics of Expertise*, Cambridge: Cambridge University Press.

Sarason, S. (1990) *The Predictable Failure of Educational Reform*, San Francisco: Jossey-Bass.

Sarason, S. (1996) *Revisiting The Culture of The School and The Problem of Change*, New York and London: Teachers College, Columbia University.

Sennett, R. (2006) *The Culture of the New Capitalism*, New Haven and London: Yale University Press.

Sergiovanni, T. (2001) *Leadership: What's in it for Schools?*, London and New York: RoutledgeFalmer.

Spillane, J. (2006) *Distributed Leadership*, San Francisco: Jossey-Bass.

Spillane, J. and Orlina, E. C. (2005) 'Investigating leadership practice: exploring the entailments of taking a distributed perspective', paper presented at the annual conference of the American Educational Research Association, Montreal.

Sugrue, C. (2006) 'Three decades of college life, 1973–1999: the old order changeth?', in J. Kelly (ed.) *St. Patrick's College Drumcondra: A History*, Dublin: Four Courts Press, pp. 225–65.

Taylor, C. (1989/1992) *Sources of The Self: The Making of Modern Identity*, Cambridge: Cambridge University Press.

Taylor, C. (1991) *The Ethics of Authenticity*, Cambridge, MA and London: Harvard University Press.

Yates, L. (2004) *What does Good Educational Research Look Like?*, Maidenhead: Open University Press.

Young, M. (1971) *Knowledge and Control: New Directions for the Sociology of Education*, edited by Michael F. D. Young, London: Collier-Macmillan.

Part II

Educational change

Lessons from home and away

4   US school reform and classroom practice

Larry Cuban

School reform is big business in the world. In the past quarter-century, policymakers have rolled out comprehensive school reform in the United Kingdom, Spain, France, Chile, Colombia, Australia, New Zealand, Israel, and the United States.

Although national contexts account for particular differences that have emerged among countries committed to reforming their educational systems, these differences should not obscure their common features. In this chapter, I will concentrate on those features that turn up again and again in these international reforms: a market-inspired definition of the educational problem, a common theory of change driving the solution to the market-inspired problem, and school and classroom outcomes (both anticipated and unanticipated) of these ambitious efforts.

I concentrate on these common features by drawing primarily from the U.S. experience with comprehensive school reform beginning in the late 1970s through the recent federal law, No Child Left Behind (NCLB). I do so because I am most familiar with the U.S. scene and, based upon my research, see these common features evident in the surge of comprehensive school reform in the U.S. and across many developed nations in the past quarter-century.

In the interest of brevity, I stipulate, as lawyers arguing a case do, certain statements about U.S. policies that are seldom disputed.[1] Should anyone quarrel with these statements, I do have supporting references and would be happy to provide them. So here is what I stipulate:

1   In the past quarter-century, a market-inspired definition of the educational problem, one strongly endorsed by media and parents and largely driven by low test scores on international tests, holds that low-performing schools have hampered economic growth, innovation, and productivity by producing graduates mismatched to the skills demanded by employers competing in a constantly changing global marketplace (see Reich, 1991; Grubb and Lazerson, 2004).

2   To solve this problem, national and state officials adopted policies that set standards for all students to achieve; mandated testing to determine if standards were being met; and held schools, students, and teachers accountable for results (see Toch, 1991).

3   To implement these policies, officials across the country encouraged competition among schools, more parental choice in schools, and better management of a public enterprise seriously deficient in each of the above. These market-inspired strategies generated an entrepreneurial marketplace of charter schools, vouchers, teacher and principal credentialing, and cyber-schools for both non-profit and profit-making organizations seeking to transform schooling, especially for urban poor children (Koldrie, 2004; Carnevale and Descrochers, 2005; Hess, 2002; McGuinn, 2005).

4   Among the many values contained within this definition of the problem and its strategies is the explicit desire to reduce societal inequalities by ensuring equal access to a labor market for those high school and college graduates who historically have been mired in poverty (Hess, 2002; Spellings, www.ed.gov/nc16/).

What I stipulate here have become operating principles in many state education laws and the federally funded No Child Left Behind (NCLB) act that President George W. Bush signed into law in 2002. President Bush in characteristic blunt language said, 'Good jobs begin with good schools' (Bush, 2002: P.A. 22). To the President and his supporters in the corporate community, NCLB was not only a jobs bill but also one that would end the 'soft bigotry of low expectations' for poor and minority children and youth (Bush, quoted in Noe, 2004). These national efforts to link public schools to the economy, however, did not begin with NCLB.

Such efforts go back to the 1890s in the last surge of globalization that led to the U.S. copying Germany and adopting vocational education as a way of ensuring that employers had skilled workers entering the industrial labor market. For our purposes, however, let me go to the immediate background of NCLB which can be located in the late 1970s (see Cuban, 2004; Grubb and Lazerson, 2004).

Then, business and civic coalitions, angered by evidence of U.S. students performing poorly on national and international tests, lobbied state legislators to increase high school graduation requirements and hold teachers and students accountable for academic achievement, They wanted schools to prepare graduates for an ever-changing economy that depended upon skills manipulating knowledge rather than industrial machines. Increasing state authority for funding schools, raising academic standards, and mandating programs, however, accomplished little, prompting President George H. W. Bush and the nation's 50 governors in 1989 to establish national educational goals that were to be achieved by the year 2000. None of the goals – including those linked to student test performance – were met or have been achieved since. Now enter George W. Bush and No Child Left Behind. This law caps the quarter-century of increased concentration of state and federal authority to govern and operate schools (see Jennings, 2003).

The federal law requires testing of all children in grades 3 through 8 in reading and math and, beginning in 2007, science. NCLB expects every single student including all minority and special needs children to make 'adequate yearly progress' (AYP) on state tests, and, by 2014, be proficient in reading, math, and other subjects, thereby wiping out the historic achievement gap between white and minority students; NCLB demands that a qualified teacher be placed in every classroom in the country and mandates that schools failing to raise test scores for two years in a row provide tutoring and other special help to low-performing children and give parents the choice to transfer them to better schools. These provisions of the law have opened up opportunities for entrepreneurs who sought to help schools before they got in trouble or schools designated by NCLB as needing improvement. If no improvement occurs in subsequent years, the school is taken over by district and state authorities or closed. Currently, nearly 2000 schools fall into that category with thousands more expected in the next few years (Associated Press, 2006).

NCLB has pushed states further in the direction that many had already moved in relation to higher academic standards, more testing, and accountability. These federal and state laws use a market-inspired definition of the educational problem and see public schooling as the high-octane fuel powering an ever-growing economy and the road toward a more just society.

What is the theory of change embedded in NCLB?

No Child Left Behind sets forth testing and accountability policies and subsequent regulations for every state and district that receives federal funds. In the U.S. system of decentralized schooling, states set policy for local districts. Local school boards hire the district superintendent who appoints principals to administer those policies in individual schools. Principals direct teachers to put federal, state, and local policies into practice in their classrooms; and teachers, the gatekeepers to classroom learning, teach students the content, skills, attitudes, and behaviors embedded in those policies. Then students take tests to display what they have learned. That is the way the chain of governance authority from federal regulations to the classroom with its many links is expected to work. NCLB contains that chain of authority and a set of assumptions about accountability and testing that adds up to a theory of change.

Within either a centralized or decentralized national system of schooling, however, this policy, its assumptions, and its desired outcomes of producing higher test scores, more high school graduates, and ultimately well-paying jobs that will close the income gap between the wealthy and the poor, must answer four critical questions:

1   Do mandated curriculum standards and accountability measures get implemented as intended?
2   When implemented, did they change teaching practices?
3   Did changed teaching practices account for what students learned as measured by the state tests?
4   Do students who have achieved proficiency on state tests go to college, graduate, and enter jobs paying solid salaries?

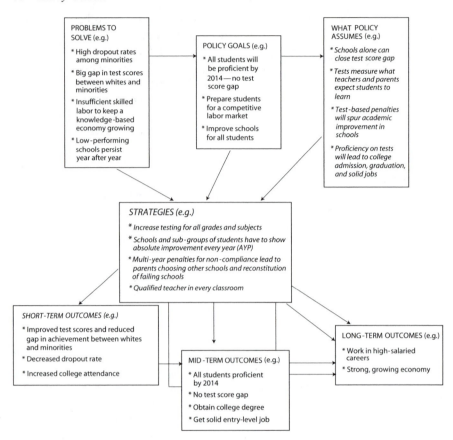

Figure 4.1 Policy logic of No Child Left Behind

The first question requires evidence that federal, state, and district policies were fully put into practice. Time again, researchers have found that state and local policies aimed at altering what occurs in schools have been selectively adapted and even ignored. Finding out to what degree the policy was implemented in classrooms is essential.

The second question builds on the answer to the first one: to what degree, if any, have those implemented practices altered routine teaching practices.

The third question asks if those changed instructional practices resulted in desired student outcomes. Even here, test score gains or losses would require close scrutiny to determine that different practices did raise (or lower) individual student's achievement over a specific period of time while controlling for their socioeconomic status and prior test performance of students. Furthermore, have test scores improved as students move from elementary to secondary schools?

Finally, the fourth question seeks to find out whether being classified as proficient on tests leads to college admission, graduation, and success in the job market – the very basis for adopting these policies in the first place.

So the potential links between federal and state policies and student achievement, much less later job performance, are both indirect and complex, challenging researchers to design studies that will capture that often zigzag path between a policy and student outcomes.

And what does the historical record reveal about federal and state policies resulting in desired teacher and student outcomes?

The short answer is that neither historic nor contemporary evidence has established a cause–effect relationship between students gaining academically and states or the federal government mandating goals, establishing uniform standards, administering tests, requiring accountability, or pushing school choice. Note that I used the phrase 'established a cause–effect relationship'. I use those words because in many large urban districts in the U.S. where these policies have been pursued aggressively there have been initial gains in elementary school students' test scores and occasional instances of closing the achievement test score gap between minorities and whites. Yet these initial gains have melted over time or settled into a plateau. None of these early positive results for elementary school students, however, have yet to touch high schools in these districts. Finally, no evidence has appeared that such school policies have reduced inequalities between poor and non-poor in the U.S. Why have these patterns emerged in urban districts?

The answer is found in the massive literature on urban schools and policy implementation. Rather than review that literature, I offer four lessons that I take away from my analysis of scores of studies.[2]

Few state and federal policies are implemented as intended

Because policy goals are intentions (some say 'hypotheses') that elected and appointed officials seek to put into practice, they use the few blunt-edged tools they have at hand. Policymakers use regulations, incentives, technical assistance, and sanctions (and mixes thereof) to prod local school boards, principals, and teachers to convert intentions into daily practices. But at each link in the policy chain, from federal and state officials' declared purposes to local school boards' actions, to principals' and teachers' behaviors, unintended adaptations and external circumstances intrude that policymakers either failed to anticipate or ignored, many of which affect student outcomes.[3]

An example might help. After three decades of U.S. officials pestering state administrators to send money to schools enrolling mostly poor students, funds finally flowed to schools with large percentages of poor children. Here is the catch, however. Federal officials negotiated with state officials a new formula that sent dollars to schools that met a minimum threshold for poverty even if nearly half the students attending were not poor. In other words, dollars went to schools; they did not follow individual poor students. Thus, the revised formula for allocating funds meant that many schools with mixes of poor and middle- and upper-income students that failed to meet the minimum poverty threshold received no federal funds. As a result, one-third of needy students (4 million in 1999) in schools not designated as eligible to receive federal funds went unserved. In short, the federal government negotiated state compliance at a cost to a substantial number of children from poor families.[4]

This process of mutual adaptation occurs at every point in the path from Washington, D.C., or a state capital to the school and classroom. Everyone's thumbprints are on educational policies as they wend their way into classrooms. Thus determining whether a policy 'works' depends on specifying exactly what was put into practice and where since even more variation results from different contexts.[5]

Context shapes implementation

A federal education policy that officials expect to be implemented uniformly in Florida and California inevitably will yield disappointment. Within a state, differences in context also matter. Los Angeles Unified School District and Beverly Hills school district may be next to one another, but their differences in size, capacity to finance schools, and children's ethnicities, race, and social classes mean that each district's students and practitioners will respond differently to state and federal policies aimed at their classrooms. The same holds true within districts. In Boston, for example, Burke High School and Boston Latin High School are very different schools in student demography, teachers, administrators, and available resources. Consequently, each will respond differently not only to district directives but also to those from the state commissioner of education and from the federal government (see Fairman and Firestone, 2001; De Bray *et al.*, 2001; Wilson and Floden, 2001).

And even within schools in the same district, contexts matter. Given their beliefs, experience, values, and expertise, teachers determine how, and under what circumstances, they will accept, reject, or modify a mandate from their principal, superintendent, school board, state legislature, Congress and, yes, the President of the United States. Teachers are literally both 'gatekeepers' and 'policy brokers' (see Wilson and Floden, 2001; Cuban, 1993; Spillane *et al.*, 2002).

If constant adaptations and context are important lessons drawn from the huge implementation literature, so are the current tools for determining student outcomes.

Assessing student learning derived from policy remains primitive

For policies intended to improve student academic achievement, effectiveness has been narrowed to gains and losses in standardized test scores. Even though most federal and state policymakers are familiar with the weaknesses of such tests, nonetheless, scores on state and national tests are used to evaluate whether standards-based reforms are successful.

In narrowing the definition of success and academic achievement to test scores, moreover, policymakers ignore the critical issue of whether the policy has been partially, moderately, or fully implemented. After all, without evidence of teachers putting all, most, or even a smidgeon of the policy into practice, the overall value of the venture can hardly be judged. For example, say a for-profit entrepreneurial organization took over a cluster of urban schools and installed different math and reading programs for teachers to use in classrooms. Explicit implementation questions have to be asked. Were teachers afforded sufficient opportunities to learn about the new approaches? Were special lessons and materials made available and demonstrated to them? Did teachers use the different ways of teaching mathematics or reading in classrooms? Were tests tied to policy aims, professional development opportunities, and classroom materials? Although some researchers have begun to construct measures that begin to answer such questions, their work, sadly, remains on the periphery of most policy research. Instead, state and federal officials hang on to slippery correlations between students' test scores and when they adopted the policies (Cohen and Hill, 2001; Porter and Smithson, 2001).

The fourth lesson I draw from the implementation literature is that *while public schools are critical actors, they alone cannot increase academic achievement among poor children and diminish societal inequalities.*

From reducing crime, unemployment, and poverty, to defending the nation against domestic and foreign enemies, and, yes, to preparing future workers for a changing labor market – reformers have turned historically to school-based solutions. Reformers seldom tried altering dominant socioeconomic and political structures, for example, to reduce the huge income gap between the rich and poor, create jobs, or end residential segregation. Instead, reformers turned to public schools for solutions to these persistent problems.

Also, political rhetoric pledging equality resonated deeply with Americans' hopes for their children. Equality of educational opportunity easily fits into the historic American Creed promising the right of each individual child not only to go to school but also exceed, through personal merit and hard work, the fondest dreams of their parents. So it comes as no surprise that egalitarian and meritocratic words have been married to policies that say schools can correct societal ills all by themselves (Myrdal, 1944).

Yet the evidence is compelling that schools alone cannot reduce poverty, end segregation, cut drug abuse and youth sexual activity – all public expectations that have been written into laws over the past century.

Both the history of using schools to solve social problems and soaring rhetoric have persuaded parents and taxpayers that schools can be miracle-producing institutions. Consider, however, that most city and state agencies offer medical, recreation, social services, transportation, food, and financial services to communities but seldom in schools. Few states, few cities, and few school districts seek tighter coordination of these services to schools to focus on improving academic achievement.

These four lessons I have extracted from the literature on current U.S. policy interventions raise serious questions about whether the long chain of policymaking that stretches from the White House through a state capital to district school board offices has impact upon a kindergarten teacher's classroom or a high school history lesson, much less the life chances of students once they leave school. Analyzing the literature, however, may be insufficient to convince advocates of centralized policymaking.

In a modest step to determine classroom effects of these policies, I gathered data from nearly 1,100 classrooms in three urban districts: Arlington, Virginia; Denver, Colorado; and Oakland, California. This study builds on a history of teaching that I had completed twenty years ago.

In that earlier study, I found that between the 1890s and the 1980s the social organization of the classroom had become increasingly informal. In the early twentieth century, dress-clad and tie-wearing teachers facing rows of 50 or more students sitting in bolted down desks controlled their every move. They required students, even little ones, to stand when reciting from the textbook or answering a question. Teacher scowled when reprimanding students for misbehaving and often paddled them.

Over the decades, however, classroom organization and teacher behavior slowly changed. By the 1980s, classrooms were filled with tables and movable desks, particularly in the early grades, so students faced one another and saw walls decorated with colorful posters and student work. Jean-wearing teachers drinking coffee smiled often at their classes and students went to a pencil sharpener or elsewhere in the room without asking for the teacher's permission. Classrooms became less fearful and more colorful, comfortable places (see Brint *et al.*, 2001).

A second conclusion I reached was about teacher-centered instruction and student-centered instruction, two traditions of teaching, each with its ardent champions. By the early 1980s, I found that most elementary and a lesser number of secondary teachers had incorporated versions of teacher-centered and student-centered practices into classroom hybrids. With the social organization of the classroom becoming increasingly informal, particularly in the primary grades, teaching practices had evolved into a blending of the two traditions.

Consider grouping. For decades, teachers taught 40 to 70 or more students as one group. Over time, the student-centered practice of dividing the whole group into smaller ones so that the teacher could work with a few students at a time on reading while the rest worked by themselves in groups or independently slowly took hold among most elementary school teachers. Small group work, however, appeared much less in secondary school teachers' classrooms although variations in grouping occurred among academic subjects (Stodolsky and Grossman, 1995).

'Activity (or learning) centers' where pairs of young students or individuals would spend a half-hour or more reading a book, playing math games, drawing or painting, listening to records or, later, tapes slowly took hold in kindergarten and the primary grades spreading to the upper elementary grades. Learning centers, however, seldom appeared in secondary schools.

Between the 1920s and 1980s, then, teachers combined two pedagogical traditions in their classrooms in imaginative ways to create hybrids. In elementary schools, particularly in primary classrooms, richer and diverse melds of the two traditions appeared with far fewer instances surfacing in middle grades and high school. In high schools – allowing for some variation among academic subjects – teacher-centered pedagogy attained it purest forms.[6]

Based on that earlier study, I fashioned a smaller inquiry and asked a policy-to-practice question: between 1993–2005, when states adopted standards-based reforms, accountability measures, and mandated testing, how did teachers in these urban districts organize their classrooms, group students, and teach lessons?

To many observers the answer would be self-evident. Classroom stories and teacher surveys have reported again and again that more lesson time is spent preparing students for high-stakes tests and the narrowing of the curriculum to what is on those tests.

A recent U.S. survey of curriculum changes revealed that in thousands of schools under threat of being closed for poor performance under No Child Left Behind, administrators have restricted students to taking only math and reading classes until their scores improve and then they can take elective subjects. Over 70 percent of nearly 15,000 districts in the nation have cut back time spent in social studies, science, art, music, and other subjects to create more time for reading and math (see Dillon, 2006).

Such stories and scattered evidence describe classroom instruction, particularly in largely poor and minority schools, as more focused on meeting prescribed state standards and raising test scores. Teachers feel pressured to drop student-centered activities such as small group work, discussions, learning centers, and portfolios because such activities take away precious classroom time from standards-based curriculum and test preparation (Firestone *et al.*, 2000; Herman, 2002; Ohanian, 1999; National Board on Educational Testing and Public Policy, 2003).

From these stories, I would expect that classroom reports I collected in the three districts to reflect a shift in instruction toward more teacher-centered practices (e.g. rows of desks facing the teacher, whole group instruction, and classroom activities dominated by much teacher talk). Further, I would expect student-centered features in classrooms such as clustering tables and desks, small group work, and activities calling for much interaction among students and between teacher and students to have diminished. Finally, I would expect that the increasing presence of teaching hybrids that I had noted in an earlier study of many districts – that is mixes of teacher-centered and student-centered practices – would have shrunk considerably in light of these state policy changes. What did I find in the three districts?

I can compress the evidence I gathered from the three districts during these years of strong state and federal backing for standards-based reform, testing, and accountability into two statements:

- The social organization of elementary and secondary school classrooms continued to be informal.

The pattern I noted in my earlier study of teaching practice across the nation had become dominant by 2005 in these three districts' elementary classrooms and more prevalent in secondary ones than in earlier decades. Classrooms filled with round tables and movable desks, particularly in the early grades, placed students in situations where they could easily converse and work in groups. Student work, colorful posters, and ceiling mobiles brightened elementary classrooms suggesting home-like settings. Teachers smiled often at their classes, used casual language, and non-physical warnings to alert students about unacceptable behavior. In the upper grades, while rows of desks were more obvious, informal relations between teachers and students were evident. For example, a firm warning embedded in a teacher-told story about one of her students who used a cell phone or ipod in class and that she confiscated it was sufficient to remind students not to use them in class.

• Pedagogical hybrids flourished.

Since I first noted in the early twentieth century, teachers exhibiting mixes of teacher- and student-centered practices in arranging space, grouping for instruction, and teaching activities, mixes of these traditions had become widespread in three districts' elementary classrooms and more evident in secondary ones.

From the many teacher reports and classroom stories over the past decade a reasonable person would have inferred that a decided shift to more rows of student desks, more whole group instruction, more seat-work, and more teacher-directed tasks such as lectures and note-taking in secondary school classrooms would have turned up in these districts. That is not what I found.

And that surprised me. U.S. administrators seldom tell teachers how to organize their classroom furniture, group students, and conduct lessons in certain ways. For those teachers who had to use mandated curriculum with scripts to follow, they tailored those lessons to the children and circumstances. In short, teachers had a degree of autonomy – some more, some less – to arrange their classrooms, group for instruction, and choose among different activities for the lessons they taught.

What is missing from this small study of classroom features is the content of actual lessons. It is, of course, likely that many teachers to varying degrees, depending upon whether they taught in low-performing urban and rural schools, did prepare students for tests and pursued specific state standards – after all many surveys and stories converge in their reports. Yet even those test-prep lessons, I need to point out, unfolded within distinctly informal settings where teachers used hybrids of teacher- and student-centered practices.

On the whole, then, the evidence I collected from reports on how teachers organized space, grouped for instruction, and the activities they designed for their students suggest that classroom informality and hybrid pedagogies I had noted evolving over the past century in many other school systems have not lessened under district, state, and federal mandates but had even become – contrary to anecdotal evidence – more pervasive in these three districts by 2005.

While I wish I could point to many other studies confirming these statements, I cannot. I have found only a few sources using classroom-based evidence beyond what I have collected that reach similar conclusions (Tepper *et al.*, 2004; Grant, 2003).

Although these few studies challenge the prevailing wisdom about effects of these policies on teaching and raise doubts about top-down policies yielding desired student outcomes, without many other in-depth and long-term classroom observation studies being done I can hardly argue that these policies have failed. At least, however, such few studies call for a reconsideration of the market-inspired definition of the problem and the theories of change embedded in the current standards-based, accountability, and testing policies.

The four basic questions I asked earlier about policies and their implementation in classrooms get to the heart of the connection between policy, research, and practice. Those questions have to be answered faithfully and completely before claims about changes in classroom practices, equity, and social justice can be assessed.

Notes

1 The legal definition of stipulations drawn from the U.S. Code is: 'Included in matters required to be stipulated are all facts, all documents and papers or contents or aspects thereof, and all evidence which fairly should not be in dispute. Where the truth or authenticity of facts or evidence claimed to be relevant by one party is not disputed, an objection on the ground of materiality or relevance may be noted by any other party but is not to be regarded as just cause for refusal to stipulate. The requirement of stipulation applies under this Rule without regard to where the burden of proof may lie with respect to the matters involved'. *U.S. Code*, 'Title 26, Appendix, Title IX-Admissions and Stipulations, Rule 91 (a)'. See: http://www.access.gpo.gov/uscode/title26a/26a_9_.html.

2 This analysis draws on the work of the following: Milbrey McLaughlin, 'Lessons from Past Implementation Research', *Educational Evaluation and Policy Analysis*, Vol. 9, No. 2 (1987), pp. 171–8; Hugh Davis Graham, *The Uncertain Triumph: Federal Education Policy in the Kennedy and Johnson Years* (University of North Carolina Press, 1984); Paul T. Hill, 'The Federal Role in Education', in Diane Ravitch, ed., *Brookings Papers on Education Policy 2000* (Brookings, 2000), pp. 11–57; Andrew Porter and John Smithson, 'Are Content Standards Being Implemented in the Classroom? A Methodology and Some Tentative Answers', in Susan H. Fuhrman, ed., *From the Capitol to the Classroom: Standard-Based Reform in the States* (University of Chicago Press, National Society for the Study of Education, 2001), pp. 60–80; James Spillane, 'Challenging Instruction for "All Students": Policy, Practitioners, and Practice', in Fuhrman, *From the Capitol to the Classroom*, pp. 217–41; Suzanne Wilson and Robert Floden, 'Hedging Bets: Standards-Based Reform in Classrooms', in Fuhrman, *From the Capitol to the Classroom*, pp. 193–216; Richard F. Elmore and Milbrey Wallin McLaughlin, *Steady Work: Policy, Practice, and Reform of American Education* (Santa Monica, CA: Rand, 1988); Michael Fullan, *The New Meaning of Educational Change* (Teachers College Press, 1991); for teachers adapting instructional policies, see Cynthia Coburn, 'Collective Sensemaking about Reading: How Teachers Mediate Reading Policy in Their Professional Communities', *Educational Evaluation and Policy Analysis*, Vol. 23, No. 2 (2001), pp. 145–70.

3 For policy as intentions and the relationship to instructional implementation, see Milbrey McLaughlin, 'Learning from Experience: Lessons from Policy Implementation', in Alan Odden, ed., *Education Policy Implementation* (SUNY Press, 1991), pp. 143–55; David Cohen and James Spillane, 'Policy and Practice: The Relations between Governance and Instruction', in Susan H. Fuhrman, ed., *Designing Coherent Education Policy: Improving the System* (San Francisco: Jossey-Bass, 1993), pp. 35–88; David Cohen and Heather Hill, *Learning Policy: When State Education Reform Works* (Yale University Press, 2001); James Spillane, Brian Reiser,

and Todd Reimer, 'Policy Implementation and Cognition: Reframing and Refocusing Implementation Research', *Review of Educational Research*, Vol. 72, No. 3, (2002), pp. 387–431.

4   Figures for unserved poor children come from *Biennial Evaluation Report, FY 1993–1994*, 'Education of Disadvantaged Children (Chapter 1, ESEA) Formula Grants to Local Education Agencies' (Washington, DC: U.S. Department of Education, Planning and Evaluation Services, 1995); and Nina Rees, 'How the Senate Can Reform Title I to Empower Parents and Help Children Achieve', *Executive Memorandum no. 659* (Washington: Heritage Foundation).

5   For further details see: Elmore and McLaughlin, *Steady Work*; Lorraine McDonnell and Milbrey McLaughlin, *Education Policy and the Role of the States* (Santa Monica, CA: Rand, 1982); Jerome Murphy, 'Progress and Problems: The Paradox of State Reform', in Ann Lieberman and Milbrey McLaughlin, eds, *Policy Making in Education* (Chicago: National Survey of Student Engagement, 1982), pp. 195–214; David Cohen, 'Standards-Based School Reform: Policy, Practice, and Performance', in Helen Ladd, ed., *Holding Schools Accountable* (Brookings, 1996), pp. 99–127.

6   In a study of socialization in 64 classrooms in four elementary schools, grades two and five in the late 1990s, Brint *et al.*, found a blending of traditional and modern values in these classrooms. 'The routine practices of classrooms similarly show a blending of the old and new' (p. 173). See John Dewey's comment from 1950s on progressivism in public schools in Dworkin, pp. 129–30.

References

Associated Press (2006) 'Rising Number of Schools Face Serious Penalties', May 10, CNN.com at http://www.cnn.com/2006/EDUCATION/05/10/school.makeovers.ap/index.html.

Biennial Evaluation Report, FY 1993–1994 (1995) 'Education of Disadvantaged Children (Chapter 1, ESEA) Formula Grants to Local Education Agencies', U.S. Department of Education, Office of the Under Secretary: U.S. Government Printing Office, available online at http://www.ed.gov/pubs/Biennial/index.html.

Brint, S., Contreras, M. and Matthews, M. (2001) 'Socialization Messages in Primary Schools: An Organizational Analysis', *Sociology of Education*, Vol. 74, p. 173.

Bush, President G.W. (2002) 'State of the Union address', *New York Times*, January 30, p. A22.

Carnevale, A. and Descrochers, D. (2003) *Standards for What? The Economic Roots of K-16 Reform*, Princeton, NJ: Educational Testing Service.

Coburn, C. (2001) 'Collective Sensemaking about Reading: How Teachers Mediate Reading Policy in Their Professional Communities', *Educational Evaluation and Policy Analysis*, Vol. 23, No. 2, pp. 145–70.

Cohen, D. (1996) 'Standards-Based School Reform: Policy, Practice, and Performance', in H. Ladd (ed.) *Holding Schools Accountable*, Brookings, pp. 99–127.

Cohen, D. and Hill, H. (2001) *Learning Policy: When State Education Reform Works*, New Haven: Yale University Press.

Cohen, D. and Spillane, J. (1993) 'Policy and Practice: The Relations between Governance and Instruction', in S. H. Fuhrman (ed.) *Designing Coherent Education Policy: Improving the System*, San Francisco: Jossey-Bass, pp. 35–88.

Cuban, L. (1993) *How Teachers Taught*, New York: Teachers College Press.

Cuban, L. (2004) *The Blackboard and the Bottom Line: Why Schools Can't Be Businesses*, Cambridge, MA: Harvard University Press.

DeBray, E., Parson, G. and Woodworth, K. (2001) 'Patterns of Response in Four High Schools under State Accountability Policies in Vermont and New York', in S. H. Fuhrman (ed.) *From the Capitol to the Classroom: Standard-Based Reform in the States*, Chicago: University of Chicago Press, National Society for the Study of Education, pp. 170–92.

Dillon, S. (2006) 'Schools Cut back Subjects to Push Reading and Math', *New York Times*, March 26, see: http://www.nytimes.com/2006/03/26/education/26child.html?ex=1301 029200&en=0c91b5bd32dabe2a&ei=5088&partner=rssnyt&emc=rss.

Dworkin, M. (1959) *Dewey on Education: Selections*, New York: Teachers College Press, pp. 129–30.

Elmore, R. F. and McLaughlin, M. W. (1988) *Steady Work: Policy, Practice, and Reform of American Education*, Santa Monica, CA: Rand.

Fairman, J. and Firestone, W. (2001) 'The District Role in State Assessment Policy', in S. H. Furhman (ed.) *From the Capitol to the Classroom: Standard-Based Reform in the States*, Chicago: University of Chicago Press, National Society for the Study of Education, pp. 124–47.

Firestone, W., Camilli, G., Yurecko, M., Monfils, L. and Mayrowetz, D. (2000) 'State Standards, Socio-fiscal Context, and Opportunity to Learn in New Jersey', *Education Policy Analysis Archives*, Vol. 8, No. 35.

Fullan, M. (1991) *The New Meaning of Educational Change*, Now York: Teachers College Press.

Graham, H. D. (1984) *The Uncertain Triumph: Federal Education Policy in the Kennedy and Johnson Years*, Chapel Hill, NC: University of North Carolina Press.

Grant, S. G. (2003) *History Lessons: Teaching, Learning, and Testing in U.S. High School Classrooms*, Mahwah, NJ: Lawrence Erlbaum Associates.

Grissmer, D. and Flanagan, A. (1998) *Exploring Rapid Achievement Gains in North Carolina and Texas*, Washington, DC: National Education Goals Panel.

Grubb, N. and Lazerson, M. (2004) *The Education Gospel*, Cambridge, MA: Harvard University Press.

Herman, J. (2002) 'Instructional Effects in Elementary Schools', *CSE Technical Report 577,* Center for the Study of Evaluation, Graduate School of Education and Information Studies, University of California, Los Angeles.

Hess, F. (2002) *Revolution at the Margins: The Impact of Competition on Urban School Systems*, Washington, DC: The Brookings Institution Press.

Hill, P. T. (2000) 'The Federal Role in Education', in D. Ravitch (ed.) *Brookings Papers on Education Policy 2000*, Washington, DC: Brookings, pp. 11–57.

Jennings, J. (2003) 'From the White House to the Schoolhouse: Greater Demands and New Roles', in W. L. Boyd and D. Miretzky (eds) *American Educational Governance on Trial: Change and Challenges*, part 1, Chicago: National Society for the Study of Education, pp. 291–310.

Kolderie, T. (2004) *Creating the Capacity for Change*, St Paul, MN: Education Evolving.

McDonnell, L. and McLaughlin, M. (1982) *Education Policy and the Role of the States*, Santa Monica, CA: Rand.

McGuinn, P. (2005) 'The Policy Landscape of Educational Entrepreneurship', paper presented at American Enterprise Institute Conference on Educational Entrepreneurship, November 14.

McLaughlin, M. (1987) 'Lessons from Past Implementation Research', *Educational Evaluation and Policy Analysis*, Vol. 9, No. 2, pp. 171–8.

McLaughlin, M. (1991) 'Learning from Experience: Lessons from Policy Implementation', in A. Odden (ed.) *Education Policy Implementation*, New York: SUNY Press, pp. 143–55.

Murphy, J. (1982) 'Progress and Problems: The Paradox of State Reform', in A. Lieberman and M. McLaughlin (eds) *Policy Making in Education*, Chicago: National Survey of Student Engagement, pp. 195–214.

Myrdal, G. (1944) *An American Dilemma: The Negro Problem and Modern Democracy*, I and II, New York: Harper and Row.

National Board on Educational Testing and Public Policy (2003) 'Perceived Effects of State-Mandated Testing programs on Teaching and Learning: Findings from a national Survey of Teachers', School of Education, Boston College.

Noe, C. (2004) 'Bush Decries Democrats' "Soft Bigotry of Low Expectations"', Newsmax. com, January 9, 2004. See: http://www.newsmax.com/archives/articles/2004/1/9/110923.shtml.

Ohanian, S. (1999) *One Size Fits All: The Folly of Educational Standards*, Portsmouth, NH: Heinemann.

Porter, A. and Smithson, J. (2001) 'Are Content Standards Being Implemented in the Classroom? A Methodology and Some Tentative Answers', in S. H. Fuhrman (ed.) *From the Capitol to the Classroom: Standard-Based Reform in the States*, Chicago: University of Chicago Press, National Society for the Study of Education, pp. 60–80.

Rees, N. (2000) 'How the Senate Can Reform Title I to Empower Parents and Help Children Achieve', *Executive Memorandum no. 659*, Washington, DC: Heritage Foundation.

Reich, R. (1991) *The Work of Nations*, New York: Alfred Knopf.

Spellings, M. (2005) 'Importance of Education for all Students Regardless of Race, Ethnicity, or Class', at http://www.ed.gov/nclb/accountability/achieve/nclb-aa.html.

Spillane, J. (2001) 'Challenging Instruction for "All Students": Policy, Practitioners, and Practice', in S. H. Fuhrman (ed.) *From the Capitol to the Classroom: Standard-Based Reform in the States*, Chicago: University of Chicago Press, National Society for the Study of Education, pp. 217–41.

Spillane, J., Reiser, B. and Reimer, T. (2002) 'Policy Implementation and Cognition: Reframing and Refocusing Implementation Research', *Review of Educational Research*, Vol. 72, No. 3, pp. 387–431.

Stodolsky, S. and Grossman, P. (1995) 'The Impact of Subject Matter on Curricular Activity: An Analysis of Five Academic Subjects', *American Educational Research Journal*, Vol. 32, No. 2, pp. 227–49.

Tepper, J. R., Stone, S. and Roderick, M. (2004) 'Ending Social Promotion: The Response of Students and Teachers', Consortium on Chicago School Research.

Toch, T. (1991) *In The Name of Excellence*, Philadelphia, PA: American Philological Association.

Wilson, S. and Floden, R. (2001) 'Hedging Bets: Standards-Based Reform in Classrooms', in S. H. Fuhrman (ed.) *From the Capitol to the Classroom: Standard-Based Reform in the States*, Chicago: University of Chicago Press, National Society for the Study of Education, pp. 193–216.

5 Community organizing for educational change

Past illusions, future prospects

Dennis Shirley

John Stuart Mill once remarked of education that 'of all the many-sided subjects, it is the one which has the greatest number of sides' (Mill, 1931: 32). We are perhaps well-advised to recall this intrinsic polyvalence of education in times such as our own, when it can appear to readers of the daily newspapers that all that really matters in education can be compressed into pupil test score results. Important as those testing data may be, an overestimation of their salience could lead one to miss out on a number of other critical social dynamics that drive contemporary educational change. Technological innovations, multicultural education, and language policies are all likely to provoke continual debates, for example, regardless of the extent to which they raise or depress test score results. The reason for this, it would appear, is that education ultimately cannot be collapsed into instrumental means, but rather entails an inextricably philosophical core that relates not only to the ends of education, but to the very wishes and dreams we aspire for in life itself. As long as this is the case – and I see no reason to think this will ever change – we would perhaps do well to remind ourselves that the ends of education are not likely to be determined through test score data alone, and that such ends can only be addressed and enacted through sustained inquiry, debate, and reflection in the public realm.

Yet a term such as 'the public realm' can be deceptive in its simplicity, presupposing what needs to be explained. Perhaps the 'public realm' is not a given, but rather a social and political achievement that allows individuals to step out of their private spheres to discover common interests in solving jointly shared problems. Perhaps even in an age of electronic chat rooms, blogging, and endless web portals, an intrinsic value remains in older forms of civic engagement that address not *virtual* but *real* educational and political problems. If this is the case, then individuals from around the world – whether citizens or immigrants, whether in developed nations or the global South, whether rich or poor – can benefit from learning about the diverse outcomes created by political strategies intended to revitalize schools as fulcrums of community engagement in our new context of standardization, testing, and measurement.

To address this topic I employ the following line of investigation. First, I provide some background on community organizing and on a specific network of schools, called 'Alliance Schools', that put what is now called 'education organizing' on the policy map in the United States. This approach to educational change – which simply did not exist two decades ago – became a significant force for improving urban schools in Texas in the 1990s. Second, I describe how recently federal legislation, as interpreted by state education policy makers in Texas, has made education organizing in that regional context so difficult for the Alliance Schools that they have been compelled to undergo a complete reorganization and are only now beginning to return as a network with real civic capacity. Developments in Texas are then, to a certain extent less hopeful than the more optimistic account of developments in California presented by Jeannie Oakes and her colleagues in Chapter 8 of this volume. Third, I indicate that growing public acknowledgment of the limitations of standards-based reforms – especially in terms of their inability to reduce escalating high school drop-out rates in the United States – is leading to a new era of 'post-standardization' that is creating new possibilities for civic engagement and educational improvement.

Community organizing for school reform: origins of the alliance schools

To begin with, one should be clear that by 'community organizing' I do not mean any effort by a group of parents or other community members to improve education in a school. Parents who make contributions to a fund to supplement school materials, or who attend a child's play, or who come to a parents' night, are not, in my sense of the term, engaged in community organizing, although they are manifesting parent involvement in education. Rather, I am using the term in a narrower sense, deriving from the social activism of Saul Alinsky in Chicago, Illinois, in the 1930s. Although space limitations do not allow one to do real justice to Alinsky's contribution, one can note that essentially he borrowed strategies from union organizing in factories and applied them to neighborhoods. He sought to build what he called 'power organizations' of diverse multiethnic constituencies – primarily first generation immigrants – that could negotiate with city councilors and business leaders to improve community conditions in some of Chicago's most squalid neighborhoods. He anchored his organizing activities in pre-existing community institutions, agitated them to question their parochialism, and built new horizontal relationships between them to project an image of popular unity and determination that wrested real concessions – in the form of sanitation, health care, and housing – from political leaders and business elites (see Alinsky, 1946; Horwitt, 1992).

Although he was successful as an organizer in numerous domains, Saul Alinsky never devoted any real attention to the improvement of schools. However, in 1940 he did start a new organization, the Industrial Areas Foundation (IAF), that originally was intended to provide an umbrella network for a wide range of community-based organizations and later created training institutes for community organizers. Alinsky died in 1972 but the IAF continued to evolve under the stewardship of his protégé, Ed Chambers. In the mid-1980s, various Texas-based IAF organizations began working with schools and attained some striking successes that caught the attention of policy makers, researchers, and the larger public (see Shirley, 1997, 2002).

How did they do it? Contrary to the dominant school reform orthodoxies of the time, the innovations piloted by the community organizations of the IAF relied not on standardized testing, marketplace models of reform such as charter schools, or 'one-size-fits-all' instructional templates. Rather, the IAF started with classic grassroots organizing based on sustained inquiry, dialogue, and reflection. In IAF parlance, organizers use 'one-on-ones' to build relational capital. In a nutshell, a 'one-on-one' is a structured conversation with a twofold purpose: to surface community issues that are foremost in the mind of citizens, and to establish a relationship with one's interlocutor.

Does it sound simple? What could be easier than put together a few needs assessment groups, administer a few surveys, code and interpret the data, and have an agenda? It makes sense on a certain level and responds to our craving for action. Yet what the IAF will sometimes do is spend up to a full year just having one-on-one conversations! Teachers talk with parents and clergy. Parents talk with small business owners and police officers. Clergy talk with bus drivers, barbers, and janitors. The goal here is *not* for the community organization to promote its pre-established agenda – rather, it is the exact opposite. The goal is for the community organization to find out what is really troubling people in a community and to ascertain if individuals can be agitated enough to take action. Simultaneously, organizers are always conducting talent searches – trying to find those individuals who aren't just concerned about their own well-being but who care for a whole community and are willing to take some risks by becoming politically involved to improve their community's conditions.

Where do 'one-on-ones' occur? Individuals talk with one another in what are called 'house meetings' that can occur anywhere, actually – typically, in someone's home, but more often in churches, schools, or the community centers of housing projects (council estates). The idea is for these house meetings to be held in settings where people already naturally convene. Gradually, 'one-on-ones' give way to group deliberations and agenda setting. Yet, throughout, the IAF does not rush agenda formation, and uses a mantra of 'power before programs' to emphasize that one has to develop a deep reservoir of relational capital before one can advance to a program that really resonates with the concerns of community residents. It isn't enough to just have one meeting, because sometimes community members need more time than that to figure out what issues really are paramount for them.

What kinds of issues then emerge from these one-on-ones and house meetings? In the poor and working-class communities where the IAF organizes, the topics are often very practical and concrete. Individuals want jobs that pay a living wage with health care benefits; they want to know that their children are safe, both in schools and on the way back and forth to them; they want affordable transportation and housing; they want access to job training programs that will prepare them for a better future. In regards to education they can be very specific: they want a crack house right across the street from a school closed down; they want to be able to understand what their children are learning in school so that they can support them at home; they want teachers who treat them with respect and dignity.

Out of a long process of one-on-ones and house meetings community organizations then begin shaping an agenda. The agenda is never aligned with that of a political party; these community-based organizations are pugnaciously insistent upon their autonomy. The community-based organizations conduct research to discover where funding might be available; stage dramatic, almost scripted encounters with elected officials in mass 'accountability sessions' in which the officials (almost always) commit to supporting the organization's agenda; evaluate their activities, and return to another round of one-on-ones, house meetings, and research actions.

These organizing strategies, of course, hardly represent a silver bullet. Teachers and parents can prove to be poor listeners, essentially defeating the purpose of a 'one-on-one'; school superintendents can stonewall or exhaust community organizations by avoiding meetings or making promises but failing to deliver on them; leadership transitions can render promising starts unsustainable as relational capital has to be rebuilt from scratch. Yet in the late 1980s and 1990s the IAF had a number of striking successes in schools throughout Texas. Some of those successes involved schools that had been veritable battle-grounds in which school principals and teachers were frightened of their students; others had suffered from low academic achievement but had settled into cultures of low expectations that needed a strong push from organized parents to become centered on teaching all pupils to high levels; still others had large numbers of Spanish-speaking immigrant parents who had felt intimidated by educators but learned through the organizing process that teachers sought genuine social partnerships with them to help their children excel in school.

By the end of the century, the IAF had put together a network of over 160 'Alliance Schools' that held annual conferences that attracted thousands of community leaders not only from Texas but all of the United States. Southwest IAF community organizer Ernie Cortes had received a highly coveted MacArthur 'genius' grant and the Alliance Schools had received millions of dollars of funding not only from liberal philanthropies like the Rockefeller and Ford Foundations but also targeted funding from the generally conservative Texas state legislature. It was a remarkable achievement that seemed to defy all of the orthodoxies of mainstream educational change in the 1990s. Nowhere else in the United States was there such a broad-based educational organizing strategy in place, projected forward by a multiracial, multi-class network of grass-roots community leaders.

Inspired by the IAF's pioneering work in Texas, similar networks of community-based organizations throughout the United States became involved in school improvement in subsequent years. These organizations have names like the Association of Communities Organized for Reform Now (ACORN), Direct Action Research and Training, and the PICO National Network. Many of these organizations are scattered across dozens of states and have highly active chapters. Their education organizing strategies are part of multifaceted progressive political campaigns that include affordable housing, jobs that pay a living wage, and health care. The organizations have web sites, send out news blasts, and, as the chapter in this volume by Jeannie Oakes and her colleagues indicates, in California have become increasingly sophisticated about finding and recruiting academic allies to support their agendas.

Unsustainable change? The impact of federal, state, and local reforms on community organizing in Texas

It would take too long to provide a full history of recent educational reforms in Texas, but one should note that beginning in the 1980s, Texas was one of a number of states that employed a 'southern strategy' of school reform. In a nutshell, the strategy was as follows: governors of states that had long lagged behind the rest of the United States in pupil achievement argued that increased taxes should go to schools, provided that educators agreed to accept new accountability measures that would document pupil achievement. This strategy was deployed by governors Bill Clinton in Arkansas, Bill Riley in South Carolina, Lamar Alexander in Tennessee, and Mark White in Texas. George W. Bush inherited these reforms when he became governor of Texas in 1996, and he used pupil learning gains documented by the National Assessment of Education Progress as an important platform in his presidential campaign in 2000.

The No Child Left Behind Act (NCLB) (P.L. 107–110), passed by the US Congress in 2001 and signed into law by President Bush in 2002, combined the continued expansion of testing, now to be monitored by the United States Department of Education, with marketplace models of reform that would enable the parents of children in low-performing schools to have the option to remove them from those schools and to send them to high-performing schools. Considerable funding was allocated to the providers of 'supplementary educational services' – including private, for-profit 'educational management organizations' – to assist children in failing schools. Combined with some of the legislation of President Bush's new Office of Faith-based and Community Services, NCLB appeared to support the devolution of school systems and auxiliary educational services to the private sector.

At the same time that NCLB supported this devolution of urban schooling along the lines of neoliberalism, it simultaneously represented an unprecedented extension of power in the educational arena by the federal government. An exception among western nations, the United States has no clause in the federal constitution regarding education, and this role historically has been allocated to states and local school districts. Now, for the first time, the federal government required three bold new reforms that would apply to all states and localities (except for those few dissidents that might be willing to forego the federal revenues that rewarded districts for compliance with the Act). First, states would be required to conduct regular tests of all public school pupils from grades three to eight in math, reading, and writing to track their progress. Second, the federal government put in place sanctions that could lead local public schools to be closed if they did not show 'adequate yearly progress' (AYP) in pupil achievement on those tests.

In the most severe cases of underachievement, those schools would be closed and their pupils dispersed. Third, the federal government encouraged the growth of educational management organizations and for-profit 'supplementary educational services' at the same time that it expanded its surveillance of virtually all of the 90,000 public schools across the country.

With passage of NCLB into law, Congress and then President Bush changed the political opportunity structure in the nation's educational system. Since the local school districts and the states had not pushed through devolution, now the federal government would do it. Since many local school districts and the states had not put in place rigorous accountability provisions with real sanctions for low-performing schools, now the federal government would do it. Power shifted in two directions simultaneously – towards market-based alternatives at the local level, and towards the monitoring capabilities of the United States Department of Education at the national level.

Who lost power in this reorganization of American education? Traditional urban public school systems, under attack for low pupil test scores and besieged with endemic infrastructural problems, appeared to be the primary losers. To address the new political opportunity structure, and to maintain as much of their traditional prerogatives as possible, they began devolving the authority to run their most troubled schools to new educational management organizations and providers of supplementary educational services. State departments of education also lost power; they would now either have to cut some services to allocate additional staff to design, administer, and report test data to the federal government, or seek new tax revenues to expand their staff to address the new mandates. Schools of education in colleges and universities, traditionally the supplier of the majority of the nation's teachers, also lost power, as NCLB provided clauses that supported 'alternative routes' – often district-based or run by start-up non-profits – into teaching. One could argue that local citizens and teachers also lost power, as local control, already shifting to the states over many decades, appeared further diminished with the rise of the new federally-mandated accountability systems.

It took local and state legislators and school personnel considerable time to recognize the full import of this new political opportunity structure. The initial passage of NCLB had been part of a broad bipartisan effort, but two years after the passage of the Act a small group of dissidents had evolved into a full-fledged revolt. By March 2004 twenty-one states had proposed or passed measures to seek changes in NCLB or to exempt themselves from the Act in its entirety. By April 2004 twenty-seven states had produced resolutions or bills calling for studies of the costs of NCLB, full funding of its provisions by Congress and the President, or for opting out of its stipulations altogether. Maine and Utah passed bills prohibiting the use of state funds to comply with NCLB; the Virginia legislature voted 98 to 1 for a resolution objecting to many parts of NCLB; and the Oklahoma House of Representatives voted unanimously for a resolution calling for the repeal of NCLB. At the time of this writing (February 2007) only three states have not sought waivers for provisions of NCLB or in other ways pushed back against the many mandates (most unfunded) that the Act imposes on their schools (see Neill *et al.*, 2004; National Education Association, 2004).

Hence, NCLB has evoked widespread anger and confusion. Part of the challenge of NCLB concerns its many different sections and ambiguities in key terms. The Act itself is over one thousand pages long, and even an abbreviated 'Desktop Reference' version opens as many new questions as it answers (US Department of Education, 2002). 'Teacher quality', for example, is a core concern of NCLB, but states are free to define teacher quality in different ways, so that comparisons between states are difficult, if not impossible. NCLB requires all schools to be able to demonstrate 'adequate yearly progress' by reducing the number of students below proficient in each ethnic group by 10 percent from the previous year – but federal guidelines defining proficiency differ markedly from those of most states, with the result that in 2004 some 317 schools in California 'showed tremendous academic growth on the state's performance index, yet the federal law labeled them as low-performing' (see Dillon, 2004). This is especially significant for educators because the overall goal of NCLB is to have all of American public school students proficient as measured on reading and math tests by year 2014, twelve years after the enactment of the law – yet 'proficiency' inevitably comes down to a best guess on where a 'cut score' on tests should be set (Rosenberg, 2004). For educators working in gateway communities with high numbers of immigrant children – and there are thousands of these scattered through the cities of the United States – one may well wonder how one should go about raising the test scores of second language learners year after year when so many children arrive in their schools lacking the most rudimentary knowledge of English.

Of separate concern are sections 1111, 1114, and 1118 of NCLB, which initially appeared to support parent involvement in education. On close scrutiny, however, one learns that beyond an unfunded mandate that districts must create parent advisory councils to promote parent involvement, the involvement primarily consists in giving parents in underperforming schools options to select supplementary educational services from outside of the public school system and in choosing charters or private schools as options for their children. For parents who are interested in improving conditions for *all* residents of a vicinity, NCLB appears to offer exit options for only a few parents rather than a strategy for uplifting *all* schools.

Yet NCLB presents daunting challenges for the public at large not only because of ambiguities in its language. At its core, it represents a fundamentally new theory of educational improvement that has won increasing acceptance by policy makers around the globe. Advocates of this approach contend that regular testing of pupils can provide valuable data about student academic achievement and teacher quality, and that in an era in which the human capital of states is increasingly important, citizens have the right to know just how well pupils are doing academically. In the United States, conservative advocates of testing have won allies on the liberal side of the political spectrum through two strategies. First, they have promised additional financial resources, especially for low-income pupils in public school systems; second, by placing a spotlight on disparities between pupils of color and white students, they have insisted that the 'achievement gap' between subgroups must be addressed as a matter of social justice (Education Trust, 2003; Skrla and Scheurich, 2004).

The unclear facets of NCLB, combined with a new federally-mandated, market-driven accountability system, have prompted some angry criticisms of the entire legislative package, especially by liberal advocates who felt betrayed when funding for low-income pupils was cut dramatically at a time of economic recession but the many sanctions of the accountability system remained in place (Meier and Wood, 2004). Further, the public at large disagrees with many key facets of NCLB. For example, more than two-thirds of adults surveyed by the Gallup poll contended that 'the performance of a school's students on a single test is not sufficient for judging whether the school is in need of improvement'; a majority of Americans would rather see more funding for struggling schools than see tax resources dedicated to outside agencies such as the 'supplemental educational services'; and 81 percent worry that 'basing decisions about schools on students' performance in English and math only will mean less emphasis on art, music, history, and other subjects' (Rose and Gallup, 2004).

To examine the impact of NCLB more closely at the grass roots level, I now turn to community-based organizations in Texas that provide some insight into the manner in which NCLB, combined with state and district level reforms, is slowly but decisively shaping educational policies in the United States today. I follow those descriptions with an analysis of the complex ecological interface between NCLB and community organizing, considering in particular the overall political framing and import of NCLB. I contend that the Act is a complicated piece of legislation that contradicts teachers' sense of best practices and endorses measures with which the public at large disagrees.

The Texas Industrial Areas Foundation

As described above, the Texas IAF created a network of 'Alliance Schools' that linked the community organizations with struggling schools in low-income urban neighborhoods throughout Texas in the 1990s. School reformers from throughout the United States and abroad attended Alliance School conferences. Yet seven years into the new century the Alliance Schools appeared to be spent at the very worst and undergoing a complete overhaul at the best. What happened?

From the perspective of the IAF's community organizers and leaders, NCLB and the entire culture of educational testing and accountability that has come to dominate schools in recent years have created a climate of fear and intimidation that have greatly increased the opportunity costs of organizing. It wasn't always this way. In the 1990s, when I lived in Houston and conducted research on Alliance Schools in cities as diverse as Houston, El Paso, Fort Worth, and San Antonio, it was common practice for the Texas IAF to convene parent academies that informed parents about the nature of the tests and why they were important in gauging their children's academic progress. Many educational groups protested against the tests, but the IAF community organizations were not among them.

At Zavala Elementary School in Austin – in many ways, the poster child of the Alliance Schools in the 1990s – the drive to improve the school began when an angry father noticed the discrepancy between his child's excellent grades and her poor results on the Texas Assessment of Academic Skills (TAAS). In this case the tests provided an external reference that gave a parent a lever to demand a higher quality of education for his daughter. Although Texas IAF organizers never explicitly endorsed the tests, their parent academies made it clear that they considered them to be one legitimate assessment tool among others for evaluating pupil progress.

I left Houston for Boston in 1998, and found on my return visits that the emphasis on testing and accountability increased greatly in the subsequent years. 'The turning point for many of us came in February 2003 at our annual Alliance School conference', Mignonne Konecny, lead organizer for the Austin IAF group recalled. 'That was when so many of our teachers and principals said that they were now getting lesson plans from their districts dictating what they should teach, that they were getting flooded with practice tests and benchmark tests to be given every Friday, and we're really getting the message that the tests had become punitive rather than diagnostic.' Organizers and leaders now found that the tests drove so many educational practices in Texas that any kind of reflection, analysis, or skill acquisition not measured on the tests was marginalized in the curriculum. 'The tests now are the curriculum in Texas', Joe Higgs, an organizer in the Houston area, commented. 'Districts are saying more and more that the test is going to be all that we teach, no matter what the cost.'

According to Texas IAF organizers, a host of unethical practices has been implemented in schools in recent years in which teachers and principals are pressed to raise test scores or face a range of punitive actions such as losing their principals or potential state take-overs. Rene Wizig-Barrios, an organizer with the IAF group in Houston, described a series of incidents that depict how extreme the new accountability measures have become:

> One of our principals was told by her district to make sure that homeless kids in a shelter shouldn't show up on testing day because they would depress the scores. Other principals have abolished free time for kids in first, second, and third grade. Principals tell us that they want to meet with us and work with us but that they're so much under the gun to raise test scores that they just can't make the time. And now we have this new law in Texas which says that if kids don't pass the TAKS [Texas Assessment of Knowledge and Skills] reading test in third grade they can be held back. That kind of pressure seems to us to be way too great to put on kids who are that little, and it's a major source of fear and stress for the teachers.

Wizig-Barrios concedes that she does not know how much of these kinds of actions were caused directly by NCLB. 'It's hard to tell what comes from the principal, the district, the state, or NCLB', she said. It is striking to note that the more extreme Texas interventions – such as not allowing third graders to go on to fourth grade unless they pass the TAKS – go far beyond anything specified by NCLB. 'Part of the pressure comes from NCLB, part of it comes from the state of Texas trying to meet the standards, part of it is the district, and part of it is from the schools, where people are scared out of their minds', Konecny commented.

In the climate of fear described by Texas IAF organizers, teachers stop collaborative work and adopt an 'every man for himself' approach to raising their test scores. In this Kafkaesque world, seventh grade teachers find that their pupils haven't learned writing since the fourth grade, because that is the last grade at which writing was assessed by the TAKS. Fifth grade teachers discover that their pupils have never had science or social studies because they were never assessed before the fifth grade – all of the emphasis was put on reading, writing, and mathematics, to get the annual TAKS scores up. 'So all of a sudden the fifth graders are getting social studies and science crammed down their throats, since that is what is tested that year', Konecny observed.

Ironically, the intense pressure put on school principals to raise test scores appears to contribute to a rapid turnover of school leaders, either because principals leave troubled schools as soon as they can or because districts are continually in search of new heads who they think can raise scores. Frightened by the prospect of losing their jobs, some superintendents have forbidden principals to leave their school campuses without prior approval, a hitherto unimaginable incursion on principals' autonomy as educational leaders. Principals in many cities in Texas are now hired on one-year contracts; if their school's test scores are low they are fired, and if the scores are high they receive bonuses. As a result, principals have very real financial incentives to press their teachers to produce high test score results on the TAKS, even when such one-sided emphasis on cognition might undermine the social, physical, and ethical development of children.

In this kind of context testing dominates all aspects of instruction and the curriculum. 'People are so anxious about testing that they try to do everything at once', Kevin Courtney, lead organizer with the El Paso Interreligious Sponsoring Organization (EPISO), said: 'We have testing going on this week in one of our schools that had forty-eight kids in a classroom for the first seven weeks of the school year; there was barely enough space for the kids to even sit on the floor. They finally got them in another class, and now they're testing them for two straight days. It's a disaster, and it isn't just in our Alliance Schools; the paper is filled with letters to the editor from angry teachers every week.'

In summary, Texas IAF organizers consider NCLB to be an incarnation of all of the worst traits of neoliberalism: an educational act that provides incentives to remove their children from traditional public schools, that gives freedoms to charter schools denied to neighborhood schools, and that provides taxpayer money to for-profit educational management organizations instead of channeling those resources into schools that have some oversight by citizens. While there is a sense that there is some value in disaggregating pupil test scores by race, ethnicity, and income, Texas IAF organizers expressed no interest in the kind of national campaign for full funding of NCLB endorsed by some liberal groups. 'There are some big businesses that are racking up on this thing, and making billions of dollars', Konecny said. 'If they took all of that money that was put into the testing regime to free up teachers to create their own assessment models, we'd be a whole lot better off.'

Given the adversarial climate in Texas, how has the IAF endeavored to confront the many anti-intellectual dimensions of contemporary reforms? The IAF's strategy has been to convene a series of 'civic academies' throughout the state to educate the public about the history of testing in the public schools and to inform the public about the millions of dollars that have gone to testing companies that could have gone to advance children's education. Of the Texas IAF's partnering schools, the strongest network has continued in Austin, and the IAF is now seeking to revitalize schools in Houston, Fort Worth, San Antonio, and the Rio Grande Valley. The IAF is in many ways attempting to reverse the historical tide of ever-increasing testing, and while it is an uphill struggle, the IAF is persuaded that the public is beginning to understand that an overemphasis on testing undermines rather than enhances education.

Transitioning to post-standardization

One of the greatest enigmas of educational change involves the curious manner in which some reform proposals never gain popular acceptance, while others are successfully institutionalized, while still others go through a period of acceptance but then lose credibility in the eyes of the public and policy makers over time. Standards-based reform is an example of a movement that began to gain traction in the late 1980s, was implemented in all fifty states in the 1990s, became federal law with NCLB in 2002, but has experienced a significant erosion of support in the following years. What happened?

For many Americans, the push to raise standards and to gather data documenting pupil learning gains has simply gone too far. From this point of view teachers lost autonomy in those instances in which the standards had gained too much detail, limiting their professional discretion. Others complained that so much time was now spent assessing pupil learning on multiple different instruments that time for purposeful instruction and in-depth learning had been sacrificed in the process. Continual testing by outside agencies hardly won much support among students themselves, who wondered why their teachers' assessments of them could not be trusted.

Among policy makers themselves, a more serious source of discomfiture came in the form of a wide variety of data sources indicating that the high number and percentage of high school students who drop out of high school has remained unchanged during the era of standards-based reforms and NCLB. While one could not *prove* that standards and the accountability movement caused high school dropouts, it seemed clear that standards and accountability did not help with this problem. A wide variety of studies, some sponsored by powerful philanthropic entities such as the Gates Foundation, indicated that many of the aspects of education most missing from the accountability movement – such as personal relationships between instructors and pupils, individualized instruction, and multifaceted and culturally responsive relationships between schools and communities – were identified by drop-outs and teachers alike as promising solutions to this 'silent epidemic' (Bridgeland *et al.*, 2006). Increasingly, even the most ardent advocates of 'data-driven decision making' had to confess that the accountability movement that promised to do so much for education had proven incapable of addressing high school drop-out rates. In many cities the percentage of students who did not graduate from high school in four years reached 50 percent.

Although at the time of this writing the term 'post-standardization' has not entered into popular discourse, the inability of standards-based reforms to address issues such as high school drop-outs indicated that a broader repertoire of change strategies would need to be cultivated to make progress in this area. In response, many cities are now showing renewed interest in community organizing strategies as one part of the broad panoply of practices intended to reach out to young people and to them to attend and to graduate from high school (Youth Transitions Task Force, 2006).

Lessons learned

This brief review of community organizing in light of the standardization and accountability movements indicates a range of responses of intermediary institutions' interpretations of this landmark piece of educational legislation in the United States.

For the IAF, the emphasis on accountability in schools has gotten out of control, and schools have been transformed from community sites with potentially democratic practices into extensions of a vast bureaucratic apparatus that values rising test scores above all else. The stance is not anti-testing, but it is critical of the idea that departments of education – whether in state capitals or in Washington, DC – really have sufficient information about the quality of learning in a school to render authoritative judgments based on pupil test scores. In this interpretation, teachers especially need to win back some professional autonomy so that they can have critical conversations with parents, their colleagues, and their pupils about instructional strategies, curricular choices, and exhibitions of pupil learning. The key vision here is that of the teacher as a democratic public intellectual, with considerable discretion over materials, informed by mindful deliberation with parents and other community stakeholders. Accountability matters, from this point of view, but accountability indicators should be shaped by the teachers, pupils, and community members who stand the most to gain or lose in the process of educational change.

For the Texas IAF, the entire emphasis on accountability has gone too far and is having detrimental effects on school climate and pupil learning. By demanding 'adequate yearly progress' as defined primarily by test scores, from this point of view, the federal government has undermined the democratic potential of local public schools and is promoting reform based on compliance with mandates that often go against educators' best judgment. Part of the repertoire of community organizations includes direct action and social protest. If there is no space for teachers to protest practices which they consider to be inimical to pupil learning, teachers will perform rituals of 'contrived collegiality' in which they give lip service to different reform models while continuing quietly with their own understanding of best educational practices (Hargreaves, 1994). Simply increasing the 'classroom press' on teachers rarely is successful, because test-driven strategies tend to focus teachers on short-term rather than long-term goals, isolate them from other adults, limit their opportunities for reflecting on their practice, and deplete their energy (Huberman, 1983). If reformers do not take the requisite time and effort to develop conjoint activities with educators who do the real face-to-face instruction with pupils, they will tend to find that the best teachers will either exit the system or engage in quiet efforts to undermine the reforms through passive resistance and general noncompliance (Hargreaves, 2003; Ingersoll, 2003; and McNeil, 2000).

These considerations are particularly important because a large percentage of teachers disagree with many of the provisions of NCLB, particularly concerning the measurement of adequate yearly progress. In one major survey of teachers recently, four out of ten teachers indicated that their school could raise test scores without improving pupil learning; nine out of ten teachers disagreed that test scores were an accurate reflection of what their pupils who learned English as a second language knew; and a substantial majority of teachers reported that their state's accountability system led them to teach in ways that were against their personal convictions of best instructional practices (Pedulla *et al.*, 2003). If Richard Ingersoll's (2003: 223) findings are accurate that on the aggregate 'the good school is characterized by high levels of teacher control', the Texas IAF's struggle to create educational activity settings in which teachers can follow their consciences and do the best teaching they can appears to be of critical importance for improving education in Texas.

The major lesson to be learned from this particular case study of educational organizing for the future of educational change is that the current accountability movement can be used not only in deleterious ways that impact pupil achievement negatively, but that further marginalize the ability of historically disenfranchised populations to participate in public education. Given the origins of public education in the United States – as a real social movement concerned above all with the development of skills of democratic civic engagement – this historic reversal requires much greater public attention than it has received thus far. Educators from around the globe need to understand that statist models of educational change such as NCLB have political as well as educational consequences. They need to understand that accountability systems can exacerbate social inequalities even as a rhetoric of equity is used to promote their widespread adaptation. Recognizing that standardization and increased testing have failed to improve high school drop-out rates, Americans are just beginning to reverse the negative consequences of the major reforms of recent years. Educators from other nations who are looking for new ways to create public roles for citizens rather than bracketing them out of the civic arena through an ideology of testing and measurement should take a cautionary note from these struggles and set-backs in education in the contemporary United States.

References

Adams, G. L. and Engelmann, S. (1996) *Research on Direct Instruction: 25 Years Beyond DISTAR*, Seattle, WA: Educational Achievement Systems.

Alinsky, S. (1946) *Reville for Radicals*, Chicago, IL: University of Chicago Press.

Alinsky, S. (1971) *Rules for Radicals*, New York: Vintage.

Anyon, J. (2005) *Radical Possibilities: Public Policy, Urban Education, and a New Social Movement*, New York: Routledge.

Association of Community Organizations for Reform Now (ACORN) (2002) *Parents Left Behind: A Study of State, Federal and School District Implementation of No Child Left Behind*, Washington, DC: ACORN.

Beam, J. M. and Sharmeen, I. (2003) *ACORN Education Reform Organizing: Evolution of a Model*, Fordham University, New York: National Center for Schools and Communities.

Berliner, D. C. and Biddle, B. J. (1995) *The Manufactured Crisis: Myths, Fraud, and the Attack on America's Schools*, New York: Perseus.

Bridgeland, J. M, DiIulio, J. J. and Morison, K. B. (2006) *The Silent Epidemic: Perspectives of High School Dropouts*, Washington, DC: Civic Enterprises.

Castells, M. (2000) *The Information Age: Economy, Society, and Culture, Vol. 1: The Rise of the Network Society*, Malden, MA: Blackwell.

Chall, J. S. (2000) *The Academic Achievement Challenge: What Really Works in the Classroom?*, New York: Guilford.

Cuban, L. and Usdan, M. (2003) *Powerful Reforms with Shallow Roots: Improving America's Urban Schools*, New York: Teachers College Press.

Darling-Hammond, L. (2000) 'Teacher Quality and Student Achievement: A Review of State Policy Evidence', *Education Policy Analysis Archives*, Vol. 8, No. 1, available online at www.epaa.asu.edu/epaa/v8n1/.

Dillon, S. (2004) 'Bad School, or Not? Conflicting Ratings Baffle the Parents', *New York Times*, 5 September, A1.

Dingerson, L., Brown, C. and Beam, J. M. (2004) *26 Conversations about Organizing, School Reform, and No Child Left Behind*, Washington, DC: Authors.

Dudley-Marling, C. and Paugh, P. C. (2005) 'The Rich get Richer; the Poor get Direct Instruction', in B. Altwerger (ed.) *Reading for Profit*, Portsmouth, NH: Heinemann, pp. 156–71.

Education Trust (2003) *ESEA: Myths Versus Realities: Answers to Common Questions about the New No Child Left Behind Act*, Washington, DC: Education Trust.

Friedman, T. L. and Wyman, O. (2007) *The World is Flat: A Brief History of the Twenty-First Century*, revised edn, New York: Farrar, Straus and Giroux.

Fullan, M. (2001) *The New Meaning of Educational Change*, New York: Teachers College.

Fuller, B. (2000) 'The Public Square, Big or Small? Charter Schools in Political Context', in B. Fuller (ed.) *Inside Charter Schools: The Paradox of Radical Decentralization*, Cambridge, MA: Harvard University Press, pp. 12–65.

Fung, A. (2004) *Empowered Participation: Reinventing Urban Democracy*, Princeton, NJ: Princeton University Press.

Gold, E., Simon, E. and Mundell, L. (2004) 'Bringing Community Organizing into the School Reform Picture', *Nonprofits and Voluntary Sector Quarterly*, Supplement to Vol. 33, No. 3: 54S–76S.

Greenstone, J. D. and Peterson, P. E. (1973) *Race and Authority in Urban Politics: Community Participation and the War on Poverty*, Chicago, IL: University of Chicago Press.

Grissmer, D. and Flanagan, A. (1998) *Exploring Rapid Achievement Gains in North Carolina and Texas*, Washington, DC: National Education Goals Panel, November.

Haney, W. (2000) 'The Myth of the Texas Miracle in Education', *Education Policy Analysis Archive*, Vol. 8, No. 41, available online at www.epaa.asu.edu/epaa/v8n41/.

Hargreaves, A. (1994) *Changing Teachers, Changing Times: Teachers' Work and Culture in the Postmodern Age*, New York: Teachers College.

Hargreaves, A. (2003) *Teaching in the Knowledge Society: Education in the Age of Insecurity*, New York: Teachers College.

Henig, J. R. (1994) *Rethinking School Choice: Limits of the Market Metaphor*, Princeton, NJ: Princeton University Press.

Horwitt, S. (1992) *Let Them Call Me Rebel: Saul Alinsky – His Life and Legacy*, New York: Vintage.

House, E. R., Glass, G. V., McLean, L. F. and Walker, D. F. (1978) 'No Simple Answer: Critique of the Follow Through Evaluation', *Harvard Educational Review*, Vol. 48: 128–60.

Huberman, M. (1983) 'Recipes for Busy Kitchens', *Knowledge: Creation, Diffusion, Utilization*, Vol. 4: 478–510.

Ingersoll, R. M. (2003) *Who Controls Teachers' Work? Power and Accountability in America's Schools*, Cambridge, MA: Harvard University Press.

Kennedy, E. M. (2003) *Press Release: Statement of Senator Edward M. Kennedy on the first anniversary of the No Child Left Behind Act*, http://nhpr.org/static/programs/specials/nclb/statements/kennedy_release.php (12 July 2004).

Klein, S. P., Hamilton, L. S., McCaffrey, D. F. and Stecher, B. M. (2000) *What do Test Scores in Texas Tell Us?*, Rand Education Issue Paper, Santa Monica, CA: Rand.

Lipsky, M. (1980) *Street-level Bureaucracy: Dilemmas of the Individual in Public Services*, New York: Russell Sage Foundation.

Manzo, K. K. (2004) 'Study Challenges Direct Reading Method', *Education Week*, Vol. 23, No. 3: 3.

Massachusetts Coalition for Teacher Quality and Student Achievement (1999) Grant Proposal to the Office of Postsecondary Education, United States Department of Education.

McNeil, L. M. (2000) *Contradictions of School Reform: Educational Costs of Standardized Testing*, New York: Routledge.

Mediratta, K. (with the community organizing research team: Norm Fruchter, Edwina Branch, Barbara Gross, Janice Hirota, Onanda McBride, Natalie Price, Beth Rosenthal, Tom Saunders, and Meryle Weinstein) (2004) *Constituents of Change: Community Organizations and Public Education Reform*, New York: Institute for Education and Social Policy, New York University.

Meier, D. and Wood, G. (1931) *Many Children Left Behind: How the No Child Left Behind Act is Damaging our Children and our Schools*, Boston, MA: Beacon Press.

Mill, J. S. (1931) 'Inaugural Address at St. Andrews', in Cavenagh, F. A. (ed.) *James and John Stuart Mill on Education*, Cambridge, MA: Harvard University Press, p. 32.

Murrell, P. C. Jr. (2001) *The Community Teacher: A New Framework for Effective Urban Teaching*, New York: Teachers College Press.

National Commission on Excellence in Education (2006) *A Nation at Risk*, retrieved 15 March, available online at http://www.ed.gov/pubs/NatAtRisk/risk.html.

National Education Association (2004) 'Growing Chorus of Voices Calling for Changes in NCLB', 22 November, available online at http://www.nea.org/esea/chorus1.html.

National Reading Panel (2000) *Teaching Children to Read: An Evidence-Based Assessment of the Scientific Research Literature on Reading and its Implications for Reading Instruction*, Rockville, MD: National Institute of Child Health and Human Development.

Neill, M., Guisbond, L. and Schaeffer, B. (2004) *Failing our Children: How 'No Child Left Behind' Undermines Quality and Equity in Education*, Cambridge, MA: Fairtest, p. 132.

Oakes, J., Hunter Quartz, K., Ryan, S. and Lipton, M. (2000) *Becoming Good American High Schools: The Struggle for Civic Virtue in Educational Reform*, New York: Free Press.

Pedulla, J. J., Abrams, L. M., Madaus, G. F., Russell, M. K., Ramos, M. A. and Miao, J. (2003) *Perceived Effects of State-Mandated Testing Programs on Teaching and Learning: Findings from a National Survey of Teachers*, Boston College, Chestnut Hill, MA: National Board on Educational Testing and Public Policy.

Rainwater, L. and Smeeding, T. M. (2003) *Poor Kids in a Rich Country: America's Children in Comparative Perspective*, New York: Russell Sage.

Rank, M. R. (2004) *One Nation, Underprivileged: Why American Poverty Affects us All*, New York: Oxford University Press.

Rose, L. C. and Gallup, A. M. (2004) *The 36th annual Phi Delta Kappan/Gallup Poll of the Public's Attitudes Toward the Public Schools*. www.pdkintl.org/kappan/k0490pol.htm.

Rosenberg, B. (2004) *What's Proficient? The No Child Left Behind Act and the Many Meanings of Proficiency*, Washington, DC: American Federation of Teachers.

Scheurich, J. J., Skrla, L. and Johnson, J. J. (2004) 'Thinking Carefully about Equity and Accountability', in L. Skrla and J. J. Scheurich (eds) *Educational Equity and Accountability: Paradigms, Policies, and Politics*, New York: RoutledgeFalmer.

Shirley, D. (1997) *Community Organizing for Urban School Reform*, Austin, TX: University of Texas Press.

Shirley, D. (2002) *Valley Interfaith and School Reform: Organizing for Power in South Texas*, Austin, TX: University of Texas Press.

Skrla, L., Scheurich, J. J., Johnson Jr., J. F. and Koschoreck, J. W. (2004) 'Accountability for Equity: Can State Policy Leverage Social Justice?' in L. Skrla and J. J. Scheurich (eds) *Educational Equity and Accountability: Paradigms, Policies, and Politics*, New York: RoutledgeFalmer.

Stein, M., Carnine, D. W. and Dixon, R. C. (1998) 'Direct Instruction: Integrating Curriculum Design and Effective Teaching Practice', *Intervention in School and Clinic*, Vol. 33: 227–34.

Stone, C. (1989) *Regime Politics: Governing Atlanta, 1946–1988*, Lawrence, KS: University Press of Kansas.

Taylor, W. L. (2000) 'Standards, Tests, and Civil Rights', *Education Week*, Vol. 15, November: 56.

U.S. Department of Education (2002) *No Child Left Behind: A Desktop Reference*, Washington, DC: U.S. Department of Education.

U.S. Department of Education (2003) *No Child Left Behind: A Parent's Guide*, Washington, DC: U.S. Department of Education.

Wayne, A. J. and Youngs, P. (2003) 'Teacher Characteristics and Student Achievement Gains: A Review', *Review of Educational Research*, Vol. 73: 89–122.

Witte, G. (2003) 'As Income Gap Widens, Uncertainty Spreads: More US Families Struggle to Stay on Track', *Washington Post*, 20 September, sec. A1.

Youth Transitions Task Force (2006) *Too Big to Be Seen: The Invisible Dropout Crisis in Boston and America*, Boston, MA: Private Industry Council.

6 Roles for systematic social enquiry on policy and practice in mature educational systems

John M. Owen

Introduction

This chapter argues that the findings of properly negotiated social enquiry can and should have a strong influence on educational change and school improvement. Drawing on the experiences of a dedicated evaluation centre at a major university in Australia, conclusions are inductively drawn about ways in which evaluators can position themselves to influence decision-making by educational policy makers and providers.[1]

For some time I have been interested in types and sources of information that are used to influence the working knowledge of policy makers and practitioners. One contribution is derived from systematic social enquiry (SSE) that, for this chapter, we can think of in terms of social/educational research and evaluation. We know that the products of enquiry are but one input to social problem solving (Lindblom and Cohen, 1979) and to policy formulation (Weiss, 1999). Even when there is enthusiasm and commitment for research, difficulties emerge because findings are not always crafted to meet the needs of policy makers or program staff (Lipton, 1992).

Taking evidence like this into consideration, my colleagues and I have been concerned to make evaluation studies useful to those who require an empirical contribution to their deliberations. This determination is also a response to contemporary criticisms that much traditional evaluation practice has failed to contribute to social betterment (Schwandt, 2002).

An implication of this criticism is to conceive of research and evaluation as a knowledge production endeavour that is considerably broader than that confined to determining worth of interventions by proving that they work. As I have indicated elsewhere, evaluation involves the production of empirically based knowledge that can be applied at any stage of policy or program delivery (Owen, 2004).

Other attempts to overcome such criticisms have been to foster relationships with program stakeholders, to ensure that SSE knowledge responds to their needs.

A third and more expansive strategy has been to act as a knowledge broker, to be on hand to provide a perspective on issues about which we have some knowledge or expertise. This is conceptual or theoretical knowledge accumulated over time due to interest in organizational improvement, and on improvements in educational policy and practice. The notion of a broker implies placing this knowledge alongside information that other interested parties bring to the table when policy and program decisions are being made (Owen and Lambert, 1998).

In the remainder of this chapter I wish to illuminate and extend these issues by presenting an example of how these strategies have influenced recent educational policy development and implementation.

This example can be thought of as a case, an examination of a series of events, in a geographical location (Australia), over time (2003–6). A reason for presenting the case is to provide grounding for the audience and to focus discussion. Being located in Australia, the implications for practice in other settings require extrapolation to other contexts. Stake and others claim that drawing these implications involves a process of 'naturalistic generalisation', which is attained by 'recognising the similarities of objects and issues out of context, and by sensing the natural covariance of happenings' (Stake, 1978: 5–8).

Case focus: developing and implementing a policy on Studies of Asia and Australia in Australian Schools (SOAAA)

The object of interest in this case is a policy encapsulated in the recent release of a document titled 'Engaging Young Australians with Asia in Australian Schools (2006).[2] State and Federal Ministers of Education, through the Ministerial Council on Educational Training and Youth Affairs (MCEETYA), have endorsed the policy. The policy is a key outcome for the supporters of Studies of Asia and Australia in Australian schools (SOAAA).

That this policy innovation has emerged from 'nothing to something' in a relatively short period of time makes SOAAA an interesting case for scholars interested in educational change. The fact that this innovation has emerged from outside existing established mature educational jurisdictions, the State education systems, adds another element to this interest.[3]

SOAAA can be traced to the formation of the Asian Education Foundation (AEF) (a foundation of the Melbourne University and Curriculum Corporation) in 1992. Over more than a decade, the AEF, with the support of the Australian government, spearheaded a national impetus for teaching about Asia through direct and indirect support for schools. The AEF has worked at both system and school level to encourage take-up of studies about Asia. The AEF had to overcome a major hurdle, that of an educational outsider, in that it was not part of the formal curriculum provision of the States, and that, for the first 10 years of its existence, no State or Federal framework explicitly supported the adoption of teaching about Asia.

However, during this period the AEF:

- was able to access some Commonwealth funds designed primarily to support studies of foreign languages, for the purposes of supporting SOAAA;
- produced extensive materials which were disseminated by the national curriculum agency – Curriculum Corporation;

- established relations with all State jurisdictions and funded (fully or partly) consultants in these jurisdictions;
- set up and supported networks of schools with common interests in SOAAA;
- arranged high quality professional development targeted at influential teachers who had interests which were consistent with SOAAA.

While the AEF had commissioned evaluations during the first decade of its existence, these had been mainly for accountability purposes, reporting successes to the Australian government to assure continuation of funding. It was not until 2003 that management of evaluation studies turned to a focus on increasing staff understanding of the effects of their initiatives and using these understandings to refine and develop their policies and services.

From 2003, I have been involved in a series of evaluative studies that contributed to this policy. Below I examine the purpose of these strategies and the knowledge products that were produced. These are reported in terms of (a) purpose of the investigation, (b) the stimulus for the study, and (c) the knowledge produced. In addition, and for the purposes of grounding the study for readers, a summary of the findings are presented.

Purpose 1: understand systemic trends that affect up-take of a policy on SOAAA

Stimulus

Extensive changes in State curriculum frameworks had commenced. AEF management required systematic knowledge of these changes to plan future strategies. To this end, the knowledge produced was an overview of existing educational frameworks and trends in provision across Australia.

Findings summary

A review of websites and interviews with key policy makers was undertaken. Below is part of the report to the management of the AEF.

As indicated (earlier), education in Australia has traditionally been the responsibility of the States. Influence on what schools do appear in many forms. The elements most relevant are:
- curriculum policies and frameworks;
- assessment of students and end-of-school examinations (Year 12); and
- support for schools through resources and professional development.

These elements affect government schools directly and also have an influence, to a lesser or greater extent, on non-government schools. Curriculum policies and frameworks provide teaching and student outcome guidelines within content areas, e.g. English, The Arts, Mathematics, Society and the Environment, that encourage schools to have the final say about how material is taught in classrooms. Nomenclature varies from State to State, for example the term Essential Learnings is used in Tasmania to refer to what is taught and how student outcomes are assessed and reported.

At the present time, some States have relatively settled frameworks, for example the Northern Territory, while others are revising their frameworks, for example, the ACT and Queensland. In Queensland syllabuses in eight learning areas for levels 1–10 have been completed and will be implemented in schools over the next three years. Still others are making concerted attempts to have their frameworks adopted. These attempts are in recognition that full adoption across all schools has been resisted in some quarters. For example, in Western Australia and South Australia, where the current versions of the frameworks have been in place for some years, additional central resources have been recently committed to ensure that all government schools use the relevant frameworks to structure what is taught. Australian curriculum frameworks exhibit a complexity often not found in educational systems in other parts of the world.

For example, the new Victorian Essential Learning Standards (VELS) is based around three 'interwoven' strands; Physical, Personal and Social Learning, Disciplined-based Learning, and Interdisciplinary Learning, designed to equip students with capacities to (i) manage themselves and their relations with others, (ii) understand the world, and (iii) act effectively in that world.

In summary, Australian schools are very busy organizations and teachers are required to make sense of complex new knowledge. On the one hand there are demands on teachers to complete routine tasks, such as extensive student assessment and reporting requirements. On the other hand, schools are in a continuous state of flux that tests the most professional and innovative practitioner. System level curriculum frameworks and policies encourage this state of flux. There is an assumption that school administrators and teachers are willing and able to decide on the detail of what is taught at a given school and how it will be taught.

The fact that most educational jurisdictions have introduced system-wide testing in these areas encourages a degree of consistency in implementation across schools. There are, however, other key learning areas, within which there is considerable flexibility and scope for the inclusion of content from various sources. All frameworks encourage interdisciplinary teaching to a greater or lesser extent, and provide opportunities for innovations in the curriculum. The above scenario leads to the conclusion that a school's curriculum can be viewed in terms of a contest among or competition for content, space and resources for non-core curriculum time.

Flexibility in curriculum decision making is consistent with a national trend to make the school Principal responsible for administrative and educational aspects of a school.

In some States, large amounts of money are controlled by Principals and used by schools or school clusters to conduct professional or staff development for teacher needs identified by a school. Observation and research has suggested that, in the past, much of this staff development has not led to sustainable change in teaching and learning settings.

To overcome this, States are moving to improve the quality of in-school professional development by appointing senior staff to oversee the quality of teacher professional development. This is consistent with pedagogical leadership applied to the whole school. As an extension of this, Victoria has introduced the *Innovations and Excellence* Program which involves the employment – for periods of up to three years – of a change agent who works with a school cluster, often one secondary school linked to feeder primary schools. The change agent usually has extensive educational experience but is not teaching while in this position.

In summary, the emerging realities of school governance in Australian schools can be characterised by the following:

- increasing emphasis on the leadership and management roles of school Principals,
- professional development controlled by and conducted at the school level,
- expectations that schools will interpret State curriculum frameworks to meet local needs,
- competition for a place in the school curriculum from a variety of pressure groups; the crowded curriculum,
- the 'internationalisation' of many schools,
- encouragement to teach to more complex student outcomes, and
- concern for assessment and reporting to parents.

Reflection

The commissioning of this review was stimulated by a need for AEF staff to develop a comprehensive overview of the rapid changes in systems that they had to deal with on a regular basis. While the staff did not have the time or capacity to undertake such a review, their existing knowledge enabled the researchers to locate important sources of information and identify key informants in the jurisdictions.

Purpose 2: understand effects of existing strategies for encouraging SOAAA in schools

Knowledge produced

Description of the implementation of SOAAA in good practice schools.

Stimulus

Little or no formalised knowledge on school and teacher responses to AEF initiatives.

Findings summary

This study used investigatory analytical techniques to:

* describe and interpret what a *commitment to studies about Asia* meant in terms of the practice of teachers and others in schools, and
* outline the strategies and conditions that encouraged and supported the development of this commitment.

Data analysis led to findings that are summarised in Figure 6.1. In commenting on Figure 6.1, we made the following statements.

A mature or sustained commitment to SOAAA has the following characteristics:

* There are two levels of implementation, the school and individual units of teaching and learning. The latter involves students directly, and leading to identifiable learning outcomes in terms of knowledge, attitudes and skills.
* A linear, and hierarchical pattern would have the school develop school policy before units of work are developed. Getting SOAAA implemented

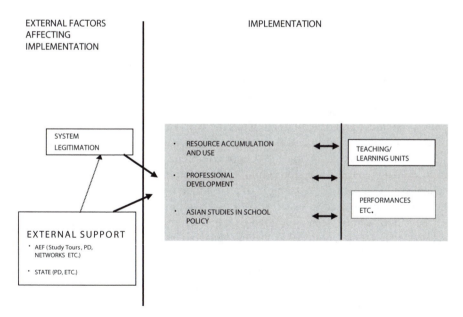

Figure 6.1 School Commitment to Studies of Asia: implementation characteristics

in schools is not like this. Instead there has been a recursive and interactive relationship between school policy and practice. From the cases, it seems that getting whole school commitment to studies of Asia was more likely to happen after a 'critical mass' of teaching practices had been implemented, often over time.

- This also applies to the relationship between the amount and nature of in-school professional development, the availability of resources, and the creation of policy. Again, of critical importance in what might be called an incremental build up of interest in SOAAA was the work and interest of passionate teachers, many of whom had been involved in extensive external professional development supplied by the AEF at the national and state levels.

- While activities such as TICFA tours (in-country professional development for teachers) were important as seeding activities, most cases in this study mentioned the ongoing support that individual teachers and schools accessed from the AEF, for example via AEF advisors and other curriculum consultants in state and Catholic systems.

The findings reinforced the view that change is a process, not an event, and that getting to a stage where a school had a commitment to Asian studies did not happen overnight. This was a finding supported by the vast literature on innovation. Another finding from this literature is that the more complex the innovation, the more time is required for its implementation, and the more difficult it is for it to become an accepted part of the work of the adopting institution. The consensus is that a major innovation takes at least three years to become sustained. By a major innovation is usually meant a single identifiable new procedure or practice, an educational example, a new method of student assessment and reporting.

A commitment to SOAAA was not like this. Securing a commitment to teaching about Asia was a complex undertaking, not merely that a unit or two across the curriculum was based around information about Asia. It was in fact multifaceted and involves school and classroom levels. At the very least it consisted of a school policy statement and/or a strategic plan, the teaching about Asia in many areas of the curriculum, and in addition, whole school activities such as a festival or school performance involving the school community. While the link has rarely been drawn, securing a major commitment to an innovation across the whole school could be seen as an example of a sustained learning activity for staff, and thus the strategies used to install and sustain a commitment to Asia in the fabric of the school can be seen as a good example of organizational learning, which acknowledges social, political as well as pedagogical dimensions.

The study also reflected on factors that affected SOAAA take-up, one of which was the AEF strategy to target a very good practising teacher in a school and support that teacher over time. This teacher usually worked initially with interested colleagues to build a basis of support, by encouraging other teachers to teach SOAAA units in classrooms. A critical mass of interest formed over time. The leader also worked on school-level strategies at the same time to spearhead whole-school commitment. Inclusion of SOAAA in formalised school plans or policies was often the last element in a school's commitment to SOAAA.

This teacher became what we called a 'pedagogical leader', variation on the idea of teacher leadership. In addition to attention to roles associated with teaching and acting as a resource for other teachers, a pedagogical leader performed important political roles in the school. These included: lobbying the Principal; working in school committee and decision-making structures to ensure more SOAAA in the curriculum; and informally influencing subject area groups when they were deciding on the content of teaching units. In effect, the AEF adopted a change model that relied on the expertise and dedication of very good teachers to achieve the changes they wanted in schools. These very good teachers could be thought of as being able to manage both 'up' and 'down' within an organizational context, and to apply their management skills as opportunities were presented.

Reflection

It would be fair to say that this study was a revelation to key AEF members. The description of key teachers as 'pedagogical leaders' hit a nerve with the AEF management. The model in Figure 6.1 was widely shared with key AEF stakeholders. The report, endorsed by the AEF Board, became a key aspect of information sessions conducted by management with teacher associations and other interest groups. The fact that the evaluators could summarise so much of what was important in a diagram was a key element in the use of knowledge produced in this strategy.

The above paragraph is mainly about reporting. A second aspect to note was that we did not use extensive referencing of the literature in documentation to the AEF. However, if it had been asked for, we had at our disposal references that could be consulted by AEF staff if required. Through the process of writing this report, we also discovered that our notion of pedagogical leadership appeared to push the boundaries of the literature. While teacher leadership has been extensively discussed (see, for example, Harris, 2003), it appears that acting as political infighters in school decision-making has not previously been included as a legitimate role for teachers as leaders. This may be due to the fact that Australian schools operate on more democratic principles than their counterparts in countries such as the United Kingdom, or that our review of the literature was not wide enough.

Purpose 3: provide directions for supporting a national policy on SOAAA

Knowledge produced

This was a framework for encouraging school principals to promote SOAA in their schools. The stimulus was: devolution of educational decision making to schools, a key development in Australian schools and the need to understand implications for SOAA.

Findings summary

This study relied on interviews with key policy and system level bureaucrats in State educational systems and group interviews with teachers and school principals.

The report included the following advice:

> A close examination of recent press articles would alert a reader to the existence of pressure groups that wish to persuade systems and schools to include their interests in the curriculum. The following are examples that have come to our attention during the past few weeks. There has been extensive publicity about the health of young people, and nutritionists and the AMA are encouraging changes to the food offered in schools. Also, we know of the extensive dissemination of a mental health curriculum resource to schools across the country. Further, a national organization is currently advertising for a researcher to undertake a national curriculum audit to determine how content about emergency management could be included in school programs. These and other like efforts are effectively in competition with SOAAA and the work of the AEF for a place in the curriculum. The strategies that are discussed in the following sections should be read in the light of this reality.
>
> In the bluntest terms, the AEF should see their mission in terms of achieving advantage over competing groups for time, space and influence in the school curriculum: *strategies* should be planned with this in mind. The AEF should not lose sight of the ultimate *outcome,* which is to provide effective and sustainable education about SOAA to students in schools across the country.
>
> Also, we recommended that a whole-school approach to SOAAA should be the goal of the AEF. We suggested strategies to achieve this could be thought of in terms of five interlocking objectives. These are:
> * persuading Principals and other key school leaders to make SOAAA a priority for school change;
> * providing the school leadership (the Principal and other leaders) with a rationale or justification for SOAAA that they could use in school level decision-making which acknowledges curriculum contestability issues discussed earlier in this chapter;
> * providing a practical model based on effective change theory that would structure high quality teacher professional development;
> * supporting teachers responsible for in-school or cluster professional development with resources by which this model could be implemented which has flexibility for use in a variety of settings;
> * continuing to provide materials and resources for teachers as the need for these resources becomes apparent.

Reflection

This report provoked interest and debate among AEF stakeholders. While there was strong support from the AEF Board, representatives from some State jurisdictions felt that some of the recommendations, such as the list of objectives above, were too direct. An implication of the report was that consultants would need to change their focus, from working directly with teachers, to one of persuading school Principals to adopt SOAAA. At some interfaces between the AEF and States, this was considered to be untenable.

However, this report did influence the national policy statement, discussed earlier in this chapter. The statement included the following indicators of progress in implementing the policy:

- active support from the school leadership;
- a team of people including the Principal, school personnel, parents and the wider school community committed to whole school across the curriculum approach to SOAAA;
- school policy which incorporates studies of Asia and Australia across learning areas and acknowledges their place in the whole school;
- a curriculum that explicitly includes studies of Asia and Australia in learning areas, that sets out a sequence including knowledge, understanding, skills and values, and that recognises multiple entry points for students. (Department of Education 2006)

Knowledge production and its influence on educational change and improvement

In this section, I would like to step back to formalise the SSE strategies used in the case example above. I have labelled this approach as *Investigator-User Linkage*. Formalising this approach provides a basis for arguing its merits relative to other models of SSE, designed to reduce the culture gap between traditional researchers and practitioners (Wingens, 1993).[4]

In the *Investigator-User Linkage* approach, initiation of the problem can come from the researchers and program stakeholders together or by the stakeholders alone. Either group can question the problem, but after it is refined, the researcher takes major responsibility for investigations, or provides technical support for users in data management processes. Diffusion of the findings is via reports and interactive techniques. Findings can be reported via academic channels but this is secondary to stakeholder reporting requirements. Studies that fit into this model are highly focused and have direct implications for implementation. They are likely to be situation specific and often on a smaller rather than larger scale.

As I have implied, policy and program evaluation at the Centre for Program Evaluation, and carried out by other specialist evaluation groups, fits within this model of SSE (Ryan, 1988). In the USA, the Evaluation Center at the University of Western Michigan undertakes similar work, but, perhaps surprisingly, there seem to be fewer university based units of this nature in Europe. However, individual academics undertake studies that fit into this category and they are well known in professional evaluation associations.

In a fully elaborated *Investigator-User Linkage* model the evaluator must attend to negotiation of evaluation design(s). This involves identification of audiences and others interested in the program, collectively referred to as the stakeholders. A key aspect of this negotiation is to focus evaluation on information needs. Thus the scope of studies based on this model tends to be localised. In addition to negotiation, a second key feature of such evaluation practice is the attention to dissemination of findings. Evaluators must possess effective reporting and other communication skills (Owen, 2006).

The effective evaluator relies on a repertoire of methodological skills to produce well-founded findings that are targeted to the specific problem defined during the negotiation stage.

The focused nature of SSE within this model implies that findings are designed to have a direct effect on policy and practice. Not surprisingly, academics and others undertaking evaluation research (research on evaluation) have carved out a major knowledge base on strategies which have led to the use of findings (see for example Johnson, 1998).

The effectiveness of the model is considerably enhanced if linkages between evaluator and clients can be extended to several studies over a longer time period, and the example in this paper is meant to show the effects of such a liaison. This requires the identification of protocols and rules of relationship between knowledge producers and knowledge users, with a deliberate resourcing of strategies for dissemination *and* assistance to agencies for translating SSE findings into action. The evaluator can enhance this by becoming closely associated with commissioning organizations, adopting a critical friend perspective.

The protocol summarised above is known in the knowledge utilisation literature as 'sustained interactivity' (Huberman and Cox, 1990). Research and evaluation groups that develop a history of collaboration with target users develop a 'user-friendly' institutional context with a corresponding reward structure. The use of informal linkage mechanisms in addition to formal ones are activated when a study is undertaken, and dissemination efforts set in motion automatically. This effort relies on a lot of dissemination and utilisation 'savviness', which Huberman maintains is probably the single most powerful influence on SSE use (Huberman, 1987).

On the basis of experiences with studies such as the AEF example above, the following strategies extend the list of important facets of the relationship between evaluator and user:

• a need for initial contacts to establish personal report rapport and an understanding of the information needs of policy makers or providers, and the capacity of researchers to undertake studies that respond to these needs;
• feedback about progress and tentative findings, and opportunity for practitioners to understand the implications for action; through this there are chances for the evaluator to correct misrepresentations;

- linkages between researchers and users enhance exchanges that can be made with a minimum of defensiveness;
- an inclination for both sides to consider, from an early stage, the implications of each phase of study for action. Initial concerns, which initially focus on evaluation design, lead, over time, towards implementation of changes based on key results.

Conclusion

The case study presented here and other work undertaken at the Centre for Program Evaluation based on this model suggests that SSE knowledge can make a strong and direct impact on policy and practice. The strength of personal relationships built up between evaluator and client affects the quality and responsiveness of the research undertaken, and utilisation of findings. Other knowledge utilisation theorists have commented that strong professional and personal rapport between evaluators and clients leads to enhanced use of SSE (Mowbray, 1988). We have found that the effort involved in setting up these relationships can later lead to increased and diverse transactions between parties at one of our sites, a large inner city school, evaluation studies have been undertaken continually for over 10 years.

In some of these studies we have observed a 'transactional' use of SSE findings. This means that organizations transform and use SSE in highly selective and strategic ways. An issue for this model is the degree of adaptation allowed before utilisation becomes less than faithful to the findings on which transformation was based.

Other commentators have suggested that practitioners should form part of the research team, and this has been incorporated in at least one study undertaken by the CPE (Hurworth and Clemans, 1996). This has led not only to the acquisition of research skills by those involved, but also increased the likelihood that practitioners acted strategically in the implementation of the findings at the local level (Vickers, 1995).

Notes

1 The evaluation group is the Centre for Program Evaluation (CPE), Faculty of Education, The University of Melbourne. The CPE undertakes commissioned research, offers a post-graduate program in evaluation studies and contributes to evaluation and knowledge development theory.
2 The policy document includes the following statement: 'Knowledge and understanding of Asia and Australia's relationship with Asia makes an important contribution to building of social capital of our nation: enriching Australian's social, creative and intellectual development by extending their skills, vocational opportunities and aspirations, and developing an understanding of themselves, their own society and the richness of human experience. Enhancing our understanding of Asian nations strengthens our ability to contribute to harmony, partnership and cooperation in the Asian region and the wider world' (p. 4).
3 Note that SOAAA is typical of a trend for outside 'pressure groups' to influence educational jurisdictions and schools to incorporate content material which they

believe should be included in the school curriculum. Two other important examples are: Mind Matters, a mental health program for secondary schools, and Emergency Preparedness Education, a program designed to assist schools to handle hazards and emergencies.

4   These are:
1   'Traditional' knowledge production
2   Investigator-controlled applied research
3   Investigator-user linkage
4   User-oriented action
5   Consultancy advice.

A discussion of these models in more depth can be found in Owen, J. M. (2002) 'Linking evaluation use to the research utilization literature', paper presented at the annual meeting of the American Evaluation Association, Washington, DC. The classification builds on the seminal work of Heller, F. (1986) 'Introduction and Overview', in F. Heller (ed.) *The Use and Abuse of Social Science*, London: Sage, pp. 4–6.

References

Department of Education (2006) 'National Statement for Engaging Young Australians with Asia in Australian Schools', Carlton South, Australia, Curriculum Corporation, Australian Government.

Harris, A. (2003) 'Teacher leadership and school improvement', in C. Chapman, A. Harris, C. Day, D. Hopkins, A. Hargreaves, M. Hadfield and C. Chapman (eds) *Effective Leadership of School Improvement*, London and New York, NY: RoutledgeFalmer.

Heller, F. (1986) 'Introduction and overview', in F. Heller (ed.) *The Use and Abuse of Social Science*, London: Sage, pp. 4–6.

Huberman, M. (1987) 'Steps toward an integrated model of research utilization', *Knowledge, Creation, Diffusion, Utilization*, Vol. 8, No. 4, pp. 586–611.

Huberman, M. and Cox, P. (1990) 'Evaluation utilization: building links between action and reflection', *Studies in Educational Evaluation*, Vol. 16, No. 1, pp. 157–79.

Hurworth, R. and Clemans, A. (1996) 'Assessing the educational needs of the older adult: an empowerment model of research', in V. Minichiello, N. Chappell, H. Kendig and A. Walker (eds) *Sociology of Aging: International Perspectives*, Fitzroy, Victoria: International Sociological Association.

Johnson, R. B. (1998) 'Towards a theoretical model of evaluation utilization', *Evaluation and Program Planning*, Vol. 21, pp. 93–110.

Lindblom, C. E. and Cohen, D. K. (1979) *Usable Knowledge*, New Haven, CT and London: Yale University Press.

Lipton, D. S. (1992) 'How to maximise utilization of evaluation research by policymakers', *Annals of the American Academy of Political and Social Science*, Vol. 521, May, pp. 175–88.

Mowbray, C. T. (1988) 'Getting the system to respond to evaluation findings', *New Directions in Program Evaluation*, Vol. 39, pp. 21–33.

Owen, J. M. (2002) 'Linking evaluation use to the research utilization literature', paper presented at the annual meeting of the American Evaluation Association, Washington, DC.

Owen, J. M (2004) 'Evaluation forms: towards an inclusive framework for evaluation practice', in M. C. Alkin (ed.) *Evaluation Roots*, Thousand Oaks, CA: Sage Publications.

Owen, J. M. (2006) *Program Evaluation: Forms and Approaches*, Sydney: Allen and Unwin.

Owen, J. M. and Lambert, F. C. (1998). 'Evaluation and the information needs of organizational leaders', *American Journal of Evaluation*, Vol. 19, No. 3, pp. 355–65.

Ryan, A. G. (1988) 'Program evaluation within the paradigms', *Knowledge: Creation, Diffusion, Utilization*, Vol. 10, No. 1, pp. 25–47.

Schwandt, T. A. (2002) *Evaluation Practice Reconsidered*, New York, NY: Peter Laing Publishing.

Stake, R. E. (1978) 'The case study method in social inquiry', *Educational Researcher*, Vol. 7, pp. 5–8.

Vickers, M. (1995) 'Knowledge for policy: what VET research can contribute to the training agenda', keynote speech at ANTARAC research in progress conference, 28 September, Sydney.

Weiss, C. H. (1999) 'The interface between evaluation and public policy', *Evaluation*, Vol. 5, No. 4, pp. 468–86.

Wingens, M. (1993) 'Towards a general utilization metaphor: a systems theory reformulation of the two-communities metaphor', *Knowledge: Creation, Diffusion, Utilization*, Vol. 12, No. 1, pp. 27–42.

Part III

Educational change

Finding new directions?

7   Schooling, curriculum, narrative and the social future

Ivor Goodson

In his recent writing on education, Zygmunt Bauman has drawn attention to the work of Margaret Mead and her life companion, Gregory Bateson. Mead said:

> The Social Structure of a society and the way learning is structured – the way it passes from mother to daughter, from father to son, from mother's brother to sister's son, from shaman to novice, from mythological specialists to explained specialists – determine far beyond the actual content of the learning both how individuals will learn to think and how the store of learning, the sum total of separate pieces of skill and knowledge ... is shared and used.
>
> (Mead, 1964: 79)

Gregory Bateson also wrote some fascinating work on learning. Learning on his analysis divides into three linked but distinct types. There is the primary learning, 'first-degree learning' of content, learning the formal curriculum so to speak.

There is also 'deutero' learning, what we might call secondary learning, the subterranean process of learning to learn. Bauman says that this secondary learning: 'Depends not so much on the diligence and talents of the learners and the competence and assiduity of their teachers, as on the attributes of the world in which the former pupils are bound to live their lives' (Bauman, 2001: 24).

Tertiary learning he summarises as learning: 'How to break the regularity, how to rearrange fragmentary experiences into heretofore unfamiliar patterns' (Bauman, 2001: 125). Tertiary learning is about living without habits and routinised learning, it's about breaking away from pre-digested, prescriptions of curriculum and moving to the definition and ownership and ongoing narration of our own curriculum.

Looking at these three types of learning should highlight the current crises of curriculum and of educational studies generally. The old patterns of curriculum development and curriculum study are utterly unsuited to the new society of risk, instability and rapid change in which we now live. They are locked into primary learning and prescription. Bauman says:

> I suggest that the overwhelming feeling of crises experienced by philosophers, theorists and practitioners of education alike ... have little to do with the

faults, errors or negligence of the professional pedagogue or failures of educational theory, but quite a lot to do with the universal melting of identities with the deregulation and privatization of the identity – formation processes, the dispersal of authorities, the polyphony of the messages and ensuing fragmentation of life which characterizes the world we live in.

(Bauman, 2001: 127)

Bauman then is clear that the crisis of curriculum and of education is not an internal matter, a question of failures of practice or research – it is a broad question of positionality: people, and in this instance curriculum people, are searching for solutions in the wrong place.

Rather than writing new prescriptions for schools, new curriculum or new reform guidelines, they need to question the very validity of pre-digested prescriptions in a world of flux and change. We need in short to move from curriculum as prescription to curriculum as identity narration, from prescribed cognitive learning to life management narrative learning. It is this shift I will try to outline in this chapter. First, I will deal with the definitive redundancy of curriculum as prescription and second I will tentatively outline the move to curriculum as narrative, which I believe marks the way to our new social future.

First then, is the established practice of curriculum as prescription on which so many of the assumptions of practitioners and researchers are based. The primacy of the ideology of curriculum as prescription (CAP) can be evidenced in even a cursory glimpse at curriculum literature. This view of curriculum develops from a belief that we can dispassionately define the main ingredients of the course of study, and then proceed to teach the various segments and sequences in systematic turn. Despite the obvious simplicity, not to say crudity of this view, the 'objectives game' is still, if 'not the only game in town', certainly the main game. There may be many reasons for this continuing predominance, but explanatory potential is not, I think, one of the factors.

Curriculum as prescription supports important mystiques about state schooling and society. Most notably CAP supports the mystique that expertise and control reside within central government, educational bureaucracies or the university community. Providing nobody exposes this mystique, the worlds of 'prescription rhetoric' and 'schooling as practice' can co-exist. Both sides benefit from such peaceful co-existence. The agencies of CAP are seen to be 'in control' and the schools are seen to be 'delivering' and can carve out a good degree of autonomy if they accept the rules. Curriculum prescriptions thereby set certain parameters but with transgression and occasional transcendence being permissible as long as the rhetoric of prescription and management is not challenged.

Of course there are 'costs of complicity' in accepting the myth of prescription: above all these involve, in various ways, acceptance of established modes of power relations. Perhaps most importantly the people intimately connected with the day-to-day social construction of curriculum and schooling, the teachers, are thereby effectively disenfranchised in the 'discourse of schooling'. To continue to exist, their day-to-day power must basically remain unspoken and unrecorded. This then is the price of complicity. The vestiges of day-to-day power and autonomy for schools and for teachers are dependent on continuing to accept the fundamental lie.

With regard to curriculum study the 'costs of complicity' are ultimately catastrophic. For the historic compromise we have described has led to the displacement of a whole field of study. It has led to the directing of scholarship into fields which service the mystique of central and/or bureaucratic control. For scholars who benefit from maintaining this mystique – in the universities particularly – this complicity is, to say the least, self-serving (for more on this argument see Goodson, 2005).

Prescription and establishment of power make easy allies. As argued in my book, *The Making of Curriculum* (Goodson, 1995), curriculum was basically invented as a concept to direct and control the teacher's licence and potential freedom in the classroom. Over the years the alliance between prescription and power has been carefully nurtured so that curriculum becomes a device to reproduce existing power relations in society. The children of powerful, resourceful parents enjoy curriculum inclusion and the less advantaged suffer from curriculum exclusion. As Bourdieu has argued, a parent's 'cultural capital' effectively in this way buys success for their student offspring (Bourdieu and Passeron, 2000).

To see how prescribed curriculum works not to include but to exclude in a powerful and insidious way let me give an example from the experience of New Labour in Britain. This should have been a government showing some commitment to social inclusion and this commitment did exist in the rhetoric of government policy.

Since the election of a New Labour government in 1997 avowedly determined to prioritise 'education, education, education', there has been a stated concern to broaden social inclusion. Given the well-established (and well-defended) patterns of social inequality in Britain, this was never going to be an easy task. But recent pronouncements from the Secretary of State for Education, Ruth Kelly, have begun to concede just how substantial the failure to broaden social inclusion has been. It would seem New Labour policies have in fact worked not to broaden social inclusion but to deepen social exclusion. Speaking on 26 July 2005 to the New Labour think tank, the Institute of Public Policy Research, she said:

> The gap between rich and poor in national curriculum test results and admissions to universities had grown. We must treat seriously the possibility that – despite all our efforts – who your parents are still affects attainment as much in 2004 as it did in 1998.
>
> (Game, 2005: 17)

The key phrase in this statement is the phrase 'despite all our efforts'. Looking at the report again should raise our suspicions. While she admits that 'who your parents are still affects attainment as much in 2004 as it did in 1998', her data actually shows that New Labour policies have worked to increase, not modify, the gap between rich and poor in educational attainment. Not so much a result 'despite all our efforts' but a result quite possibly 'because of all our efforts'. The data shows that New Labour policies are not working towards social inclusion but actually furthering social exclusion.

Now a cynical reading of New Labour policies might argue that this government has been following a policy of fine-tuning social exclusion by stealth. I do not take this view. Rather I suspect we have a government with broadly good intentions that approaches the task of social inclusion as a Christian and philanthropic duty. The educational background of the major players in government and their advisers and civil servants pre-dispose them to believe in social inclusion as a process of distributing elite educational categories more widely. They forget that as members of the elite their educational experiences were founded on the social exclusions of others. What counted as education for them was designed for the few at the price of exclusion for the many.

As a result they have, quite possibly unknowingly, employed educational strategies built around well-established foundations of exclusion to try to deliver social inclusion. This is not as illogical as an informed educational research reading might imply. Most of us equate 'education' with our own educational experiences and we accept as 'givens' basic educational phenomena such as 'traditional' school subjects or 'academic' examinations. These are part of the widely accepted 'grammar of schooling'. A layman's view would be that since 'these things equal good schooling' let's try and include more pupils in this kind of educational experience and thereby we will deliver social inclusion. Seems like common sense and certainly this was the way New Labour proceeded. In fact the truth is far more complex and contradictory. We need to understand a little of the history of schooling to see why New Labour rushed so far and fast up an exclusionary cul-de-sac in pursuit of social inclusion.

To outline a section on the history of schooling, I want to draw on the studies I have been undertaking for the last thirty or so years. They too have attempted to answer the question as to why social inclusion and 'fair education for all' seems so perennially elusive. Broadly, what these studies show is that many of the traditional curriculum building blocks of schooling are themselves devices for social exclusion not inclusion. Let me take as an example that unproblematic 'given' in every school: the 'traditional school subject'.

Exclusive pursuits: the invention of school subjects

To begin with let us commence with an episode in the invention of one school subject: science. I choose this example to show the relationship between school subject knowledge which is accepted, and becomes therefore 'traditional', and subject knowledge which is disallowed. This is the interface between school knowledge and powerful interest groups in society. School subjects are defined not in a disinterested scholastic way but in close relationship to the power and interests of social groups. The more powerful the social group the more likely they are to exercise power over school knowledge.

In his book *Science for the People*, David Layton (1972) describes a movement in the initial development of the school science curriculum called the 'Science of Common Things'. This was an early attempt to broaden social inclusion through relating the science curriculum to ordinary pupils' experience of the natural world, of their homes, daily lives and work. This curriculum was delivered in the elementary schools set up for predominantly working class clienteles. There is clear evidence provided by Layton and in contemporary government reports that the Science of Common Things worked successfully in classrooms and extended science education. A successful strategy for social inclusion in school knowledge was therefore put in place.

We would however be wrong to assume that this was seen as a desirable development – far from it. Other definitions of school science were being advocated. Lord Wrottesley chaired a Parliamentary Committee of the British Association for the Advancement of Science on the most appropriate type of science education for the upper classes. Hodson argues that the report 'reflected a growing awareness of a serious problem: that science education at the elementary level was proving highly successful, particularly as far as the development of thinking skills was concerned, and the social hierarchy was under threat because there was not corresponding development for the higher orders' (Goodson, 1987: 36). Lord Wrottesley's fears were clearly stated as regards moves to further social inclusion:

> ... a poor boy hobbled forth to give a reply; he was lame and humpbacked, and his wan, emaciated face told only too clearly the tale of poverty and its consequences ... but he gave forthwith so lucid and intelligent a reply to the question put to him that there arose a feeling of admiration for the child's talents combined with a sense of shame that more information should be found in some of the lowest of our lowest classes on matters of general interest than those far above them in the world by station.

Wrottesley concluded:

> It would be an unwholesome and vicious state of society in which those who are comparatively unblessed with nature's gifts should be generally superior in intellectual attainments to those above them in station.

> (Ibid.: 36–7)

Soon after Wrottesley's comments in 1860, science was removed from the elementary curriculum. When science eventually reappeared in the curriculum of elementary schools some twenty years later it was in a very different form from the science of common things. A watered-down version of pure laboratory science had become accepted as the correct and 'traditional' view of science, a view which has persisted largely unchallenged to the present day. School subjects it seems have to develop a form acceptable to the 'higher orders' of society – being a mechanism for social inclusion naturally does not recommend itself to the higher orders whose very position depends on social exclusion. School subjects thereafter become in themselves not only 'accepted', 'given', 'traditional', inevitable, but also in their academic form exclusionary devices.

Fast forwarding a century or more I began to study a new subject, 'environmental studies', not unlike the science of common things in that it grew from its origins as a working class inclusionary subject to begin to claim the status of 'a proper subject'. In the book, *School Subjects and Curriculum Change* I show how this new subject highly suited to comprehensive schools and with real inclusionary potential was systematically blocked from becoming a broad-based A level 'academic' subject (Goodson, 1993). In Britain only a subject accepted as 'academic' can be resourced as a high status 'proper subject'.

This position of hierarchy for 'academic' subjects in fact represented a history of subjects linking to social hierarchy and social exclusion. The dominance of academic subjects goes back to the battle over which subjects should be prioritised in the new secondary schools at the start of the twentieth century. In 1904 the government's 'Secondary Regulations' handed victory to the public school cum grammar school vision of education and school subjects. Hence the academic subject was built on a clear foundation of social exclusion, for such schools never catered for more than 20 per cent of pupils. In effect the 'bottom' 80 per cent were sacrificed and the top 20 per cent promoted by the prioritisation of the 'academic tradition'. A contemporary noted of the 1904 Regulations that the academic subject-centred curriculum was 'subordinated to that literary instruction which makes for academic culture, but is of no practical utility to the classes for whom the local authorities should principally cater'.

In the comprehensive schools whilst new curriculum initiatives developed new subject categories such as environmental studies, but also community studies, urban studies, women's studies and social studies, the stranglehold of the academic tradition remained. This effectively blocked other traditions in subjects which stressed those vocational and pedagogic traditions likely to promote social inclusion. The very process of becoming a school subject therefore purges subject knowledge of its inclusionary characteristics. Layton shows this exclusionary effect with his evolutionary profile of the traditional subject. In the first stage.

> The callow intruder stakes a place in the timetable, justifying its presence on grounds such as pertinence and utility. During this stage learners are attracted to the subject because of its bearing on matters of concern to them. The teachers are rarely trained specialists, but bring the missionary enthusiasms of pioneers to their task. The dominant criterion is relevance to the needs and interests of the learners.

In the interim second stage:

> A tradition of scholarly work in the subject is emerging along with a corps of trained specialists from which teachers may be recruited. Students are still attracted to the Study, but as much by its reputation and growing academic

status as by its relevance to their own problems and concerns. The internal logic and discipline of the subject is becoming increasingly influential in the selection and organisation of subject matter.

In the final stage:

> The teachers now constitute a professional body with established rules and values. The selection of subject matter is determined in large measure by the judgements and practices of the specialist scholars who lead inquiries in the field. Students are initiated into a tradition, their attitudes approaching passivity and resignation, a prelude to disenchantment.
>
> (Layton, 1972: 9)

The central place of 'academic' subjects is ensconced in our British schools, so there is an in-built pattern of social prioritising and exclusion. The process outlined above shows clearly that school subject groups tend to move progressively away from social relevance or vocational emphasis. High status in the secondary school tends to focus on abstract theoretical knowledge divorced from the workaday world or the everyday world of the learner. To these high status academic subjects go the main resources in our school systems: the better qualified teachers, the favourable sixth form ratios and the pupil deemed most able. The link is now strengthened by New Labour initiatives in terms of targets, tests and league tables. In this way a pattern of social prioritising built on exclusive pursuits found itself at the heart of a programme of social inclusion. Such a central contradiction and a range of other exclusionary devices inherited unknowingly or unthinkingly, have contributed to the abject failure of New Labour policies to further social inclusion. It is urgently to be hoped that the next time policies are formulated relevant educational research in the area will at least be consulted and considered.

The underpinning prioritisation of academic school subjects effectively strangled new attempts to develop a more inclusive curriculum in comprehensive schools. This pattern of social prioritising was finally consolidated in the new 'National Curriculum' of 1988 which almost exactly re-established Morant's Secondary Regulations of 1904 – the public school and grammar school curriculum was firmly re-instated. A pattern of subject knowledge based on selective exclusion became the lynchpin of the curricula to be offered in comprehensive schools.

Into this stratified and exclusionary terrain came the New Labour government preaching social inclusion and missionary morality. Their focus was on tightening up delivery on targets, tests and tables. But they never even questioned the exclusionary foundations on which their policies were to be built. In Britain there were the leading researchers in the world on the history of school subjects and on the patterns described above. Not one of these researchers was ever consulted by the government. They pursued social inclusion employing a wide range of well-honed exclusionary devices. The results were precisely as Ruth Kelly recorded

– the pronouncements in favour of social inclusion produced results that further extended social exclusion.

Curriculum as prescription and powerful interest groups are then locked in a potent historical partnership which structures curriculum in basic ways and effectively subverts any passing innovations or reforms. The prescriptions provide clear 'rules of the game' for schooling and finance and resources are tied into these rules. Curriculum research, with a few honourable exceptions has also tended to follow the 'rules of the game' by accepting curriculum as prescription as its starting point even when in the odd case advocating resistance or transformation. The reason for hope now comes because whilst the rules of the game for curriculum and for reproducing the social order are well established, the wider social order and associated rules of the game are now undergoing seismic change. This will destabilise the cosy alliance of power and prescription in unpredictable but definitive ways. The curriculum game is about to experience pulverising change but often seems blissfully unaware of what the future holds.

In the new era of flexible work organisation, workers face unpredictable and constantly changing assignments.

> The types of skills required to practise flexible occupations do not on the whole demand long-term and systematic learning. More often than not, they transform a well-profiled logically coherent body of skills and habits from the asset it used to be, into the handicap it is now.
>
> (Bauman, 2001: 132)

Long-established and prescribed courses of study therefore become a handicap to the new flexible work order. Curriculum as prescription might provide residual patterns of social reproduction but its increasingly economic dysfunctionality calls its continuity into question by powerful economic interests and global pressures. Bauman stated the dilemma with exquisite precision and with utter clarity for our curriculum futures. 'In our increasingly flexible and thoroughly deregulated job market all prospects of arresting the rot, let alone restoring the fast-vanishing framework of prospective planning grow bleaker by the hour' (Bauman, 2001: 131–2).

'Prospective planning' of learning, curriculum as prescription, is then colossally inappropriate to the flexible work order – on this analysis it is doomed and will require rapid replacement by new forms of learning organisation. Let us therefore look at some new notions of curriculum such as narrative learning, a form of learning being explored in a range of new research projects.

Curriculum as narration

In this section I want to give an example from research projects that I am currently involved with. The main project that addresses the issue of narrative learning is the Learning Lives project. Learning Lives is a four-year longitudinal study which aims to deepen our understanding of the meaning and significance of informal learning in the lives of adults and aims to identify ways in which that adult learning can be supported and enhanced. It is funded, as part of the British government's 'Teaching and Learning Programme', by the Economic and Social Research Council. As well as informal learning the project has begun to focus on what we call 'narrative learning'. 'Narrative learning' is the kind of learning that goes on in the elaboration and ongoing maintenance of a life narrative or identity. The kind of motifs that emerge in narrative learning are those such as: the journey, the quest, the dream – all of them central motifs for the ongoing elaboration of a life mission. We have come to see this kind of narrative learning as central in the way that people learn throughout the life course and it requires a different form of research and elaboration to understand this kind of learning as opposed to the more traditional kinds of formal and informal learning. In investigating narrative learning it is at this point that we begin to develop the concept of narrative capital.

To explain the meaning of narrative learning and narrative capital I want to provide an example of how this new mode of education works from different assumptions to those modes of learning which accept curriculum as prescription.

As noted in an earlier section the established modalities of education and learning depend on curriculum as prescription and link closely to existing patterns of power and cultural capital. For Bourdieu, cultural capital and indeed symbolic capital represent those aspects of dominant interest groups which can be commodified and credentialed as successful learning (Bourdieu and Passeron, 2000). In Britain cultural capital is best evidenced in the high status public schools which are in fact the schools where the parents privately pay for their children to be educated. Schools such as Eton and Harrow would be classic examples of cultural capital where the cultural domination of the group and the social networks to which the schools afford access, provide enormous cultural capital for students learning in these schools. In the traditional pattern of social reproduction students with cultural capital effortlessly move into social elites and work with those that share similar patterns of cultural and social capital. Hence curriculum as prescription, cultural and social capital and existing forms of social reproduction through schooling and education form a tripartite alliance of enduring power. But this power as Bauman intimates in his own analysis is now subject to considerable challenge in a new world of flexible work organisations. Here the power of defining an organisational mission or life narrative becomes enormously important and can at certain times even in this initial phase undercut old patterns of cultural capital and social elitism.

Nothing illustrates the shift from old hierarchies of cultural and symbolic capital towards something we might call 'narrative capital' better than the case of David Cameron, the new leader of the Conservative party in Britain (see Goodson, 2005).

In previous generations his Old Etonian and Oxford connections would have provided an authoritative narrative through which to promote his political ambitions. The cultural and symbolic capital of such an education would then have come with an implicit and very powerful storyline. These places traditionally produced those who govern whilst the symbolic and social capital is still largely intact. But Cameron has become worried about constructing an acceptable life narrative. The dilemma is outlined in this interview with Martin Bentham, undertaken before he became leader:

> But as Cameron insists, it is not just his preference for racy television programmes that calls into question the stereotyped image that others have placed upon him. He cites his liking for the 'gloomy left-wing' music of bands such as the Smiths, Radiohead and Snow Patrol, which brings ribbing from his friends, as a further example of his divergence from the traditional Tory image, and also, perhaps rather rashly for a newly appointed shadow Education Secretary, admits to regularly misbehaving 'in all sorts of ways' while at school.
>
> Most importantly, however, he says that what keeps him connected very firmly in ordinary life is the job of representing his constituents in Witney, Oxfordshire, and life at home with his wife, Samantha, and their two children, three-year-old Ivan, who suffers from cerebral palsy and epilepsy, and Nancy, who is aged 14 months.
>
> 'Am I to posh to push?' he quips, before determinedly explaining why he rejects the criticism of his background. 'In the sort of politics I believe in it shouldn't matter what you've had in the past, it's what you are going to contribute in the future, and I think that should be true of everybody, from all parts of society, all colours and ages and races, and I hope that goes for Old Etonians too.'
>
> (Bentham, 2005: 10)

What I think Cameron has noted is that if he re-crafts his life narrative, 'it shouldn't matter what you've had in the past'. In other words he is worried that his life experience of sustained systematic privilege will interfere with the narrative he is trying to create for himself and his party where there is a 'genuine care and compassion for those who fall behind' and where what 'people really want (is) a practical down-to-earth alternative to Labour'. He ends, 'Am I too posh? It shouldn't really matter where you come from – even if it's Eton'. While Eton then may have massive historical claims to cultural and symbolic capital, the narrative capital it provides is clearly a little more difficult to present and cash in. Cameron's honest appraisal of the dilemma elegantly illustrates the seismic shift towards narrative politics and how this is likely to feed through into new educational modes for acquiring narrative capital.

In the Learning Lives project we have the chance to see how life history can elucidate learning responses. What we do in the project is to deal with learning as one of the strategies people employ as the response to events in their lives. The great virtue of this situation of our understanding of learning within the whole life context is that we get some sense of the issue of engagement in learning as it relates to people living their lives. When we see learning as a response to actual events then the issue of engagement can be taken for granted. So much of the literature on learning fails to address this crucial question of *engagement,* and as a result learning is seen as some formal task that is unrelated to the needs and interests of the learner, hence so much of curriculum planning is based on prescriptive definitions of what is to be learnt without any understanding of the situation within the learners' lives. As a result a vast amount of curriculum planning is abortive because the learner simply does not engage; hence to see learning as located within a life history is to understand that learning is contextually situated and that it also has a history, both in terms of the individual's life story and the history and trajectories of the institutions that offer formal learning opportunities, as well as the histories of the communities and locations in which informal learning takes place. In terms of transitional spaces we can see learning as a response to incidental transitions such as events related to illness, unemployment and domestic dysfunction, as well as the more structured transitions related to credentialling or retirement.

The way that our Life History Interviewees describe learning often eloquently states the shift from traditional patterns of curriculum as prescription and learning by content into a more elaborated notion of narrative learning. The following quote which I give at length provides us with a clear evaluation of the different forms of learning given by one of our life history subjects.

> Well I suppose the first thing that comes is, is the different kinds of, of learning that's, that I've done in, in my life from acquiring skills or acquiring languages – which, which entails something that you, you had absolutely no idea before and when you learn you *can* actually *do* it and you didn't know that you would be able to in the beginning and it really gives you a sense of empowerment. That's, I think that's, I mean, that's lifelong, a lifelong process because I'm still, I'm still learning how to play the violin, and I will be until, until the end and I'm still acquiring hopefully new languages, so that's, that's two things that, that I know that I'll continue, hopefully progressing in. And then there's, there's learning about, about how to be a social person in a, in a given environment, which entails in my case because I have to kind of translate myself from country to country, learning how the rules function in any given, given space, or given space that you live in, and they change, it's like goalposts that change, keep changing, so you have to translate your behaviour in certain ways. And you learn that something that you, something that's fine in one society, how you perceive completely differently. That is definitely a process of, of learning, and it's a two-fold thing because you learn about the society that you are in but you also learn about yourself and how you react to it. And then I guess the third thing is, would be, learning about yourself as a person and how you deal with, with life as, you know, in general, and that's also a lifelong, lifelong process, of how to, how to become what you think a person should be, a good person or a bad person or whatever person, whatever sort of person, and you work, you work on that. Try to examine your, your own behaviour and your relationship with, with the world and try to make sense of why things happen to you, why your reaction has brought

up a certain, certain thing, and how the circumstances affected you in reacting a certain way, so it's a self examination I suppose, but that's maybe the third kind of level of, of learning. I think, I think that's it. I think that's basically the three, the three things that I can think of off the top of my head.

(Learning Lives interview, 02.11.08)

The narrative learning defined by our life story subject 'learning to be a social person in a given environment' and learning about yourself as a person and defining an identity project comes close to the notion of tertiary learning defined by Bateson. The curriculum shift we are seeing is from primary learning and curriculum as prescription to tertiary learning and curriculum as narration. This shift will accelerate rapidly as the move to flexible economic organisation takes place. The contextual inertia of a content-based curriculum of prescription will not endure in the fast-changing global world order.

Bauman puts it this way: 'Preparing for life – that perennial, invariable task of all education – must mean first and foremost cultivating the ability to live daily and at peace with uncertainty and ambivalence, with a variety of standpoints and the absence of unerring and trustworthy authority' (Bauman, 2001: 138).

No better warning against the supreme inadequacies of the authoritative prescription of curriculum could be given: the qualities that are needed are 'fortifying critical and self-critical faculties', developing people's capacities to define and narrate their life purposes and missions in a fast changing environment.

Bauman notes: 'The point is ... that such qualities can hardly be developed in full through that aspect of the educational process which lends itself best to the designing and controlling powers of the theorists and practitioner of education through the verbally explicit contents of curriculum' (Bauman, 2001: 138).

Curriculum as prescription and primary learning of predetermined content, he is telling us, is a game that is coming to an end. He says: 'Educational philosophy and theory face the unfamiliar task of theorising a formative process which is not guided from the start by the target form designed in advance' (p. 139).

If curriculum as prescription is ending, the new era of curriculum in the new social future, we have to admit, is yet far from clear. In the sketches provided here of narrative learning and narrative capital is, I believe, the beginning of a new specification for curriculum. We are only at the beginning. It is a beginning which provides hope that we can finally heal the 'fundamental lie' that sits at the heart of curriculum as prescription. In the new social future we must hope that curriculum will engage with the life missions, passions and purposes which people articulate in their lives. Now that would truly be a curriculum for empowerment. Moving from authoritative prescription and primary learning to narrative empowerment and tertiary learning would transform our educational institutions and make them live out their early promise to help in changing their students' social future.

References

Bauman, Z. (2001) *The Individualized Society*, Cambridge: Polity Press.

Bentham, M. (2005) 'Tories' young pretender insists on a fair chance for all', *The Observer*, 15 May 2005.

Bourdieu, P. and Passeron, J. C. (2000) *Reproduction in Education, Society and Culture* 2nd edn, London and Berverley Hills, CA: Sage.

Foot, M. (2001) 'Best foot goes ever forward', *The Observer*, 4 March.

Game, R. (2005) 'Educational reforms and the better off', *The Independent*, 2 June.

Goodson, I. F. (1987) *The Making of Curriculum: Essays in the Social History of Schooling*, London: Falmer

Goodson, I. F. (1993) *School Subjects and Curriculum Change*, 3rd edn, London and New York: Falmer.

Goodson, I. F. (1995) *The Making of Curriculum*, London and New York: Routledge Falmer.

Goodson, I. F. (2005) *Learning Curriculum, and Life Politics*, London and New York: Routledge.

Hudson, D. (1987) 'Science curricula change in Victorian England: a case study of the science of common things', in I. F. Goodson (ed.) *International Perspectives in Curriculum History*, London: Croom Helm, p. 36

Layton, D. (1972) *Science as General Education*, London: HMSO.

Layton, D. (1973) *Science for the People*, London: George Allen and Unwin.

Mead, M. (1964) *Continuity in Cultural Evolution*, New Haven, CT: York University Press.

8 Research and community organizing as tools for democratizing educational policymaking

Jeannie Oakes, Michelle Renée,
John Rogers and Martin Lipton

Education reforms have failed to disrupt persistent schooling inequalities that disadvantage the nation's low-income students and students of color. In this chapter, we argue for processes by which members of low-income communities of color define education problems, develop solutions, and press for action. We also argue that these groups and processes require research capacity that is responsive to their needs.

We elaborate this argument in three ways with evidence from the United States. First, we observe (as have many others) that the elites who dominate education policymaking have, for the most part, accepted a social ideology advanced by far-right foundations and think tanks. Of particular significance is that these conservative groups have sponsored and marketed policy-relevant research that is aligned with their ideology.

Second, we question whether knowledge that is useful for solving intractable social problems can be produced by 'experts' who are removed from the people most affected by those problems. Rather, policymaking and the research knowledge that informs it must also draw from 'non-elites'' actions and deliberations about how public institutions can best serve the public good. Here, we look for guidance to John Dewey's work in the 1920s and 1930s, a period when he was concerned about corporate interests and experts having eclipsed public deliberation in social policymaking.

Third, we draw on empirical evidence from our four-year study of grassroots and advocacy groups who engage directly in California education policymaking. We found that their engagement with research strengthened their activist campaigns by equipping them with countervailing facts and persuasive arguments, helped them to garner new cross-interest and cross-class allies, and generated a more vibrant education policy debate. The result of this engagement is that the organizers and advocates counter the dominant ideology and democratize the education policymaking process.

Elite domination of education policy and social research

Often, education policymaking is neither democratic nor egalitarian. Elites and influential interests have the financial and social resources to create, frame, and leverage common (popular) understandings about the likely causes and solutions of social problems, which problems warrant policy attention, and the merit of various policy choices. The result is a political process that appears to be guided by knowledge and majoritarian preferences, claims to be deferential to all interests, but nearly always confers disproportionate advantages to elites.

Elites, ideology, research, and *social* policy

Over the past 50 years, research has been invoked as a good way for social policy to be shaped by scientific knowledge, rather than by exclusionary values, discredited traditions, or crass politics. Researchers have responded with relevant studies that inform policymakers. Many researchers have sought to remain above the policy fray, making clear their commitment to being both non-partisan and non-ideological (see Rich, 2004).

However, even in the most bi-partisan and ideologically neutral contexts, policy research tends to serve elite interests – those of well-educated and well-off Americans. Because these elites have the considerable financial, institutional, and intellectual resources that social policy research requires, it is not surprising that their perspectives become the common-sense starting points for most research on contentious social issues, including education. Increasingly, however, some of the most influential and visible policy research organizations also increasingly align their work with particular political ideologies and agendas.

Political scientist Andrew Rich notes in *Think Tanks, Public Policy, and the Politics of Expertise* that the number of 'think tanks' grew from 70 to more than 300 between 1970 and 2000. Two thirds of these new institutions eschewed earlier traditions of ideological and political neutrality, and most of these set out to advance a conservative agenda of limited government and free markets (Rich, 2004). The Heritage Foundation, the Manhattan Institute for Policy Research, and the Heartland Institute are three prominent examples.

These conservative research organizations aggressively market their ideas to shape public opinion and policymakers' decisions. Well-funded by conservative foundations, these think tanks spend heavily on government relations and media, in comparison to mainstream research organizations. For example, the Heritage Foundation spends 20 percent of its budget on marketing, which they believe to be a core part of their mission (Rich, 2004). In such instances, social research becomes more than the production of knowledge; it becomes a commodity marketed to a particular audience for the benefit of a particular constituency.

Over the past thirty years, conservative think tanks have successfully advanced explanations for social problems that challenge the historical and structural explanations that emerged from the liberal civil rights movement. The theories of conservative economist Milton Friedman have been at the core of this shift.

Friedman's 1962 book, *Capitalism and Freedom*, argued that political and social freedom required limiting the role of government in a free market economy and expanding individual choices and responsibilities (Friedman, 1962).

For example, 'big government' interventions such as housing and health care assistance, unemployment insurance, minimum wage guarantees, need-based financial aid for higher education, affirmative action, and so forth are seen to cause rather than to mitigate social problems. Rather than social safety nets and compensatory relief from past injustices, these interventions are characterized as ill-conceived programs that foster dependency, undermine families, and erode the work ethic of their beneficiaries. Consistent with this new diagnosis of society's problems, an entirely different set of social policy solutions has come to the fore. Government must get out of peoples' lives, allow room for market-driven improvements and economies, and restore self-sufficiency, individual responsibility, family values, and hard work (Rich, 2004; Berliner and Biddle, 1995; for additional details on conservative philanthropy and conservative think tanks, see the Media Transparency website http://www.mediatransparency.org).

Elites, ideology, research, and *education* policy

At the risk of oversimplifying a very complex landscape, we summarize below the convergence of elite interests, conservative-sponsored and promoted research, and education policy, beginning with *A Nation at Risk,* published in 1983.

High test scores mean educational quality

The authors of *A Nation at Risk* framed the nation's primary educational crisis as one of low standardized test scores, particularly relative to those of other nations. Of the thirteen 'indicators of the risk' that the report listed, nine were standardized test scores (*A Nation at Risk*, 1983). They framed the solution to the crisis as 'reform and excellence throughout education', achieved, in part, by 'rigorous and measurable standards' assessed with a 'nationwide (but not Federal) system of State and local standardized tests' (*A Nation at Risk*, 1983). Test scores were to be the metric of excellence.

Lacking a thorough and critical analysis of standardized tests, policymakers accepted the nation's 'low' test scores as 'evidence' that the education system was putting the country's economic well-being at risk. A next logical step was to focus specifically on African American, Latino, and low-SES students – those with the lowest scores. Not only did their low scores contribute to the nation's overall risk, the students were portrayed as contributing to the full range of social and economic ills plaguing low-income communities and communities of color – i.e. high rates of unemployment, crime, family instability, etc. Better school performance (test performance) for these students was seen as directly, if obscurely, related to improving the lot of the nation's poor.

Accordingly, elements of *A Nation at Risk* appealed both to conservative and progressive sensibilities and formed an illusory basis for common cause both at the time and years later in *No Child Left Behind*. Many liberals believed that an appeal to the country's overall security and economic viability would compel attention to equalizing educational resources and opportunities. Conservatives believed that market-based approaches to education replicated the equal chances all Americans had to succeed via the dynamics of unfettered commerce.

Inequality is 'the achievement gap'

It was not a huge leap from *A Nation at Risk* for both conservatives and liberals to frame the most serious educational *equity* problem as the 'achievement gap' between African American, Latino, and low-SES students and their white and middle-class counterparts. Understanding and closing this test-score gap quickly became the dominant focus of equity policy research and equity policy. In the process, however, the 'achievement gap' evolved from being an *indicator* of systemic social and educational inequalities to being the problem itself. Under the influence of conservative ideology, the gap became portrayed as a problem amenable to direct intervention, even in the absence of attention to a whole constellation of social, economic, and educational causes.

Although many liberals argued for attention to broader inequalities, there was really no contest when it came to the political and legal wherewithal to prevail in this ideological struggle. Using the logic of limited government, conservative policy researchers had, by this time, pronounced as failures prior efforts to ameliorate unequal educational opportunities through court-ordered school desegregation and the educational programs of Lyndon Johnson's 'War on Poverty' (see, for example, Armor, 1995; Hanushek and Somers, 2001) and they cited a growing number of econometric studies showing that increasing educational 'inputs' would not increase students' test scores (Hanushek, 1986, 1997). The harshest explanation of that failure came in the early 1990s, with the publication of Richard Herrnstein's and Charles Murray's (1994) *The Bell Curve: Intelligence and Class Structure in American Life*. They argued that the failure of social interventions in the 1960s and 1970s was inevitable, given that the cause of low achievement lay in race-related disparities in cognitive abilities (Hernstein and Murray, 1994). This book in essence reiterated the conservative deficit paradigm in the seemingly neutral guise of research.

Liberals were outraged at the suggestion that compensatory education programs had failed because of racial or cultural deficits of students. However, most were ill-equipped or disinclined to contest the idea that high standardized test scores, alone, constituted educational quality. They argued that 'all children can learn', and that test-score 'gaps' would close when poor children and children of color received equitable schooling, but these were weak assertions in the face of prevailing racial attitudes and easy cultural explanations that blamed mismanaged schools, individual deficits, lack of motivation for education, and so forth.

Equity is closing the 'achievement gap'

The political right has had the upper hand in framing the policy solutions to the 'achievement gap', just as they did in framing the gap itself. They eschewed remedies seeking to equalize students' social and economic circumstances or that sought to equalize or increase the schooling opportunities such as well-trained teachers; safe, healthy, uncrowded, facililities, sufficient learning materials, and more. Instead, they focused on what the second Bush administration would later call 'the soft bigotry of low expectations'.

Conservatives and many liberals would join the call to elevate expectations and to place greater academic and behavioral demands on schools, on children, and poor families. The prevailing theory for how *expectations* worked was reminiscent of mid-twentieth century behavioral psychology: effective policies would install incentives and sanctions to *motivate* whole schools, as well as individual teachers and students, to achieve at much higher levels. Free-market approaches, including competition, choice, and privatization, conservative scholars argued, were especially useful for providing rewards to those energetically pursuing a good education and for discouraging would-be failures. Relying heavily on conservative scholars' narrow definition of 'scientifically-based research', the current Bush administration insists that most proposals which shift the balance from 'outputs' (i.e. tests) to 'inputs' (i.e. opportunities to learn) are simply unsupported by research and therefore wasteful.[1]

Both, conservative and liberal policymakers have so thoroughly accepted the achievement gap ideology that the dominant policy debate no longer focuses on core education problems. Rather, the arguments are over what particular technical mix of standards-based and/or market-based reforms is most likely to provide the most productive and efficient incentives for narrowing the 'achievement gap'. Liberals tend to favor curriculum standards, test-based accountability, and public school choice, and conservatives prefer free-market solutions in which test-scores inform individual parents' choices, with public and private schools competing for students.

This convergent policy thinking is most clearly evidenced in the bi-partisan support for the *No Child Left Behind* Act, which includes a mix of standards-based reforms and choice. The debates are largely over whether the improvement targets are set properly and whether the funding is adequate; few challenge the fundamental logic of seeking just the right incentives to motivate educators and students to produce higher achievement, as measured by standardized tests.

A limited education policy dialogue

So successful have conservative arguments been that many believe there are simply no progressive alternatives – or, worse, that the prevailing agenda *is* progressive. As a result, genuinely progressive proposals languish at the far margins of the education policy debate. These include proposals that some schools be given disproportionate resources to balance the out-of-school resources in middle-

and upper-income communities, or link educational inequality to inequalities in other social arenas, such as housing, health care, and access to living-wage employment.

A core problem (the proverbial 'elephant in the room') is that, even if material or non-material resources, opportunities, and privileges are not taken away from more advantaged students (although in some cases they could be), inherent in reforms aimed at improving poor children's education is that more students – and different students – will have access to the advantages that are currently the purview of fewer students. Elsewhere, we have written about the role of *scarcity* in maintaining middle-class worry that their children must be positioned on the advantaged side of the education gap, so they and not other children will benefit from the higher educations and incomes that not all can obtain (Oakes *et al.*, 2006). Liberal elites are as susceptible to these worries as are conservatives.

Moreover, elites – both liberal and conservative – work at a considerable distance (geographically, culturally, and economically) from the schools for which they make policy. For these policymakers, poor teaching, inadequate learning conditions, and low expectations are often abstractions that lack the vital urgency of daily crises felt by students who attend the schools and by the students' parents. Their distance from local teachers also creates a desire for teacher-proof remedies. They are more likely to devalue educators' professional knowledge by controlling the curriculum, by advocating for lower teacher-qualification standards, by demonizing teachers' and other public sector unions, by identifying teachers' lack of motivation as the primary cause of students' poor achievement, and more.

The distance between policymakers and low-income communities also makes it easier to dismiss parents and students as unmotivated. Thus, policies pit some groups of parents against others by suggesting that some care more than others about their children's success. These effects are often compounded by policymakers' own elite experiences. Liberal as well as conservative elites sometimes ignore their own positionality and privilege in an unequal education system and take their own success in using market choices to secure 'good' education for their own children as evidence that market-based reforms should work for all.

The absence of powerful, progressive, public voices

Progressive policymakers lack both intellectual and political counter forces to the dominant conservative ideology. They have little access to advocates and researchers who challenge the dominant perspective. Most mainstream foundations are reluctant to fund work that appears to have a progressive political agenda, perhaps conflating *agenda* with empirical work and scholarly analyses that can be anticipated to give support to one side of a controversial issue. Partly as a result, researchers in universities and mainstream think tanks often lack the resources and capacity to insert into the political arena work that challenges the prevailing ideology.

Those researchers who have raised such challenges, such as Richard Rothstein and David Berliner whose studies link the educational problems of low-income communities to cultural norms, rules, values, and power relations that perpetuate economic inequality and structural racism (Berliner and Biddle, 1995; Rothstein, 2004) have been praised in the research community. However, well-resourced conservative advocates have blunted the impact of this counter evidence by characterizing it as simply echoing not only failed attempts at education reform, but as consistent with the entire panoply of failed liberal social arguments.

In spite of these grim descriptions of the educational-political landscape, America has never lost the makings of a constituency for a just, democratic, and equitable distribution of educational opportunity. Although the country lacks a *powerful* public constituency that presses for adequate and equitable educational and social opportunities, widespread public sentiment for equitable opportunities does exist.

Although, public opinion resonates with the conservative ideology,[2] most people are also very concerned (78 percent in a 2004 survey) about the lack of money available to schools in low-income communities in their area. Nearly half of all Americans say that they would like a public education finance system that either spends the same amount of money on each student (46 percent) or a system in which low-income and special-need students can receive more money (48 percent) (Hart and Teeter, 2004).

However, looking only at the aggregates can mask some clear differences among communities. For example, a 2005 poll found that more Black and Latino parents (50 percent) than whites (33 percent) consider a lack of money 'to do the job' at their local schools as a very serious problem. Black and Latino parents also reported serious problems with classroom overcrowding at almost twice the rates of white parents, and they complained two or three times more often than whites that their children were taught too little math and science. Minority parents are also far more likely to reject the views that their children's problems begin and end at the schoolhouse door and that either high-stakes tests or educational markets will rectify the many social and educational inequalities their children face. In brief, those parents and community members who bear the brunt of educational inequality are also most opposed to conservative policies. These are communities who, even more than the public at large, believe that government is unresponsive to their concerns.[3]

Harvard sociologist Theda Skocpol suggests that the decline in public participation and influence over policymaking results partly from the rise of 'professionally managed advocacy groups' and non-profits dependent on support from philanthropy. Such groups have taken the place of large civic organizations with local chapters and a broad membership base, that, in earlier times, played significant roles in pressing for social policies that benefit the less affluent. Skocpol argues that this shift has 'diminished democracy' by lessening the exercise of public power through the mobilization of communities and individuals and, increasingly, lobbying by a professional/business elite that is more likely itself to support policies that favor elites (Skocpol, 2003). As Skocpol puts it:

Scholars have established that a combination of resources, motivation, and mobilization explains who participates in public life, how, and at what levels. Individuals from privileged families have advantages of income and education, gain civic skills at work, and also tend to be regularly contacted by civic organizers and election campaigns. Nevertheless, civic disparities can be partially counteracted if popularly rooted political parties, unions, churches, and associations spread skills and mobilize and motivate average citizens.

(Skocpol, 2004: 125)

Other sectors that traditionally have opposed social inequalities are also losing power in their struggle to curb socioeconomic disparities. Trade unions, organized providers of social welfare 'safety nets', and the public schools themselves suffer diminished presence in policy debates. Or, when these groups are included, they may take a narrower stance that focuses on stemming the decline of their members' more parochial concerns including working conditions, salaries, and survival of jeopardized local programs and jobs. Finally, as the economic stakes of having a good education seem higher (as evidenced by the growing wealth and income gaps), education is seen increasingly as an individual, private good to be competed over by individual families. The net effect is that communities deliberating about constructing schools that will advance the collective public good have been eclipsed by parents engaged as educational consumers seeking advantages for their own children.

Guidance from John Dewey

Our struggle to imagine how the U.S. might break through the current narrow, ideological and political lock on education policymaking led us back to John Dewey's political and educational writings from the 1920s and 1930s.[4] Dewey saw the new science of public relations, which emerged following World War I, leaving the public unable and often uninterested in looking beneath the superficial presentation of social issues to grapple with the deeper realities (Dewey, 1922, MW 13:331). Dewey also warned about elites' domination of knowledge about social issues. He argued that, when a 'class of experts' is 'removed from common interests', it 'become[s] a class with private interests and private knowledge, which in social matters is not knowledge at all' (Dewey, 1927, LW 2:364). In addition to creating a new 'intellectual aristocracy', this elevation of experts 'shut[s] off' the social intercourse so crucial to the problem solving process (Dewey, 1927, LW 2:362–3).

Without a public informed about social conditions and engaged in shaping them, Dewey worried that the economic interests of big business would swamp attention to the collective social good. His response was to call for more public intelligence and a revitalized public. He pointed to the values inherent in the scientific process – willingness to constantly test beliefs, openness to alternative ideas, and systematic analysis – as general principles for guiding the work of publics. These values, he hoped, would encourage skepticism about the source and distribution of knowledge and power in society.

Dewey encouraged publics to adopt the 'method' of science in assessing social policies. He called for groups of citizens to treat 'policies and proposals ... as working hypotheses ... subject to constant and well-equipped observation ... and ready and flexible revision'. This experimental approach – and more important, an experimental attitude – could educate the public, providing them with the 'tools ... of observing, reporting, and organizing ... [which] can be evolved and perfected only in operation' (1927, LW 2:340). Similarly, Dewey attributed an educative role to the direct 'consultation and discussion' that occurs within participatory social inquiry (1927, LW 2:364, 367). Like Tocqueville, he points out that public dialogue 'forces a recognition that there are common interests ... [and it] brings about some clarification of what they are' (1927, LW 2:364).

Although the publics that Dewey envisioned are inherently populist in their composition, he marked out a limited role for experts. Experts could support lay publics by 'discovering and making known facts' (1927, LW 2:364). Dewey did not dismiss expert knowledge, but sought close relationships between experts and common citizens so each could inform the other in the process of inquiry. Such inquiry, he argued, would create new and useful systems of knowledge, accessible to all.[5] Accordingly, experts should join lay publics in dialogue about both problem and method and treat these sessions as serious consultations from which they might learn (Dewey, 1927, LW 2:364).

Dewey's hope for equitable social policy turned on the intellectual capacity and political participation of common citizens. He argued that citizens engaged in public, social inquiry would better connect educational inequalities to their social, cultural, and political contexts and account for the sense of entitlement that sustains and provides a moral grounding for those inequalities. The result could be more progressive public policies (Dewey, 1935a, LW 11:64).

Policy advocates and grassroots activists using research to democratize policymaking

Inspired by Dewey, we sought out sites where we might observe, participate in, and document instances of participatory social inquiry around the educational problems that low-income students of color experience and about potential solutions to those problems. What we found were grassroots and advocacy groups working for (what many call) 'educational justice'.[6] Some groups emphasize generating new information to inform policy debates; some protest unjust policy by holding rallies, marches and meetings; others use litigation and legislative advocacy to compel equitable change; others work to ensure that the equity intent of laws is maintained in practice. Nearly all work directly to build the power of low-income students, parents, and community members of color in order to expose and disrupt schooling inequalities.

This new activism responds to the severe educational crisis in California. A decades-long decline in the quality of the state's educational system has coincided with demographic shifts reducing the number of households with school-aged children, and increasing the proportion of school-aged children who are low-income, Latino, and/or immigrants. Today, California education ranks near the bottom of the states in everything from per-pupil expenditures to student achievement to matriculation of high school graduates into four-year colleges. Those most burdened by these conditions are low-income students of color, many of whom are still learning English. So it's not surprising that groups around the state previously engaged in campaigns for living-wage jobs, affordable housing, quality health care, immigrant rights, and affirmative action are also seeking better schooling.

Evidence from our four-year-long study of these groups gives us considerable confidence that research in the context of organizing can democratize the education policymaking process and challenge the dominant policy ideology. Through processes like the participatory social inquiry that John Dewey envisioned, we at UCLA's Institute for Democracy Education and Access have worked with these policy advocates, large statewide grassroots groups, small local organizations of parents and students and others in a social design experiment we call the Education Justice Collaborative. In this setting, we've supported these groups' efforts to construct new knowledge about education problems and policy solutions and use research as a tool to inform and legitimize their participation as they increasingly sit at the tables where education policy is made.[7]

The Education Justice Collaborative (EJC)

At the time of this writing, the EJC is nearly 30 organizations strong. Several of the EJC groups are local, multi-racial, grassroots groups that organize low-income communities of color. The members of Californians for Justice are high school students in five cities; CADRE and Parent U-Turn bring together South Los Angeles parents; the Community Coalition and Inner City Struggle organize both adults and young people; the Coalition for Educational Justice connects progressive teachers with parents and students. Other grassroots groups are state affiliates of large national networks, including ACORN (Association of Communities Organized for Reform Now) with 24,000 member families in neighborhood groups in 19 cities across the state, and PICO California Project, a faith-based network of 350 member congregations representing 400,000 families. Although most of the grassroots groups are staffed by professional 'expert' organizers, the groups' issues and strategies always reflect members' concerns and preferences.

Other EJC groups are advocacy or research organizations. So, as grassroots organizations build powerful bases and develop movement strategies, research groups like California Tomorrow and Justice Matters Institute share information and research capacity, and groups like MALDEF, Public Advocates and PolicyLink have legal and policy expertise that is very important to the collective whole. This means, of course, that there are many experts and information providers in the EJC. In fact, one of the dynamics most valued is that the groups' contributions are both unique and overlapping, and expertise across the partners develops reflexively as skills and knowledge from different sectors (the university, the community, schools, etc.) co-mingle.

EJC's participatory social inquiry

As a 'site' for participatory social inquiry the EJC members identify problems worthy of investigation, delve into extant research, search publicly available data bases, collect and analyze new data, and craft new ways to represent the knowledge so that it is accessible to multiple audiences. This inquiry occurs in the context of EJC groups exchanging ideas and strategies; learning to reach and make their work compelling to policymakers and the media; and collaborating voluntarily and opportunistically on one another's campaigns. Inquiry serves several purposes in the groups' activism for educational justice.

Collectively the EJC engages in multiple aspects of the policy process, but each organization recognizes its unique role. For example, we researchers play a role in studying education problems and developing solutions, but limit our engagement in actual policy debates to serving as experts in official legislative testimony. The grassroots partners with an active membership base advocate for specific policies, but are also community partners in the research process.

Research and education policy process

John Kingdon (1995) explains that policy agendas arise through the interaction of three major streams of action: problem definition, policy development, and political advocacy. Specific issues reach the policy agenda when these three streams collide and form a policy window. This framework is useful for describing the multiple streams of work within the Education Justice Collaborative. Together, the EJC defines and documents education problems, develops policy alternatives, and advances those policies through the legislative process. Member groups also engage in policy implementation – ensuring that the equity intent of laws is actually applied in practice. In this next section we describe the work of the EJC in these streams of education policy.

Problem definition

As discussed above, low-income communities of color often have explanations of education problems that differ from the dominant conservative ideology. A key part of the EJC work is building definitions and identifying evidence of education problems. For example, in the course of working with local parents and young people, Californians for Justice (CFJ) became aware Long Beach students could not take all the high school courses that the state's four-year public colleges required. Their inquiry was iterative, beginning with their knowledge of college expectations, moving to local research on course availability, and frequently accessing experts' knowledge and methods.

But in order to change policies, CFJ knew their data needed to be systematically collected and credible both to their own communities and to policy makers. CFJ asked us to help them access data bases to learn about the availability of college preparatory courses in different schools and students' rates of participation in them. We worked with them to create graphics that would make the information easy for students and parents to understand. We also helped them find other studies so they could speak authoritatively about the kind of learning opportunities low-income students of color might need to succeed in college preparatory courses.

Californians for Justice's research contributed directly to a citywide campaign to pass a school board policy to provide all students the sequence of college-preparatory courses, and to support students' success in these courses with additional instructional time, summer bridge classes, after-school tutoring, and more. The powerful cycle of learning and action that occurred is of particular note. As CFJ members learned and gained policy experience, they began new investigations that required further research, knowledge, and interactions with their constituencies and with elites. In sum, they engaged in more informed activism and a more confident fight for higher quality schooling.

Policy development

For our partners, documenting evidence of problems is not an academic exercise in 'knowledge production'. Community organizing thrives on the urgency of winning policy battles in order to solve those problems. In addition to challenging how education problems are defined, participatory social inquiry generates new policy ideas that policymakers might not conceive of (or have the political capital to suggest!) in the elite policy arena.

One such idea emerged from the EJC's examination of the disparities in resources and opportunities between schools in advantaged and disadvantaged communities. The groups produced a document that specified what every student deserved simply by virtue of their residence in a state that guarantees a right to education. Both inspirational and daunting, their 'Bill of Rights' named widely accepted basic resources and conditions, such as safe and clean school facilities, qualified teachers, sufficient textbooks and instructional materials, and so forth. They also included the right of English Learners to learn in the language they are most fluent, fair assessments, and in the right of parents to attend regular 'open forums' to discuss education issues at their schools. With the Bill of Rights, the groups called attention to the tremendous gap between what one should find in a democracy and what California's children actually have.

The Bill of Rights was advanced as a viable policy idea. Two EJC groups, California ACORN (Association of Communities Organized for Reform Now) and MALDEF (Mexican American Legal Defense and Education Fund) campaigned to have the California Legislature adopt the Bill of Rights. At first, it looked as though a policy window might open as the groups brought their definition of problems, solutions and policy alternatives to the Legislature.

An Assembly member introduced legislation that addressed several Bill of Rights provisions, including guarantees of adequate instructional materials, safe school facilities, qualified teachers, and reasonable class sizes. The bill included a formal complaint mechanism that families could use if schools did not provide these basic educational resources. The Assembly Education Committee approved the bill, but the Appropriations Committee later determined that the legislation would cost 'in excess of a billion dollars', so the bill went no further.

In spite of the defeat, EJC's inquiry and action produced a policy proposal that generated serious policy debate. It forced the state to place a dollar figure on the extent to which California fails to provide basic educational resources to all. It introduced the idea of a 'complaint process' that was later incorporated into the settlement of *Williams v. California*. Finally, the statewide grassroots and advocacy work had the exhilarating effect of engaging new policy actors and their progressive ideas in policy deliberations inside the formidable Capitol walls.

Political advocacy

One of the greatest challenges to progressive education change is showing how the immediate problems of low-income communities reflect economic, historical, and political forces, rather than those problems being the 'fault of those who suffer'. To reveal these connections, community members seek to answer *critical* contextual questions about the education policy issues they are investigating. Who makes decisions, and who is left out? Who benefits and who suffers? Why is a given practice fair or unfair? What are its origins? What alternatives can we imagine? What is required to create change?[8]

Carefully researched answers to such questions can become powerful tools in the hands of grassroots and advocacy actors who use this knowledge to thwart the blaming of social misery on those who suffer from it most. For example, a coalition of EJC groups across the state have disrupted the dominant frame underlying the California's High School Exit Exam by combining their empirical analyses with critical understandings of history and structural conditions. Documenting the lack of educational opportunities available (severe shortages of fully credentialed teachers, significant overcrowding, etc.) at the schools with the lowest pass rates on the exam, they argued that these shortages and disparities were not random occurrences, but developed out of systematic neglect and biased policy decision-making. Doing so, the groups identified concrete and remediable *structural* reasons why many students failed the test, and these reasons were not the commonplace explanations of low academic aspirations or effort. Their research report, 'First Things First: Why We Must Stop Punishing Students and Fix California's Schools', strategically reframed the exit exam as a distraction from attending to the lack of educational opportunity failing students experience.

Students and their allies in other activist groups used the report to explain the exit exam issue to members of the California State Legislature and the State Board of Education in one-on-one meetings. They brought 450 members to protest at a State School Board meeting, where thirty representatives of the Campaign for

Quality education testified. Their pressure helped convince the State Board of Education to delay implementation of the exit exam's 'diploma penalty' for two years. Their research also laid the groundwork for new funding for schools with high exam failure rates and later litigation challenging the constitutionality of withholding diplomas. Most important, the research demonstrating the absence of basic education resources generated vigorous debate in the media and public forums. Their data added a competing perspective to the previous elite argument that if teachers and students just worked hard enough, everybody could pass this easy test.

Activists' 'actions' are the key medium for bringing their messages to those who have the power to effect change. These actions include strategies to impress their adversaries with the large number of people they can mobilize around an issue, to disrupt business as usual, and to tell their personal stories so that social harms enter into the consciousness of the broader community.[9] Yet, they are more likely to challenge the prevailing conservative ideology successfully when they add to these strategies solid research drawn from processes that have begun with the critical questioning we referred to earlier. When those most impacted by inequality use their research to frame policy problems and solutions, they create a new 'story' of communities who want and deserve high quality education and who know what education can and should be.

Policy implementation

Historically judges, legislatures and school boards have pressed for equity-focused education reforms, but often the equity intent is lost as the enactment trickles down to the school level (Oakes *et al.*, 1998; Welner and Oakes, 2005). Because grassroots organization members can have direct connections to schools, they can participate in and oversee the implementation of education change.

As one example, in spring 2005, several EJC groups piloted a process for accessing and reporting about school conditions. They had several goals: to know about their schools, to inform the *Williams Settlement* monitoring and implementation process, and to develop collaborative relationships with local education officials. Each group examined one school's existing 'School *Accountability* Report Card' (emphasis added). As California's official means of communicating to the public how schools and students are doing, these report cards were all but useless to most parents. They were formulaic and contained stock paragraphs, supposedly about each school's unique circumstances, that principals copied from one another or copied from district boilerplates. Many reports were incomprehensible and had missing or untrue information.

By contrast, the groups conducted surveys and focus groups with youth and parents to learn their perceptions of the schools; they interviewed school leaders, they tracked complaints; and they accessed state data. Equipped with all this information, the groups developed, with our collaboration, a 'School *Quality* Report Card' (emphasis added) for each pilot school. These locally developed 'School *Quality* Report Cards' became the foundation for school-based public forums where the groups made the information public and engaged with school officials about solving problems.

Both CADRE and Parents for Unity, two relatively small parent organizations, reported that going door to door, interviewing parents and youth, and analyzing their data, helped their members develop confidence, leadership and research skills. They also became more visible to others in the community and gained new members. In this way, the report card was a powerful organizing tool. Additionally, the groups' data-collection interactions with school officials and reporting findings in public forums fostered a different climate for public accountability by showing public officials, as well as the groups themselves, that organized youth and parents can call education officials' attention to school conditions needing improvement.

Creating knowledge, space, and accountability for equitable education policy

We conclude from our analysis that challenging the current elite ideological lock on education policymaking and shifting the stale debate into vigorous, democratic deliberation requires social activism by those who are most negatively affected by educational inequalities. There is a unique and vital political role for such 'outsiders'. They can widen the ideological spectrum to enable policymakers to position a more progressive agenda as 'moderate'. Those favoring the *status quo* will no longer have exclusive claim to the center. Only with the presence of vigorous activist pressure for greater equity can policymakers effectively *balance* multiple legitimate, if conflicting, public demands.

The benefits of this activism to democratic policymaking, we believe, extend far beyond education. Although elite policy experts can and sometimes must remain in the constrained arenas of their 'fields', community members' lives are not so neatly parceled. They live in complex communities; they confront multiple challenges that are associated with low wealth and underserved neighborhoods. As such, the power they gain in any one social domain such as education can also address other systemic problems – the lack of decent housing, living-wage jobs, health care, etc.

A democratization of research is central to such social policy activism. Such research helps marginalized groups acquire political power and redefine common sense so that it does not automatically advantage elite interests. New identities as public actors and intellectuals, new ideas grounded in the best of American democracy, new relationships to create collective power – these are the real generative formulations that occur when community members combine knowledge and participation to work for a just and equitable society.

Activist groups are eager for this sort of democratized research and for relationships with 'experts' who can help them navigate the policy system. Several groups responding to our statewide survey said that they contact researchers at the earliest stages of their need for information about a new issue. They also say that, if a researcher they trust and have a long relationship with recommends a particular piece of research, they are far more likely to read it and believe it. Inner City Struggle's Director Luis Sanchez explained:

> Researchers bring a wealth of information to the partnership. They're always finding new research that helps support the work that we are doing. IDEA [UCLA's Institute for Democracy, Education, and Access] can give us the answer to questions within a day that would take us two weeks to figure out. It matters, on some level that we are working collaboratively with UCLA. When you're trying to move an equity focused policy agenda with parents and students, a lot of them ask where this information came from. It helps to tell them that we've been working with professors at UCLA to show that it is something we haven't made up.
>
> (Flapan *et al.*, 2005: n.p.)

On the other hand, placing the onus on poor people to initiate 'participatory social inquiry' and find researchers with whom to collaborate, calls on them to surmount the material and political asymmetries that underlie their current disadvantages – not the least of which is a lack of financial resources and social capital, major factors in building power and mounting successful social and political campaigns. We and many of the EJC groups have been fortunate to have the backing of private foundations and of our university colleagues, but we appreciate the uniqueness of our setting.

A final challenge is that relationships between community activists and researchers nearly always cross race and social class lines. Many well-meaning white and middle-class researchers are oblivious to the privilege and racism they bring with them to these initiatives and how these can easily undermine the very democratization of research and policymaking they seek (Anner, 1996). Even those of us who flatter ourselves as being 'not-oblivious' can still be ignorant. Engaging in the democratization of research as a researcher in an elite institution means simultaneously finding strength in your privilege and your limits. It is about sharing your capital – funding, technical expertise, political access, and knowledge – while also being humble enough to realize that this is not everything. One must actually believe, respect, and trust that the power and knowledge of low-income communities are essential to creating democratic and equitable social polices.

Acknowledgments

We wish to acknowledge the important contributions to the thinking and research reported here of our UCLA colleagues, Gary Blasi, Rocio Cordoba, Julie Flapan, Christine Senteno, and Claudia Vizcarra-Barton.

Notes

1   In a quite recent example of this line of analysis, conservative scholars Abigail and Stephan Thernstrom argued in *No Excuses: Closing the Racial Gap in Learning*, that misguided educators have used students' cultural and economic problems as excuses to allow their continued low achievement and, as a result, provided them with undemanding, low-level curriculum and teaching.

2   For example, a 2005 Gallup Poll on education reveals widespread public acceptance of standardized achievement testing as a measure of school quality. While respondents placed blame for the gap on factors outside of school (especially on parents), they also felt that the achievement gap is an important policy issue.

3   For example, in a 2004 study, less than half of American adults reported that they believe that the government 'listens to people like me;' and half agrees that 'public officials don't care much what people like me think'. Notably, however, although 56 percent overall saw government as being run by a 'few big interests looking out for themselves', rather than 'for the benefit of all', a full 71 percent of Black Americans held this view.

4   Material in this section is elaborated in more detail in Oakes and Rogers, *Learning Power*, 2006.

5   In his conclusion to *The Public and Its Problems,* Dewey argues that 'It is outside the scope of our discussion to look into the prospects of the reconstruction' of publics. *The Public and Its Problems,* 1927, LW 2:368. Similarly, he closes his other major work in political philosophy, *Liberalism and Social Action*, by noting: 'It is no part of my task to outline in detail a program for renascent liberalism'. *Liberalism and Social Action,* 1935, LW 11:64. 'Setting new goals at 70', 1931, LW 6:407; 'Is there hope for politics', 1931, LW 6:188.

6   Our recent survey found sixty-four organizations in the state that seek to represent the interests of low-income communities of color in the educational policy process.

7   See Oakes and Rogers, with Lipton (2006), for an account of this earlier work and the basis for our moving outside schools for promising sites of inquiry.

8   The progressive education group, *Rethinking Schools,* offers these examples of critical questions that they believe should be adopted with age-appropriate modifications for classroom use. See, 'Editorial: Teaching Against the Lies', Volume 18, No. 4, Summer 2004 (http://www.rethinkingschools.org/archive/18_04/edit184.shtml).

9   These various forms of action used by the groups are explained in more detail in Renée (2006).

References

Anner, J. (1996) *Beyond Identity Politics: Emerging Social Justice Movements in Communities of Color*, Boston: South End Press.

Armor, D. J. (1995) *Forced Justice: School Desegregation and the Law*, New York: Oxford University Press.

Berliner, D. C. and Biddle, B. J. (1995) *The Manufactured Crisis: Myths, Fraud, and the Attack on America's Public Schools*, New York: Addison Wesley.

Center for Political Studies (2004) American National Election Study, available online at http://www.umich.edu/~ne /nesguide/gd-index.htm#6.

Dewey, J. (1922) *Education as Politics*, MW, Vol. 13, p. 331.

Dewey, J. (1927) *The Public and Its Problems*, LW, Vol. 2.

Dewey, J. (1931) 'Setting new goals at 70', LW 6:407..

Dewey, J. (1935a) *Liberalism and Social Action*, LW:11:64.

Dewey, J. (1935b) 'Is there hope for politics?', LW 6:188.

Flapan, J. (2005) 'Building Knowledge, Building Schools: Community Groups Look to Researchers for Help', paper presented at the Annual Meeting of the American Educational Research Association, Montreal, CA.

Friedman, M. (1962) *Capitalism and Freedom*, Chicago: University of Chicago Press.

Hanushek, E. (1986) 'The economics of schooling: production and efficiency in public schools', *Journal of Economic Literature*, Vol. 24, No. 3, pp. 1141–77.

Hanushek, E. (1997) 'Assessing the effects of school resources on student performance: an update', *Educational Evaluation and Policy Analysis*, Vol. 19, No. 2, Summer, pp. 141–64.

Hanushek, E. and Somers, J. A. (2001) 'Schooling, inequality, and the impact of government', in F. Welch (ed.) *The Causes and Consequences of Increasing Inequality*, Chicago: University of Chicago Press, pp. 169–99.

Hart, P. D. and Teeter, R. M. (2004) *Equity and Adequacy: Americans Speak on Public Funding*, Survey commissioned by the Educational Testing Service (ETS).

Hernstein, R. and Murray, C. (1994) *The Bell Curve: Intelligence and Class Structure in American Life*, New York: The Free Press.

Kingdon, J. (1995) *Agendas, Alternatives, and Public Policies*, New York: HarperCollins College Publishers.

Media Transparency website http://www.mediatransparency.org.

National Commission on Excellence in Education (1983) 'A nation at risk: the imperative for educational reform', a report to the Nation and the Secretary of Education, United States Department of Education, April.

Oakes, J. and Rogers, J. (with Martin Lipton) (2006) *Learning Power: Organizing for Education and Justice*, New York: Teachers College Press.

Oakes, J., Welner, K., Yonezawa, S. and Allen, R. (1998) 'Norms and politics of equity minded change: researching the "zone of mediation"', in M. Fullan, A. Hargreaves, and A. Lieberman (eds) *International Handbook on Educational Change*, London: Kluwer.

Public Agenda (2006) *Reality Check, Issue No. 2: How Black And Hispanic Families Rate Their Schools*, a Report from Education Insights at Public Agenda, available online at http://www.publicagenda.org/research/pdfs/rc0602.pdf.

Renée, M. (2006) 'Using research to make a difference: learning from social movement organizations in California', unpublished doctoral dissertation, University of California, Los Angeles.

Rethinking Schools (2004) 'Editorial: teaching against the lies', Volume 18, No. 4, available online at http://www.rethinkingschools.org/archive/18_04/edit184.shtml.

Rich, A. (2004) *Think Tanks, Public Policy, and the Politics of Expertise*, Cambridge: Cambridge University Press.

Rose, L. C. and Gallup, A. M. (2005) '37th annual Phi Delta Kappan/Gallup poll of the public's attitudes toward the public schools', *Phi Delta Kappan*, available online at http://www.pdkintl.org/kappan/k0509pol.htm.

Rothstein, R. (2004) *Class and Schools: Using Social, Economic and Educational Reform to Close the Black–White Achievement Gap*, New York: Teachers College Press.

Skocpol, T. (2003) *Diminished Democracy: From Membership to Management in American Civic Life*, Norman, OK: University of Oklahoma Press.

Skocpol, T. (2004) 'The narrowing of civic life', *American Prospect*, June 7.

Thernstrom, A. and Thernstrom, S. (2003) *No Excuses: Closing the Racial Gap in Learning*, New York: Simon and Schuster.

Welner, K. and Oakes, J. (2005) 'The limits of conventional reform strategies', in J. Petrovitch and A. S. Wells (eds) *Bringing Equity Back In*, New York: Teachers College Press.

9   Improving city schools

Who and what makes the difference?

Kathryn A. Riley

Introduction

The story of urban education is often presented as one of crisis: tales of disruption, stories of children running riot, accounts of young people failing to achieve basic skill levels. But this is only part of the reality. While the concentration of social and economic disadvantage in urban contexts can have damaging effects on children's beliefs about learning, and on their experience of education, there is a buzz and sense of possibilities in many of our city schools not found elsewhere. The children and young people are lively, resourceful and creative. Many of our city schools are places where teachers want to stay, not necessarily easy places to work, but exciting and rewarding ones.

I have chosen to write not about our *urban* schools but about our *city* schools. Semantics matter. The choice of word shapes our understanding and expectations. For me, the term *city* has many more positive connotations than that of *urban*. It suggests opportunities and possibilities, not just problems. I think about the buzz in my own home city of Manchester, as well as the efforts of Manchester's Founding 'Fathers' to create educational and social welfare opportunities for its citizens. I think too of the renaissance and resilience of other cities such as Liverpool and Dublin, with their cheekiness and energy; or London, my home for many years, with its vibrancy and cosmopolitan communities; or Chicago with its new approaches to schooling; or São Paulo with its flamboyance; or New York re-surfacing from the traumas of 9/11.[1]

Our city communities can change fast. Impoverished downtown areas become gentrified in relatively short periods of time: new populations move in and out, influenced by global events and the movement of refugee populations. A reality of our cities is the ever altering nature of their communities.

In this chapter I want to focus on the pivotal role of the leaders of our city schools in relation to this kaleidoscope of change. My basic argument is that the leaders of our city schools need to be vanguards of educational change, committed to building connections between schools and communities and creating shared beliefs about what can be achieved for, and by, the young people of our cities. By working with parents, young people and staff in new ways, they can establish a fresh dialogue about schools and community. This dialogue will only emerge, however, if school leaders learn to view parents as co-educators; come to recognise that young people hold the key to unlocking the knowledge and information which they, as school leaders, need to transform schools; and understand how to unleash the talent and enthusiasm of staff in their schools.

Enabling staff to make the difference

Some years ago I carried out a study for the General Teaching Council for England, on what makes a good teacher. In a period of a prescriptive national agenda, I concluded that every staff room probably contained two distinctive groups of teachers: 'glow-worms' and 'skylarks'. The 'glow-worms' were locked into a painting-by-numbers approach to teaching; the 'skylarks' knew how to fly but had had their wings clipped. Nevertheless, the 'glow-worms' could be re-energised and the 'skylarks' encouraged to soar (Riley, 2003). Delving back to my own experience in the 1970s and 1980s as a teacher in a challenging inner-city school, I have concluded that three critical elements made a difference to how teachers could work most effectively with the children and young people from our cities: (i) collegiality; (ii) aspirations and expectations, hopes and dreams; and (iii) connecting to the community context: cities in all their richnesses, as well as the local community context.

I began teaching in inner-city schools in 1973 when I joined Peckham School in South London, having first spent two years as a volunteer teacher in Eritrea. Peckham was a large ten-form entry girls' comprehensive school with some 1,500-plus students, serving an established white working-class community – some of whom made their living on the stalls of East Street Market off the Old Kent Road – as well as long-established, and more recent, immigrant communities from the Caribbean, East Asia, China, Vietnam, Greece, Cyprus, Ireland and many other parts of Europe. It was a lively and challenging place to work, and there was a certain cachet attached to teaching in a school which was designated as being in an Educational Priority Area.[2]

The school had two striking architectural features: an over-abundance of stairwells (popular with reluctant students) and a surfeit of windows which resulted in frequent visits from young male window cleaners: tantalising to the hormones of young female adolescents and disruptive of even the best planned lessons.[3] Peckham was a glass-house with its own micro-climate, a winter gulag and a tropical greenhouse in summer. Nevertheless, in the sweltering heat wave of 1976 I was reprimanded for not wearing stockings. Whatever the temperature, certain proprieties had to be maintained.

The 1970s was a period of exploration and creativity in education, and also one in which deeply held ideological differences surfaced. There was a growing right-wing critique of state education, which emerged in the wake of student unrest in the UK, France and the USA.[4] Views became polarised around the goals and outcomes of education. Was the purpose of schools to liberate children or to create the workforce of the future? Who should decide what happens in our schools

– teachers or government? Should access to schools be determined by market forces, or by local direction? (*Whose School is it Anyway?* Riley, 1998).

In 1975, William Tyndale School in Islington, North London, burst into the media limelight, becoming a cause célèbre as the battleground between opposing forces: the liberal and child-focused 'progressives' and the standards and system-based 'traditionalists' (Riley, 1998).[5] Events at Tyndale reinforced the views of the Labour Prime Minister of the day, James Callaghan, that the government needed to challenge teacher domination of schools and of the curriculum,[6] and helped legitimate the educational reforms of successive UK Conservative and Labour Governments of the 1980s and 1990s. Producer control (by teachers and local education authorities) was to be replaced by a more market-orientated approach, greater public accountability and more national direction (Riley, 1998).

In my second year at Peckham (1974–5), we were visited by a research team led by Michael Rutter.[7] The team was seeking answers to the following question Are some city schools more effective than others? Their answer to that question was 'yes'. Rutter and his colleagues argued that, once differences in pupil intake had been accounted for, schools had a differential impact on behaviour and attainment. Not only were pupils influenced by the ways in which they were dealt with as individuals, but 'there was a group influence resulting from the ethos[8] of the school as a social institution' (Rutter *et al.*, 1979: 205).[9] The book which emanated from this study, *Fifteen Thousand Hours*, was to become famous in education research annals. At the time, it was a fillip to London teachers. At Peckham, it reinforced our own beliefs that what we did mattered, and that there was a pay-off for the effort and pressure of working in an inner-city school.

Looking back, I saw that three things, in particular, could make a huge difference. It was in my pastoral role as Deputy Year Head, and under the leadership of the urbane Head of Year, Eileen Wellard, that I began to understand those lessons. The first lesson was what later came to be called *collegiality* (see Hargreaves, 1994) but which we then experienced as mutuality, sharing, team-work, support – and fun. Under Eileen's guidance, we developed a strong identity as a group. Woe betide anyone who missed the Thursday evening Year Meetings in the hut at the back of the Humanities Building. We talked about individual pupils, tracked their behaviour and performance before those terms became fashionable, shared our anxieties and always left on an upbeat note. This was helped by the ways in which the social and professional aspects of our relationships interlocked.

The second was about *aspirations and expectations, hopes and dreams*. Eileen demanded the best from us. In our turn, we demanded the best from the children. Her aspirations for us were paralleled by our aspirations for them. Our solidarity as a group of staff included solidarity for the children in our care. Through that solidarity, we also gained confidence to challenge the small minority of other staff who were dismissive in their attitudes towards our pupils.

The third lesson was about *community context*. There were two aspects to this, the wider London context with all its rich resources and opportunities, and the local communities. As a group of youngish staff we dipped into London's theatre culture, the Royal Shakespeare Company in its heyday at the Aldwych, the mime art of Marcel Marceau, experimental music and theatre at the Roundhouse.

We took otherwise feisty South London pupils into central London which, for some of them, meant crossing the River Thames for the first time. As exuberant, if occasionally noisy members of theatre or cinema audiences, they were fascinated by codpieces and men in tights. We took them to Amsterdam. We took them to the countryside – Box Hill in Surrey – where one large girl decided to roll down the steep incline. Aided by the forces of gravity and her considerable girth, her descent to the bottom was rapid.

The other aspect of community was the school's local community. As a Year Group, we shared our understanding about our students, recognising that our Afro-Caribbean pupils were not a homogenous group but came from many islands, not just Jamaica.[10] Our pupils were not just Cypriot, but Greek and Turkish Cypriot. We tried to understand where the culture and values of pupils born in London were at variance with those of their parents. We drew on our own experience of having worked in different cultures. We also tried to make sense of the views and aspirations of the local white working-class community. In response to a pre-Christmas truancy problem, we took ourselves to East Street Market off the Old Kent Road in South London, agreeing with parents that working on the market stall could improve the numeracy skills of their children but arguing, nevertheless, that there was something to be gained from encouraging their offspring to attend school. We worked to take that knowledge about pupils' lives into the curriculum and into our daily encounters and practices.

Understanding children's lives and experiences

In 2002, a group of pupils made history in the United Kingdom by appearing before a Parliamentary Group examining whether the UK should create a Human Rights Commission. They used the occasion to articulate their experiences of discrimination and violations of human rights, and to urge that a Children's Rights Commission should be appointed (*Guardian*, 2002; Riley and Docking, 2004). The case for involving school students and young people in decision-making that affects their education and welfare has been made on moral, physiological, social, educational, pragmatic and democratic grounds (MacBeath *et al.*, 2001; Levin 1999; Pollard *et al.*, 2000). As part of that debate, Rudduck and Flutter (2000) pose an important question: 'Are we "using" pupils to serve the narrow ends of a grades-obsessed society rather than "empowering" them by offering them greater agency in their schools?' (p. 82).

My response to that question is that school leaders need to find new ways of learning from and about young people that will enhance children's learning and their opportunities for self-development and growth. To do this successfully, they need to take themselves out of the daily box of activities in which they usually find themselves.

In 2002 I became involved in the project *Leadership on the Front-line* (Riley *et al.*, 2004, 2006). The project set out to equip school leaders to understand more about the complexities of city schools, and to develop their capacity to respond to the array of challenges.[11] We wanted to explore the benefits of our city schools (their cultural and community diversity; the creativity, energy and exuberance of the children), as well as the challenges' contexts (social disadvantage, poverty and ill health). A key element of the investigation was an exploration of the lives and experiences of the young people.

Working with nearly 500 children aged 3–17 in 49 of the schools in the project, we asked two broad questions: What is it like living round here? What is it like being in this school? Our interviews enabled us to understand more about the intricacies of young people's lives: the disjuncture between school and community; issues to do with safety, space, culture and belief; and issues about territory. We asked pupils to draw pictures which illustrated their experience of life within the wider community. These images are vivid, and looking at young people's lives in new ways is enabling school leaders involved in the project to understand the totality of children's lives and the complexities of community.

Our city children may encounter poor street lighting, rubbish, threats of violence, lack of stability on a daily basis. Their lives may be constrained by lack of play space, fears for safety, worries about gangs or stolen cars. They may meet prejudice and low expectations, but they also experience different languages, cultures, foods, beliefs, expectations and have opportunities for sports, cultural events and a range of other activities. Many have the support of friends and families. And many have a resilience which will be invaluable in tackling life's uncertainties. Nevertheless, what young people can experience can be a shock to their school leaders.

Figure 9.1 demonstrates a vivid contrast in the life of a London student. Within the school (left-hand side of the illustration), there is friendship and opportunities. The area around the school (the right-hand side of the illustration) is experienced as unsafe and restrictive. There are problems about travel and gangs but this young woman also enjoys the warmth and support of her own home culture.

Figure 9.1 My multiple environments

Figure 9.2 is drawn by a child from Manchester. Once again there is a stark contrast between the world of school and the world of the locality, in which there is a strong gun culture. The text of a similar drawing by a London child reads, 'I hate gunshots' and 'I hate the sun getting in my eyes'. Both the image and the text had a powerful impact on school leaders.

The children whom we met experience their area of the city in all its complexities. They are likely to know about drugs and violence but equally too – with the encouragement of their schools – they will probably also know about the opportunities. Children in Newham (which is in east London, an area undergoing regeneration as part of the UK's Olympic site) relish the opportunities which will be on offer to them. City regeneration can be a source of stimulation and opportunity. Nevertheless, children's lives are also constrained by their views of what is familiar and safe territory. This is as true for the children in the white working-class estates of south London (Eltham), South Manchester (Wythenshawe), Birmingham, Dublin and Cardiff. City estates can be isolated, with limited transport and infrastructure.

Territory becomes very important and children and young people have a clear and sophisticated understanding of how to manage and survive in particular localities.

Issues about space and territory are finely nuanced in Northern Ireland. Figure 9.3 is drawn by a young person from Londonderry. On seeing this, a Derry Principal commented:

> Our schools are on either side of the community divide but the problems are the same. The kids are fearful, the lawlessness of the town, certain areas they don't feel safe – these are the issues that are coming out for us. Dealing with that is the brutal truth, and to do something constructive about that. I'm at quite a loss to think about it.

Figure 9.2 Be safe: be unseen

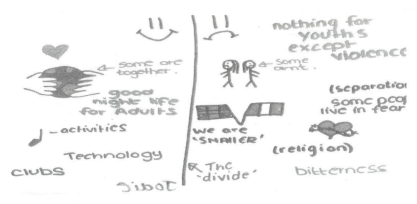

Figure 9.3 Divided society: segregated schools

Children told us that transport can be dangerous: for example, going upstairs on one particular bus in Newham in the direction of Waltham Forest is not advised; drug dealers operate near the tubes at particular times. London children's fears of travelling have increased since the July 2005 bombings. Many of our city children do not travel any significant distance from their homes, often feeling unsafe and vulnerable outside the known and familiar areas. However, once again the issue is complex. London children living close to a tube line also experience a sense of possibilities and opportunities, as do young people living near the city centre in Manchester or Birmingham. Yet proximity and access can be different. Children living on the city estates in Dublin may travel to the city centre, but only for limited city centre shopping. Undoubtedly there are issues about whether the Celtic tiger has left some of them, or their families, behind.

When we asked pupils what it was like for them in their school, it became clear that issues of space and territory are as important in school as out of it. What matters for them is that the school provides them with the opportunity to be themselves: to run around; to play with friends; to explore; and to develop – their thinking and their skills. For many children, particularly young children, the playground is one of the most important aspects of their school life: one of the few places where they can run around and play with their friends and be safe (see Figure 9.4). Schools may underestimate the importance of this, but those schools which have created exciting and explorative areas for children have massively enriched children's lives.

Friendships are another important element of schooling for children of all ages. For older children in mixed gender schools, an enjoyable aspect of being at school is the opportunity to be friends with someone of the opposite sex – an issue raised by a number of Asian children. Children in those schools which are very mixed racially, ethnically and socially, value that diversity. Students' drawings demonstrate the importance and value they attach to diversity and to school-based friendships across cultures and communities: see Figure 9.5, drawn by a Birmingham child.

Figure 9.4 Playground: playing around

Figure 9.5 Enrichment: schools for diversity

Taking on the learning

In 2005 at a Summit Conference for the *Leadership on the Front-line*, school leaders reflected on the project and highlighted the insights they had gained about community context and children's lives and the powerful learning which had enabled them to develop a broader perspective on leadership. This perspective was about being able to reach *beneath, beyond* and *within* the micro-politics of their life as school leader.

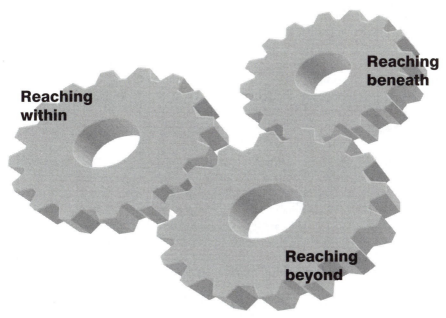

Figure 9.6 Dynamics of leadership on the front-line

Reaching beneath was about understanding the forces, experiences and relationships which influence children or staff to act in a particular way. The focus in *Leadership on the Front-line* on children's lives, and on the complexities of the communities in which they live, had been a spur to many participants to become more proactive in connecting to their local communities, and to find new ways of bringing their knowledge about children's lives back into school. Project participants identified particular actions they planned to take in response to this sharper focus on community, for example:

> We need to actively cultivate parental involvement within schools and do more to engage the community and earn their respect. The increased awareness of community (which has been part of the project) has led to an enhanced curriculum offer to meet community needs.
> We need to share the understanding of community context with staff to enable the breaking of the cycle of deprivation.
> We don't always look into our children's knowledge of the community. We need to ask children more and listen more. We need to create the time, space and opportunity to listen to children, to enable them to speak to us, and to each other.

They reflected that there is 'less turmoil in our lives than in children's and that, as school leaders, it is important 'to appreciate the resilience of students and staff and recognise that experience forces many children out of childhood'.

Reaching beyond was a striving to recognise the wider picture: what it is that children and young people can achieve, experience and be in their life – and who can help them do this. For the school leaders involved in *Leadership on the Front-line* this reaching beyond has been a reaffirmation of the importance of working with parents and communities, and a determination to find new ways to do this. For some, involvement in the project as a research activity had reaffirmed the need for focused and active research to support school improvement planning. Children's images had brought home the importance and centrality of schools:

> There is so much confusion and haphazardness in our students' lives and we have to create that stability and security.
> Schools matter more than we think. They are often a sanctuary. Children want and like the stability and order that schools provide. Significant numbers of young people do not experience stable communities. We need to identify how we can support children more. Pupils value meeting each other. Schools don't always appreciate that. We've come to recognise that children's needs in urban schools in many different contexts are very similar.

The school leaders also reflected on the benefits of having the space and opportunity to take stock of their community context, and to reflect on their role in relation to it:

> There is a dearth of quality support (such as this project) for headteachers that will reduce isolation, develop networking and build trust. It is a lonely job and there is an absence of 'training' that will enable headteachers to understand the issues about diversity, for example, and work with communities more effectively. There is also little that equips us to deal with the kinds of critical incidents we have discussed in the project.

For them, 'reaching beyond' was about connecting to the wider political agenda: drawing attention, for example, to the need for 'massive extra investment in city schools'; for programmes which develop pupils' self-esteem and self-confidence; for a broader agenda on young people. 'Reaching beyond' was also about recognising the importance of their own learning: the need to be open and continue exploring, inquiring and developing. As one headteacher observed: 'Urban leadership is like a fixed gear bike – you stop pedalling and you fall off!'

Reaching within was about reconnecting to the inner drivers: the values which shaped their core attitudes and beliefs. Participants in *Leadership on the Front-line* shared a common view that they needed to revisit these core purposes, and make them more explicit in their day-to-day encounters and actions. They acknowledged the importance of reaffirming their personal values, commenting, for example, that:

> We need to revisit our values and core purposes and draw on these to steer practice more purposefully. The link between vision, values and everyday

actions needs to be constant. We need to hold true to our own vision and values and be very clear and explicit in these.

We chose the challenge of being urban leaders. The project has reaffirmed the importance of that decision. To make a difference to children's lives, we have to go out and make more contact with the community. We need to develop the freedom to enjoy pupils without all the baggage associated with the head's role.

As leaders, they were motivated by understanding what could be achieved:

'I knew I could make a difference to the lives of our students.'

'I saw that I could have a garden in an urban school – flowers in a concrete jungle.'

They articulated their deep rooted beliefs as being about:

- vision and passion;
- hope and optimism;
- a belief that all children can achieve;
- social justice;
- love and respect for children;
- high expectations.

We asked participants at the *Leadership on the Front-line* Summit about the pluses of the job: What got them out of bed? What kept them going? They responded with humour and passion (see Figure 9.7).

Reflections

My work in recent years on city schools, and on the leadership of those schools, has led me to conclude that there is something distinctive about urban leadership. This is about pace, complexity and the day-to-day challenges, in community contexts which are demanding and volatile. And while there is not a set of unique characteristics which distinguish urban schools leaders from their colleagues elsewhere, there are a number of unifying elements. These are to do with:

- *Motivation to make a difference:* wanting to make a meaningful contribution to the lives of children and young people.
- *Commitment to learning*: a deep and profound commitment to learning – their own learning and that of others.
- *Professional Identity:* a strong sense of professional identity which may lead them to challenge conventional wisdoms.
- *Energy and creativity:* a determination to maintain the momentum and to seek creative solutions to complex problems.

Making the difference
- The opportunity to work with and make a difference to/for the lives of so many young people: helping them achieve what you know and believe they can – and sometimes against the odds.
- We can make things happen, as long as we stick with it.
- We make a difference to the WHOLE school community.
- The quiet satisfaction of knowing we're great/good.

The joys
- Accessing the goodness in our communities.
- Watching young people succeed.
- Everybody tells you everything, no matter how hard it is to tell.
- The magic of giving 'HOPE' to children and parents.
- Having the chance to have faith in the possibilities for the children.
- Giving children a chance to have experiences of 'awe and wonder'.
- The chance to develop strong teams and see colleagues develop and become leaders.

The buzz
- It is like being on a roller coaster. It can be full of highs and lows. It is full of teamwork and feels very supportive. The sense of volatility and the unexpected is addictive.
- You never know what is going to happen. Every day is different: from unblocking the loo; to getting wasps out of rooms; to managing parents; to raising standards; to influencing national policy.
- It's good fun.
- Taking risks and being innovative.
- Change is an imperative and we get the chance to change.

Other people.
- The trust of children and parents.
- Nutty, diverse, challenging, exciting kids.
- Fast moving communities where much is possible.
- Celebrating together.
- A chance to influence (positively) colleagues.
- Meeting so many teachers who are committed to our children and are massively skilled in handling them.

Figure 9.7 The most amazing thing about being an urban leader is … apart from still being here!

It has also re-affirmed my views about how important it is for schools and their leaders to understand more about context, community and children's lives, as well as the ways in which city communities can and do change. The challenges for school leaders are *how* to develop strategies which will draw on children's knowledge and experience, and *how* to create a closer alignment between schools and communities.

However, it is important not to underestimate the difficulties of engaging in a very different dialogue and debate with communities. This goes beyond reaching out to help the community and is about learning from, and making better use of, existing resources in the community – an issue which Karen Seashore and I explored in a review of schools and community leadership (Riley *et al.*, 2004).

We found that while the leadership implications of aligning schools and communities are largely unexplored in the literature, there is evidence to suggest that communities – including poor communities – are full of untapped resources that go beyond cohesive social relationships that provide caring support for children (see, for example, Bauch, 2001). The assumption that all multi-ethnic cities have low social capital because of divisions and tensions is unwarranted.[12] If communities have untapped resources, school leaders need to find out where and what they are, and encourage relationships that may help schools to gain access to them. Yet, as we acknowledged, school leaders cannot do everything.

> If they currently teach, manage school finances, coordinate professional development, and work with new governing boards, they are already pressed. Working to engage disparate community groups that may have resources to buttress the school's goals is very time consuming and may have little short-term payoff. The notion that school leaders have community responsibilities that go beyond educating students is so new that current school leaders have few role models or honed skills to help them begin these tasks.
>
> (Riley and Seashore, 2004: 23)

To support them in doing this, and to enable them to reap the benefits from being a leader of a city school, as well as weather the storms, they will need to develop a sense of wholeness. What I have argued elsewhere is that this sense of wholeness is gained by bringing together the different realities they inhabit: the physical day-to-day realities; the social and political; the emotional; and the spiritual or ethical (Riley *et al.*, 2006). Through developing this sense of wholeness, it becomes more possible for school leaders to acknowledge the challenges and the joys: the children themselves, their liveliness and exuberance; the support of staff and senior teams; the pleasure in seeing a child or a member of staff enlivened by experiencing learning in new ways.

This chapter is only a partial representation of the ways in which schools can contribute to the rich mosaic which makes up the education experience of young people in our city schools. My primary focus has been on school leaders and the ways in which, through gaining sharper insights into children's lives and experiences, they can re-attune their leadership. A key aspect of their role is to re-affirm values about the richness of diversity and to develop staff beliefs about the capabilities of our city children. This is not, of course, something that they do in isolation, but in partnership with pupils and communities – and of course staff.

I want to end the chapter where I began – with the staff – and illustrate the potential for growth. In a current development programme, 'Developing the Urban Leaders of the Future', I have been working with a group of middle leaders: the school leaders of tomorrow.[13] I wanted them to make the critical link between schools and community and, at the end of the first working session I set them the task shown in Figure 9.8, Rethinking community. The group departed with some trepidation. Returning some weeks later, they presented their ideas with some diffidence. But what they had come up with were inventive proposals, based on a new conceptualisation of the richness and diversity of their school and community contexts.

The middle leaders' group had created guided walks around the locality to show the diversity (the food, the shops, the places of worship); they had interviewed children and young people about their lives and connected this information to knowledge about local communities in the area (where they came from, what was important for them); and they had drawn on the skills and expertise of young people to produce lively videos. As a group, they had become fired with a belief in

---

Activity: devise an induction programme which focuses on school and community.

The purpose of this induction programme is to enable new staff (teachers and support staff) to find out more about the school and its community context in ways that will enable them to:

- Develop a greater understanding about children's lives and experiences;
- Connect this learning to curriculum and learning opportunities;
- Make stronger links with communities.

Don't be afraid to experiment.

Use the tools that we have provided, if you want to.

Things to think about:

- To what extent are staff in your school aware of the changing nature of the community?
- If so, which staff?
- To what extent does the school draw on pupils' own knowledge of the community context/s in which they live?
- Are there any cultural stereotypes?

Figure 9.8 Rethinking community

the richness of children's lives, moved and motivated by a deeper understanding of what many children and young people in our cities have to contend with on a daily basis. What I had done was touch a nerve, a vein of enthusiasm which ran deep within them. The process of reflection had enabled a committed group of teachers, potential leaders of the future, to strengthen their understanding of the children and young people in our cities.

There is a *potential* for change and engagement in many of our city schools. However, we also need to recognise that our city schools, by their very nature, are fragile and volatile organisations. Whether the broad swath of staff can be energised; whether school leaders can make those critical connections to communities; whether schools will be granted the resources and political support needed to make those changes happen remains to be seen. Reflecting on my work in schools, with those school leaders of the future, as well as with current school leaders, I am struck by an emerging dynamic about teacher learning, by a language and commitment which shifts professional development from an individual teacher activity, to one which involves staff within and across schools, and by a growing awareness of the importance of understanding children's lives. When this happens, the staffroom is no longer a retreat from reality but a powerhouse for change, and our city children gain the opportunities they so richly deserve.

Acknowledgements

With thanks to all the headteachers and school principals who participated in the project *Leadership on the Front-line* and to the supporting Institutions, School Boards and Local Authorities in Belfast, Birmingham, Cardiff, Dublin, Greenwich, Hammersmith and Fulham, Liverpool, Londonderry, Manchester, Newham and Tower Hamlets. All contributed their knowledge and experience with openness and energy. Many thanks, too, to other members of the project team:

- *Centre for Leadership in Learning, Institute of Education, University of London*: Jane Reed, Dr Karen Edge, Jenny Griffiths, Dr. Carol Campbell and Yvonne Beecham
- *Northern Ireland Regional Training Unit*: Dr Tom Hesketh (co-leader), Sean Rafferty and John Young
- *Drumcondra Education Centre, Dublin*: Eileen O'Connor and Dee Coogan
- *Leadership Development for Schools, Dublin*: Zita Lysaght, Ciaran Flynn and Paddy Flood
- *Consultants*: Estelle Currie, Gillian Jordan and Paula Taylor-Moore.

Notes

1 A parallel publication (Riley, forthcoming) explores the changing nature of city contexts and the implications of this for schools.
2 An area identified as presenting particular challenges. Teachers in EPA schools received a small additional payment in recognition of the challenges.

3 Since my time at Peckham Girls, the school has metamorphosed into Warwick Park (a co-educational comprehensive which was an amalgamation of three secondary schools) and, more recently, into Peckham Academy, part of the government's glittering school regeneration strategy.

4 Foremost amongst the academics who proffered this critique were Brian Cox and Tony Dyson who edited a small but influential journal called the 'Critical Survey'. Disillusionment about state schools, and comprehensive education in particular, found a voice in what came to be known as 'The Black Papers'. Critics included Rhodes Boyson who was headteacher at Highbury Grove School in Islington, close to William Tyndale. Boyson later became a Conservative MP and Junior Education Minister (Riley, 1998: 17).

5 To supporters, Tyndale was the school in which left-wing teachers had tried to give working-class children real choices and opportunities (Ellis *et al.*, 1976). To detractors, it was a school out of control, in which teachers had become too powerful and the local authority, the ILEA – the Inner London Education Authority – had failed in its responsibilities. The ILEA subsequently set up a Public Inquiry on events at Tyndale headed by Robin Auld, then QC, now a senior judge (ILEA, 1976).

6 When I interviewed James Callaghan in 1997, he told me that the thinking behind his famous 1976 Ruskin Speech on education stemmed from a general concern about education (he had been Home Secretary in 1968, at the time of the student sit-ins in the UK and student riots in France and thought that students were wasting their time), as well as from a particular concern about schools. 'Some parents were expressing disquiet as to whether their children were being taught or not … There was a feeling of dissatisfaction … The Tyndale school was rattling on getting a lot of publicity and that wasn't doing the teaching profession any good … The government had to take responsibility' he told me (Riley, 1998: 58–9).

7 Peter Mortimore (later to become head of research at the ILEA and then Director of the Institute of Education, London) was a member of the research team.

8 The 'ethos' of a school was defined as, 'the values, attitudes and behaviours which will become characteristic of the school as a whole' (Rutter *et al.*, 1979: 179).

9 It had supporters, as well as critics. For example, contributors to a major critique of the study argued that the study was technically flawed and philosophically questionable (Tizard *et al.*, 1980).

10 Some years later I was to explore the issues of race, class and gender more fully in my researches for my PhD (Riley, 1985).

11 Over 60 headteachers and principals from a range of schools in challenging urban contexts – Belfast, Birmingham, Cardiff, Dublin, London (Greenwich, Hammersmith and Fulham, Newham and Tower Hamlets), Londonderry, Liverpool and Manchester – have taken part. The schools are cross-phase and reflect the range of types of schools in urban contexts.

12 Cities with similar demographics vary significantly in their civic capacity to support schools and to connect to communities (Stone, 2001).

13 I have been joined in this work by a colleague from the London Centre for Leadership in Learning, Mary Dawe.

References

Bauch, P. (2001) 'School-community partnerships in rural schools: renewal and a sense of place', *Peabody Journal of Education*, Vol. 76, No. 2, pp. 204–21.

Ellis, T., Haddow, B., McWhirter, J. and McColgan, D. (1976) *William Tyndale the Teachers' Story*, London: Writers and Readers Publishing Cooperative.

Guardian Newspaper (2002) 11 June, p. 5.

Hargreaves, A. (1994) *Changing Teachers, Changing Times: Teachers Work and Culture in the Post-modern Age*, London: Cassell.

Hargreaves, A. (2003) *Teaching in the Knowledge Society: Education in the Age of Insecurity*, Maidenhead and Philadelphia: Open University Press.

ILEA (1976) *The William Tyndale Junior and Infants Schools, Report of the Public Inquiry conducted by Mr Robin Auld, QC into the Teaching, Organization and Management of the William Tyndale Junior and Infants Schools Islington, London N1*, London: Inner London Education Authority.

Levin, B. (1999) 'Putting students at the centre in educational reform', *Journal of Educational Change*, Vol. 1, No. 2, pp. 155–72.

MacBeath, J., Myers, K. and Demitrou, H. (2001) 'Supporting teachers in consulting pupils about aspects of teaching and learning, and evaluating impact', *Forum*, Vol. 43, No. 2, pp. 78–82.

Pollard, A. and Triggs, P. with Broadbent, P., McNess, E. and Osborn, M. (2000) *What Pupils Say: Changing Policy and Practice in Primary Education*, London: Continuum.

Riley, K. A. (1985) 'Black girls speak for themselves', in G. Weiner (ed.) *Just a Bunch of Girls*, Buckingham: Open University Press, pp. 63–6.

Riley, K. A. (1998) *Whose School is it Anyway?*, London: Falmer Press.

Riley, K. A. (2002) 'Leading challenging urban schools: demands, dilemmas and dreams', paper presented at the Annual Meeting of the American Educational Research Association, San Diego, April 2004.

Riley, K. A. (2003) 'Redefining the profession – teachers with attitude', *Education Review*, Vol. 16, No. 2, pp. 19–27.

Riley, K. A. (forthcoming) 'Leadership and urban education', in B. McGaw., E. Baker and P. P. Peterson (eds) *International Encyclopaedia of Education*, 3rd edition, Oxford: Elsevier.

Riley, K. A. and Docking, J. (2004). 'Voices of disaffected pupils: implications for policy and practice', *British Journal of Educational Studies*, Vol. 52, No. 2, pp. 166–79.

Riley, K. A. and Seashore, L. K., with Currie, E. (2004) *Exploring New Forms of Community Leadership: Linking Schools and Communities to Improve Educational Opportunities for Young People*, Nottingham: National College for School Leadership.

Riley, K. A., Currie, E., Edge, K., Flynn, C., Hesketh, T., Jordan, J., Lysaght, S., Rafferty, S., Reed, J. and Taylor-Moore, P. (2006) *Bringing Leaders Together to Learn Together*, London: Centre for Leadership in Learning, Institute of Education, University of London.

Riley, K. A., Hesketh, T., Rafferty, S., Young, J., Taylor-Moore, P., Beecham, Y. and Morris, S. (2004) *Urban Pioneers – Leading the Way Ahead: First Lessons from the Project Leadership on the Front-line*, London: Institute of Education, Issues in Practice Series.

Ruddock, J. and Flutter, J. (2000) 'Pupil participation and pupil perspective: craving a new order of experience', *Cambridge Journal of Education*, Vol. 30, No. 1, pp. 75–89.

Rutter, M., Maughan, B., Mortimore, P., Ouston, J., with Smith, A. (1979) *Fifteen Thousand Hours: Secondary School and their Effects on Children*, London: Open University Press.

Stone, C. (2001) 'Civic capacity and urban education', *Urban Affairs Review*, Vol. 36, No. 5, pp. 595–619.

Tizard, B., Burgess, T., Francis, H., Goldstein, H., Young, M., Hewison, J. and Plewis, I. (1980) *Fifteen Thousand Hours: A Discussion*, London: Institute of Education.

Part IV

Educational change

Linking research, policy and practice

10 Beyond 'misery research' – new opportunities for implementation research, policy and practice[1]

Milbrey McLaughlin

Reflecting on a litany of failed expectations and dashed hopes, Swedish scholar Bo Rothstein dubbed implementation research 'misery research, a pathology of social sciences'.[2] Today, the complex, multi-faceted and often unpredictable nature of the policy implementation process is taken for granted among researchers and policymakers. However, in the mid-1960s and early 1970s, when the US federal government began to extend its policy reach across and into state and local jurisdictions, implementation was not considered in problematic terms; policy was expected to be more or less self-implementing, given necessary resources, regulation and resolve.

This chapter first takes a look at the domains of 'misery research' generally and in education in particular to draw lessons from the experiences of researchers, policymakers and practitioners during the 25 year period from approximately 1970–95. It then looks beyond misery research to consider how the lessons of that period offer opportunities to understand better implementation and the process of change in education, and how that understanding might lead to more effective education policies and practices. Although this analysis is rooted in US experience, the themes and lessons will resonate with education reform experiences in other settings.

The birth of misery research

Many consider the 1973 publication of Pressman and Wildavsky's *Implementation* the 'birth announcement' of implementation research and first account of the 'ruined hopes' that gave rise to a stream of sober research findings about policy effectiveness, the possibilities of reform, and conclusions in some quarters that policy can affect practice only with the greatest difficulty, especially in education.[3] As discouraging (and often surprising to reform proponents) as these accounts were, they also generated many lessons about implementation problems, processes, and outcomes. The past quarter century of research on policy implementation provides some solid conceptions of how to consider and support implementation and points to areas in which understanding is still evolving. These developing perspectives raise some new questions and considerations for implementation research.

Lessons from past research

Overarching lessons from past implementation research feature ways in which early analysts and reformers underestimated or misunderstood implementation. Problems associated with narrow problem conceptions, dichotomous notions about the 'most effective' location of authority, decontextualized models of implementation paths and cost/benefit assessments surfaced once policy analysts began to tackle implementation as a topic of study. Lessons from this experience implicate all elements of policy implementation research – conceptions of the policy problem, the implementation site, actors, the process and outcomes.

What's the problem?

One of the first things students of policy implementation discovered is that problem framing – what a policy concern is assumed to be a 'problem of' – arguably is the most important decision taken as a policy is developed. For example, is persistent poverty a problem of societal resource allocation, one of individual agency, or one of macro shifts in the economy? Specification of the problem sets the course for both policy and practice and pushes alternative conceptualizations of an issue off the table. Assumptions about the nature of the policy problem anticipate the policy solutions pursued and the logic of action adopted by a policy. And notions about preferred solutions determine how policies are formulated – the policy target, the nature of policy implements, level of support and regulatory structures, for example. Early implementation studies seldom made the problem problematic. Policy researchers soon saw, however, how competing formulations of policy problems were just that – alternative ideas about the root causes of a social issue.

Nowhere is contention about the 'problem of the problem' more prevalent than in education because of the sector's 'people dependent' nature, its 'soft' core technology and the contested terrain of governance, voice and authority. Is disappointing student achievement a problem of inadequate standards, shoddy curriculum, poorly prepared teachers, or an overly bureaucratic education system? Waves of reformers stitched various problem statements into policy banners to champion reform initiatives as diverse as charter schools, standards-based accountability, and school decentralization. Reformers associated with the 'effective schools' movement in the United States saw school failure in terms of inadequate leadership and organizational structures. Others defined the problem of poor student outcomes in terms of teachers' skills and expertise and pursued scripted instructional programs such as 'Success for All'. The most recent broad-based education reform in the United States, *No Child Left Behind* (NCLB), features testing and 'evidence-based' curriculum and touches every state and district in America. For NCLB, a core problem underlying disappointing student outcomes is insufficient school-level accountability for their achievement. Heated debates about NCLB's problem statement rage in the US education literature and in political forums.

The field has learned that most education policy problems, like issues in other social sectors, defy once-and-for-all solutions and that problems themselves shift over time. For one, problems and solutions are often ephemeral because the contexts within and through which they function change constantly – and so alter both the effectiveness of the policy response as well as the policy problem itself. Additionally, policy problems in education are rarely 'solved' because even successful policy responses create new issues. For example, an effective strategy for meeting teachers' professional learning needs may address an immediate need, but also generate new ones if demand for these resources outstrips supply. Similarly, the rush to develop new small schools builds on research that supports the strategy but has created a crisis in staffing – the pool of qualified principals is insufficient to meet demand. Or, the high-stakes testing and accountability programs featured in many regions perhaps can claim increased student achievement, but associated with these gains are increased student drop out and 'push out' rates.

A basic lesson, then, is that problem statements cannot be taken for granted. Instead both problems and the solutions attached to them have the same status as theories – theories of change. As such they present an important area for empirical investigation – research that examines alternative formulations of problems and solutions, and attends both to context and down-stream implications.

What's the relevant implementation site?

Early implementation studies focused on the endgame – the organization or agency ultimately responsible for carrying out policy directives. However, as Pressman and Wildavsky (1973) detail, policy directives and resources travel through many levels and agencies on their way to the 'bottom' of the system. 'Successful implementation' in the Pressman and Wildavsky case depended on the cooperation of many semi-autonomous agencies – from the Economic Development Administration in Washington, D.C., to city agencies in Oakland, California. In the tradition of misery research, Daniel Moynihan (1970) characterized the consequences these policy responses as *maximum feasible misunderstanding*, observing how the meaning various actors assign policy diverged in fundamental ways from policy makers' intent. As we soon learned from Moynihan, Pressman and Wildavsky and legions of succeeding implementation researchers, policy implementation is a multi-layered phenomenon, and each layer or level acts on the policy as it interprets intention, resources and regulatory framework.

The strategic role played by each implementation site highlights the endogenity of policy making and has important implications for implementation research. Many implementation studies take the policy as formulated as the policy 'input', and examine consequences in light of this official expression. However, hundreds of implementation studies testify to variation across and within implementing systems and sites and underscored the point that the 'policy' that matters ultimately is the one enacted within the system, not the one originated outside it.

Analysts now recognize at least five system levels that directly and indirectly shape the character and consequence of public policies: national, regional or multistate, state, substate areas and local (Scott and Meyer, 1991: 126). Each level through which a policy must pass makes policy in a fundamental way as it translates and filters intent and regulatory language and so serves as an implementation site in its own right. However, even levels of the system not directly named in policy design can affect policy outcomes. For example, shifts in federal preferences regarding instruction and curriculum filter down to states, and influence state-level choices. State-level adoption of high-stakes accountability structures has pushed other, locally-preferred assessment strategies off the table at the local level. These inter-level relationships have made their way into contemporary implementation research, though few researchers have focused explicitly on how implementation decisions at one level influence those at another.

Taking policy as wholly exogenous fundamentally misrepresents implementation realities in education. Amanda Datnow (2006), for example, details the co-constructed nature of Comprehensive School Reform policy and how school innovations supported by this federal initiative were negotiated by distinctive features of the school setting. Similarly, Spillane *et al.* (2002) describe how district personnel modify policy intent and principles as they interpret them through their own frames of experience. Likewise, an implementing agency's internal administrative structures, capacity and norms of action affect choices and outcomes. Agency design and institutional setting interact with policy design to produce a site-specific response. Relatively uncomplicated policies typically can be carried out more or less uniformly within and across levels of the system – laws specifying school-leaving age, for example, are relatively easy for agencies to implement. When policies are administratively or technically complex, however, variation in policy response becomes an inevitable result of broad variation in implementing sites' administrative arrangements, funding, professionalization and political authority. For example, Title I of the 1965 Elementary and Secondary Education Act (ESEA), an ambitious federal effort to improve educational opportunities for disadvantaged children, operated significantly differently in states across the country (McDonnell and McLaughlin, 1982). Title I functioned as a tightly controlled state program in states like New York, which had a highly professionalized, well-staffed and proactive state department of education. In so-called 'local control' states such as Iowa, however, Title I operated more or less as a pass-through program to local districts. Iowa and similar states possessed neither the administrative apparatus nor the state level authority to assume a dominant role in this federal program. This interaction between policy design and agency characteristics represents an important source of variation in policy implementation and a fruitful, but currently understudied, area for implementation research. It counsels policy analysts to consider elements of formal policy – regulatory frames, resources, timelines – as building blocks for implementers' responses, not road maps for action.

Who are the critical actors?

Organizations do not act, people do. 'Street-level bureaucrats' entered the policy research vernacular shortly after *Implementation* was published (Weatherley and Lipsky, 1977). Weatherley and Lipsky's classic analysis of the pivotal role of implementers at the 'bottom' of the system led to an appreciation that change is ultimately a problem of the smallest unit: street level bureaucrats' role as interpreters of and responders to policy is as critical as that of policymakers at the 'top' of the system who formulate policy. This research taught that implementers' incentives and identities matter – that street level bureaucrats have professional and personal motivation to comply or carry out policy directives, or not.

Subsequent researchers focusing on individual implementers featured different explanations for the variable responses to policy goals and strategies seen at the street level. David Cohen's well-known narrative about 'Mrs. Oublier', a California mathematics teacher carrying out the state's new math framework, showed how an implementer's knowledge and experience matter (Cohen, 1990). Though 'Mrs. O' was dutiful in her efforts to implement the state's math curriculum, she failed in fundamental ways to do so because she did not comprehend the framework's basic precepts for instruction. Mrs. Oublier could only do what she understood, and build upon the expertise she possessed. California's math framework provided no opportunity for her to gain the knowledge she needed to make the assumed changes in her classroom practice.

Spillane, Reiser and Reimer's distributed cognition framework extends Cohen's analysis (Spillane *et al.*, 2002). They show how district leaders viewed reform proposals through their own experience and so missed policymakers' core intent and deeper principles for action. District administrators didn't refuse, resist or retard reform policies – they simply didn't understand policy intent or strategies.

Each of these researchers elaborates how the oft-heard response from educators to reform strategies – 'I'm already doing it' – many times reflects lack of under-standing rather than any correspondence between their practices and reform strategies. Research into the actions, values and thoughts of implementers shows that implementation is not about mindless compliance to a mandate or policy directive, and that implementation shortfalls are not just issues of individual resistance, incompetence or capability, but also a process of sense making that implicates the implementer's knowledge base, prior understanding and beliefs about the best course of action. Early implementation research focused on the technical properties of policy and individuals' ability to carry it out – what was to be accomplished and by what means – to the general neglect of institutional elements that affected how and whether individuals responded – their norms, values, beliefs.

Researchers also generally overlook questions of policy salience to on-the-ground implementers. Both policy makers and researchers often impose their own categories or parameters around policy issues and fail to consider how important or relevant they are to the contexts in which street-level bureaucrats operate. For example, the lack of attention paid by faculty of a high-poverty middle school to a reform initiative that featured inquiry and evidence-based decision making had little to do with the focus or goals of the reform, *per se*, but rather with the pressures competing for time and attention in their school setting. Crises associated with school violence, deteriorating facilities and attendance issues pushed evidence-based decision making off the table in terms of faculty time and attention (McLaughlin and Mitra, 2004). 'Inquiry' as imagined by the reform effort underway in their school was not just salient given faculty realities.

Contemporary researchers acknowledge how these normative, cognitive and contextual factors may trump technical components of a policy. However, while these lessons about institutional contexts are key for both research and policy, policy research models include these factors with great difficulty since they are difficult to access and assess by means of standardized instruments but require more costly site-based, qualitative research.

What does the implementation process entail?

Researchers' early observations that policy implementation did not proceed in a straightforward, unidirectional fashion across and through levels of the policy system – *ipso jure* – generated alarmed surprise in national policy circles. Early implementation theorists took a similarly simple stance, basing their analytical starting point in a policy's regulatory language, ignoring both deals made earlier in the policy making process and adjustments made as the policy made its way through the implementing system.[4] These analyses, based in the old public administration model, separated administration from politics and took the policy as a given. This analytical stance leaves implementation context and actors in the shadows. Implementation in this view was an 'efficiency' problem and about 'carrying out' policy directives, an administrative and apolitical process, as opposed to 'getting something done' and all the messiness that implies.

Researchers and reformers are much more sophisticated today about the implementation process. We understand that disconnections occur up and down the system. We understand that bargains struck can shift as aspects of the context change. And we know that these bargains are likely to change over time, as policy is *re*formulated in light of shifting expectations or normative assumptions or learning based in on-the-ground experience.

Power is an essential dimension of the implementation process; contemporary implementation analysts figure considerations of power and politics into the process, focusing on how power is assigned to different groups. Anne Schneider and Helen Ingram elaborated the ways in which political power determines the 'social construction of target populations' as weak or strong, as dependent or deviant (Schneider and Ingram, 1993). This perspective provides insight about why some populations are the targets of punitive, coercive policies whereas others receive supports. Political power enables those possessing it to impose their will on others or, where power is more equally distributed, demand a process of negotiation.

Implementation research also is beginning to move beyond linear or staged conceptions of the process assumed by early policy models and policy research designs. Both the implementation process and the policy making process itself typically have been formulated in terms of discrete phases that follow one another. Models of change efforts or innovative programs, for example, generally have been depicted as a three-stage process – adoption (getting started), implementation (carrying it out), and continuation (carrying on once special project funding or oversight has ended). This conception represents implementation tasks as separate and sequential. Yet experience shows that the process is neither linear nor discrete, certainly not at the 'bottom' of the system as new actors enter the scene, demands shift, resources change and competing pressures divert attention.

Excepting education policy implementation tasks involving narrow surface structures such as schedule changes or calendar modification, we have learned that implementation, broadly conceived, often implicates all of these tasks simultaneously. For example, teachers new to a school or district are 'new adopters' of a reform initiative even though the program may have been in place for some time, while veteran teachers are working to deepen its practices in their classrooms. Or, districts acting to extend an effective initiative to new sites confront the challenge of providing supports for sustaining change in original sites, while at the same time providing start-up supports and resources in others. On the ground, implementation involves interplay of change and continuity, getting started and going deeper, learning and relearning as mid-course corrections are made. Despite this understanding, though, too many implementation research designs continue to adopt a discrete step-wise model, rather than deal directly with the actual simultaneity of different implementation tasks.

In line with this understanding about how the process unfolds, ideas have changed about the role of ambiguity in implementation directives and conflict in the process. Public management models tended to view ambiguity and conflict as policy flaws and something to be ironed out of the process, rather than inherent features to be anticipated or even exploited as opportunities. Experience documents the potentially dysfunctional efforts of 'goal clarity' and prescribed implementation procedures and shows the benefits of ambiguity that allows positive local adaptation and negotiation about strategies, indicators and priorities.

How to understand implementation outcomes?

What is 'effective implementation?' Within both research and policy communities, disagreement exists about what constitutes 'implementation' and when it might be deemed 'successful'. This seemingly straightforward question obscures several issues. One is whether or when success means fidelity to reformers' intent and specific directives or instead considers what occurred as a result of implementers' action. A related question is the extent to which an 'output' or an 'outcome' can be equated with a sought-after 'impact' or positive, significant policy consequence. Do visible results signal policy success? For example, a restructuring effort may result in the desired construction of small learning communities – but did those learning communities result in improved teaching and learning, or, might higher academic standards have been adopted? But are they associated with changes in classroom instruction?

Another outcomes consideration involves assumptions about relevant timelines. When short-term successes or bumps in performance persist, does that signal implementation success? Or, conversely, do findings of 'no significant difference' underestimate the longer-term policy gains or significant delayed effects? Teachers' professional development programs exemplify policy efforts whose payoffs may appear down the road in terms of teachers' knowledge base, motivation and sense of professionalism, rather than in terms of students' more immediate achievement gains. Similarly, reforms seeking significant change in practice often take time to mature and become established. To this point, Paul Sabatier argues that implementation should be studied in cycles of ten years in order to consider maturation and policy learning (Sabatier, 1991). Likewise, it is difficult to assess in the short span of most special projects whether change, where it is observed, is evolutionary or revolutionary. Often small changes, such as localized efforts around voucher models of school reform or privatized education models, seemed to make only marginal change in the public school landscape. Over time, however, these incremental changes may be revolutionary for America's system of schooling. Or, policy changes which at the time seemed radical or revolutionary – curriculum realignment or merit pay for teachers, for example – over time have added up to little significant change in the everyday business of the public schools.

Assessment of implementation outcomes also implicates context. How do outcomes look when viewed from the perspective of the broader implementing system? A highly-touted art program in a mid-western American school district, for example, resulted in outstanding student accomplishment; however, resource requirements for the effort drained supports from other arts programs in the district, and so deprived students unable to participate in this special project. Was it a success, all things considered? Another example: a new reading initiative boosted student scores in a high-poverty school district. While these increases were statistically significant, students still performed substantially lower overall than did students in more advantaged settings, and significantly below the state average. How should this effort be judged – did it succeed in its ultimate goal of preparing competent, skilled students? Or, what is the assessment of success when a high school is able to boost graduation rates, the ostensible policy goal, but the high school diploma awarded by the school – the ultimate education standard – in fact means little in terms of academic accomplishment?

Concerns about sustainability pose different questions about relevant outcomes. Implementation research examining the extent to which innovative practices were continued after special funding went away generally found low levels of continuation (Berman and McLaughlin, 1978). One explanation for this disappointing observation centers on implementers' learning (McLaughlin and Mitra, 2001). Often reform efforts focus on activity structures, materials and project routines, to the neglect of the knowledge principles that motivated the innovation. Lacking this knowledge, teachers risk 'lethal mutations' of the project in their classrooms as they modify or extend the practice. Or, teachers are unable to continue a project once special supports are withdrawn because they never learned *why* they were carrying out particular activities or routines. Teachers require knowledge of a reform's 'first principles' if they are to sustain project activities on their own. This knowledge of foundational theoretical constructs comprises an essential implementation outcome and extends beyond the activity structures assessed to determine degree of project implementation. Likewise, important questions feature the relationship between individual and system capacity. What system supports are necessary for individual learning to continue and deepen, and how does individual learning become established in system routines and knowledge?

Important implementation outcomes, then, involve not only the consequences associated with project activities, but also the individual and system capacity developed to sustain, extend and deepen a successful initiative. Just as problem formulations cannot be taken for granted, lessons learned about the complexity of implementation outcomes also direct researchers to make outcomes problematic and issues for empirical analysis.

Beyond misery research: reframing connections between research, policy and practice

The understandings generated by misery research prompt researchers to move beyond reliance on linear models or cause and effect conceptions of change to contemporary models that assume bidirectionality (that is change can move from small to large agencies, or up the system, as well as from top to bottom or big to small), a process that is dynamic (not fixed), lumpy, often unpredictable and highly interdependent in both 'cause' and 'effect.' Moving beyond a linear perspective on policy implementation highlights timeframe and pathway issues and enables an expanded view of implementation. Once that analytical shift is made, alternative conceptions of the appropriate 'unit of analysis' come into play, frameworks that feature links within and across levels of an implementing system and its context.

Timeframes matter

While policymakers' and politicians' timeframes typically are short – often constrained by a budget or an electoral cycle – the policy and program implementation process proceeds at a pace complicated by context, challenges, resources, and goals for change, as misery research testifies. However, timeframe presents a critical consideration when assessing consequences of a program or policy. Whether a change is seen as incremental, significant or revolutionary often depends on *when* you look. As discussed earlier, what might appear an insignificant or marginal change in the short term may, with a longer range perspective, be understood in terms of fundamental shifts to policy or practice.

Will the small schools movement significantly restructure American education or will conservative tendencies support the status quo? Our evaluation of the Bay Area School Collaborative (BASRC) covered a ten year period. Had we reached conclusions about the level and consequences of the Collaborative's reform implementation after five years, we would have drawn incorrect conclusions in many instances. At midpoint, evaluators found ineffective or insufficient school-level implementation of the 'engine' of BASRC's model, a cycle of inquiry; after a decade's implementation, however, these same schools exhibited positive outcomes, institutionalized commitment and significant change in school norms of practice and culture of professionalism (Young, 2005).

For all that timeframes matter, however, they have been virtually ignored as issues for research, and generally disregarded by policy makers looking for a quick fix or easy win. Timeframes are particularly important to implementation research because questions of stability, persistence and extent of change cannot be addressed in the short term.

Conceptions and assessments of timeframe and patterns of change also may differ depending on the *level* of policy or practice under consideration – ground-level, local, state, national, or global (see Campbell, 2004). Relevant timeframe depends on *where* researchers and reformers look for evidence of change. Past research taught, for example, that timeframes and levels of analysis can be interrelated and that change often is more likely to show up at the micro level than in macro-level factors such as state or federal policy initiatives or agency configuration (see Campbell, 2004). Change often happens first at the micro level for a number of reasons. We learned in the years of misery research that change ultimately is a problem of the smallest unit, and that street level bureaucrats can frustrate change in policy and practice for reasons of capacity, beliefs or feasibility, especially when change is 'top down'. However, we also saw that much of the innovative practices and models of effective educational change have come from the 'bottom' of the system – from classrooms, schools and districts. Some examples. The AVID program (Advancement via Individual Determination) began in 1980 with a single class of 32 students in a San Diego, California, high school.[5] Developed in response to court-ordered integration of the city's schools, AVID aimed to provide underachieving students of promise the support and preparation they needed to get to and achieve in college. The program has evolved into a fifth-through-twelfth grade system that operates in approximately 2,300 schools across the US. The National Writing Project, the demonstrably effective and longest-lived professional network in the US, likewise had modest beginnings. Begun in 1974 as a summer institute convened by James Gray and colleagues at the University of California, Berkeley (see Gray, 2000; and Lieberman and Miller, 2004), the NWP currently receives $21.5 million dollars in federal funds and operates 195 writing projects across the country. Or, we saw how the experience and expertise of BASRC leadership schools successfully implementing a Cycle of Inquiry to inform instructional change 'traveled' up the system to change district level practices around data, inquiry and district supports for school inquiry efforts.

Creative educators at the micro level operate a kind of 'skunkworks' for education reform;[6] both the type and pace of change often is different at this level of the system since it can occur at the margins and outside the formal policy system. The next generation of implementation researchers can provide important contributions to policy and practice by looking at the rate and pace of change across system levels.

Pathways matter

Implementation pathways, like timeframes, have received only incidental attention from researchers, policymakers or practitioners even though all acknowledge that starting places matter. Education reform efforts enter a setting that has particular history, expertise, predisposition and constraints, factors that affect the pace, rate and nature of change associated with an initiative. For example, the BASRC schools that had participated previously in a California initiative focused on evidence-based decision making, or in the Coalition of Essential Schools inquiry sessions, were among the only schools to implement fully BASRC's cycle of inquiry within the first five years of the initiative. These schools possessed the experience and capacities needed to make solid progress with the BASRC reform effort. Their successes need to be understood in terms of 'BASRC-plus', the institutional history that enabled them to make effective use of BASRC resources (McLaughlin and Mitra, 2004).

Ignoring pathways as essential to an implementation process risks not only incorrect conclusions. A *de novo* approach to reform can derail implementation. For instance, San Diego, California reformers – district outsiders – generally ignored institutional histories when the comprehensive, ambitious district-wide school reform 'blueprint' was developed (Hess, 2005). The consequence not only was widespread ill-will among district educators, negative attitudes that contributed ultimately to the reform's demise, but also missed opportunities to capitalize on the experience and expertise that existed within the system.

Policy and program implementation is path dependent. Institutional history – experience gained, bargains struck, choices made – feature prominently in how an implementation process plays out, the extent of change that occurs, and its long term stability. A pathway viewpoint enables researchers, policymakers and practitioners to move beyond a decontextualized, independent assessment of a particular program or policy to take a 'value-added', interactive view of an initiative's contribution in the context of other resources and opportunities. Implementation research of this stripe would contribute far more useful information to policy and practice than has the traditional 'special project' or policy research models that feature decontextualized assessments of 'treatment effects'.

A societal sector framework

With lessons about the essential complexity of policy implementation and the multiplicity of relevant system and nonsystem actors come conceptual and practical challenges for researchers. If implementation is not a straight-line process bound by the formal policy system, how might researchers draw meaningful borders around the process, places and players? Complexity and expanding conceptions of influence are difficult to wrap empirical or theoretical arms around.

The evolving model of a *societal sector* provides a promising theoretical frame to guide this next generation of implementation research by providing a unit of analysis that assumes relational complexity. The societal sector paradigm, as developed by W. Richard Scott and John Meyer, incorporates lessons learned from past implementation research about narrow constructions of problems, actors, implementation settings, and logics of action to include all organizations, actors, and relationships within a sector associated with a particular activity or service, such as education (Scott and Meyer, 1991).

This framework represents the convergence of implementation research and institutional theory as applied to organizational fields. It emphasizes function not geography or bureaucratic affiliation to include all relevant system and nonsystem relationships, existing and new organizational actors, formal and informal relationships. It features the wider interorganizational systems that are involved in policy implementation and bounds them by sector function. A societal sector framework permits researchers to pursue lessons learned about relationships, contexts and outcomes, while also pursuing opportunities associated with new actors and associations created in response to contemporary understanding about policy implementation or revealed by this broader frame.

A societal sector framework draws boundaries by function, and so enables researchers to look outside the formal policy system. Yet, contemporary implementation researchers, with few exceptions, generally train their lens on the formal policy system under study to the exclusion of nonformal relationships that extend across categorical or functional boundaries – such as those with nongovernmental organizations, professional organizations or the private sector. Implementation research that considers broader societal influences on education policy and practice has much to contribute to our understanding of the depth and complexity of policy issues and the implementation process.

Considering system learning

A societal sector frame provides boundary for research; it features relationships and a functional view of policy implementation. It provides less assistance, though, in understanding *processes* of change within a sector. Particularly important are questions of how the enacting systems and interorganizational networks that define the sector learn from experience, acquire and use new knowledge, adapt and sustain positive outcomes.

The system focus has been largely missing in implementation research, especially in education. Organizational theorists have examined questions of organizational learning (Argyris, 1993; Brown and Duguid, 1991; March, 1991); policy researchers have paid episodic attention to how ideas travel, but relatively unexamined are questions about how systems within the public domain learn. In part this lack of attention to system learning within education reflects the fact that only recently has the system been considered as a unit of change. In particular, within education, implementation researchers are beginning to highlight the essential role of the local district – the system – as critical to how policies are interpreted, carried out and sustained (Hightower *et al.*, 2002; Marsh *et al.*, 2005; Spillane *et al.*, 2002). Prior education policy research typically followed categorical policy streams, for example, or focused on particular policy domains such as teacher professional development or standards based reform. It focused on 'trees' to the neglect of the 'forest'.

A key focus for future implementation research involves a system perspective on enacting system responses to exogenous policy goals and structures. Implementation researchers are beginning to broaden conceptions of relevant unit of analysis at local and state levels and to incorporate considerations of agency design.

Longer-term and more fundamental issues, though, implicate questions of system learning. Ambitious policies generally seek sustained change in practice and culture, not episodic attention to goals or targets. However, innovation in public policy rarely is the consequence of radical shifts but rather the result of incremental improvements that are incorporated into existing routines and norms. As Lee Cronbach so aptly put it: there are few 'slam bam' policy effects (Cronbach, 1982). Incremental improvements, organizational learning theorists demonstrate, require opportunities to examine practice regularly, consider alternatives and make adjustments informed by experience. Similarly, change that is sustained and deepened assumes coherent and consistent supports within the enacting system – what Weick and Roberts call a 'collective mind', a condition practitioners might describe as 'everyone being on the same page' (Weick and Roberts, 1993).

Yet neither policy makers nor researchers have paid much attention to how systems would learn these new behaviors or acquire the knowledge necessary to a collective mind. How can systems learn from experience? How can policy systems generate and use new knowledge in ways that further reformers' goals? How does individual learning connect to system learning? For example, when education policy targets change in teachers' capabilities and practices, what are assumed connections between individual and district system learning? Currently, both policy and research usually overlook this essential link and so neglect the relationship between individual learning and organizational improvement.

Or, by and large the accountability and evaluation structures associated with education policy situate 'learning' outside the implementing system, as compliance measures and assessments of policy investment. This stance, while valid from the perspective of a social account, overlooks the importance of the system as its own source of learning and in many instances displaces opportunities for system learning. How might education policy at all levels be more intentional about facilitating system learning? For instance, learning theorists stress the importance of 'situated learning' and context-specific interpretation of experience (Brown *et al.*, 1989, for example). Helen Simons and colleagues (Simons *et al.*, 2003) similarly highlight what they call 'situated generalization', the opportunity for teachers to translate information from their environment in terms specific to their students, subjects and classroom settings. Scholars contributing to the burgeoning 'knowledge management' literature likewise underscore the importance of learning by doing, integrating learning and practice on a continuing basis (see, for example, *Harvard Business Review*, 1998).

Implementation research aims to investigate the structures and processes that move policy goals into practice, and the field can take advantage of theoretical developments that inform these objectives from another perspective. A productive viewpoint for the next generation of implementation researchers would integrate lessons from implementation research with current ideas about learning systems and knowledge management to understand how enacting systems can learn as part of policy implementation.

Notes

1 A version of this chapter appeared as a chapter in Honig (2006).
2 This assessment was based on his review of the implementation literature, cited in Hill and Hupe (2002: 79).
3 The full title of Pressman and Wildavsky's book conveys the tone and perspective of the account: *Implementation: How great expectations in Washington are dashed in Oakland; or, why it's amazing that federal programs work at all, this being the saga of the Economic Development Administration as told by two sympathetic observers who seek to build morals on a foundation of ruined hope.* Pressman and Wildavsky's book named the complex and often unpredictable process that other observers of the policy described as Kennedy-Johnson era Great Society social programs rolled out of Washington, D.C. in the 1960s. Daniel Moynihan's 1970 *Maximum Feasible Misunderstanding*, which details the huge variation in state and local responses to federal poverty initiatives and Martha Derthick's 1972 portrayal of the federal government's inability to order other governments' compliance with the conditions of a new federal housing program, *New towns in town: why a federal program failed,* also stand as early challenges to conventional ideas about policy implementation.
4 Van Meter and Van Horn (1975) and Mazmanian and Sabatier (1983) exemplify this early implementation research. See review in Hill and Hupe (2002) and Matland (1995).
5 Information about AVID can be found at: https://www.avidonline.org/.
6 'A skunkworks is a group of people who, in order to achieve unusual results, work on a project in a way that is outside the usual rules. A skunkworks is often a small team that assumes or is given responsibility for developing something in a short time with minimal management constraints.' Downloaded June 6, 2006 from http://whatis.techtarget.com/definition/0,289893,sid9_gci214112,00.html.

References

Advancement via Individual Determination, available online at https:www.avidonline.org.
Argyris, C. (1993) *Knowledge for Action: Overcoming Barriers to Organizational Change*, San Francisco, CA: Jossey-Bass.
Bardach, E. (1977) *The Implementation Game: What Happened after a Bill Becomes a Law,* Cambridge, MA: MIT Press.

Berman, P. and McLaughlin, M. W. (1978) *The Rand Change Agent Study, Vols 1–8*, Santa Monica, CA: The RAND Corporation.

Brown, J. S. and Duguid, P. (2000) *The Social Life of Information*, Cambridge, MA: Harvard Business School Press.

Brown, J. S., Collins, A. and Duguid, P. (1989) 'Situated cognition and the culture of learning', *Education Researcher*, Vol. 18, No. 1, pp. 32–42.

Campbell, J. L. (2004) *Institutional Change and Globalization*, Princeton, NJ: Princeton University Press.

Cohen, D. K. (1990) 'A revolution in one classroom: the case of Mrs. Oublier', Educational *Evaluation and Policy Analysis*, Vol. 12, No. 3, Fall, pp. 327–45.

Cronbach, L. J. (1982) *Designing Evaluations of Educational and Social Programs*, San Francisco, CA: Jossey-Bass.

Datnow, A. (2006) 'Connections in the policy chain: the case of comprehensive school reform', in M. I. Honig (ed.) *New Directions in Policy Implementation*, Albany, NY: State University Press.

Derthick, M. (1972) *New Towns In-Town*, Washington, DC: Urban Institute.

Gray, J. (2000) *Teachers at the Center*, Berkeley, CA: The National Writing Project.

Harvard Business Review (1998) *Harvard Business Review on Knowledge Management*, Cambridge, MA: Author.

Hess, F. (2005) *Urban School Reform: Lessons from San Diego*, Cambridge, MA: Harvard Education Press.

Hightower, A., Knapp, M., Marsh, J. and McLaughlin, M. (2002) *School Districts and Instructional Renewal*, New York: Teachers College Press.

Hill, M. and Hupe, P. (2002) *Implementing Public Policy*, London: Sage Publications.

Honig, M. I. (ed.) (2006) *New Directions in Education Policy Implementation*, Albany, NY: State University Press.

Lieberman, A. and Miller, L. (2004) *Teacher Leadership*, San Francisco, CA: Jossey-Bass Publishers.

March, J. G. (1991) 'How decisions happen in organizations', *Human–Computer Interaction*, Vol. 6, No. 1, pp. 95–117.

Marsh, J. A., Kerr, K. A., Ikemoto, G. S., Darilek, H., Suttorp, M., Zimmer, R. W. and Barney, H. (2005) *The Role of Districts in Fostering Instructional Improvement: Lessons from Three Urban Districts Partnered with the Institute for Learning*, Santa Monica, CA: The RAND Corporation.

McDonnell, L. M. and McLaughlin, M. W. (1982) *Education Policy and the Role of the States*, Santa Monica, CA: The RAND Corporation.

McLaughlin, M. and Mitra, D. (2001) 'Theory-based change and change-based theory: going deeper, going broader', *Journal of Educational Change*, Vol. 2, pp. 301–23.

McLaughlin, M. and Mitra, D. (2004) *The Cycle of Inquiry as the Engine of School Reform: Lessons from the Bay Area School Collaborative*, San Francisco, CA: Bay Area School Collaborative.

Matland, R. E. (1995) 'Synthesizing the implementation literature: the ambiguity-conflict model of policy implementation', *Journal of Public Administration Research and Theory*, Vol. 5, No. 2, April, pp. 145–74.

Maxmanian, D. A. and Sabatier, P. A. (1989) *Implementation and Pubic Policy*, New York: University Press of America.

Moynihan, D. P. (1970) *Maximum Feasible Misunderstanding*, New York: Free Press.

Pressman, J. and Wildavsky, A. (1973) *Implementation*, Berkeley, CA: University of California Press.

Sabatier, P. (1991) 'Toward better theories of the policy process', *PS: Political Science and Politics*, Vol. 24, No. 2, pp. 129–68.

Schneider, A. and Ingram, H. (1993) 'Social construction of target populations: implications for politics and policy', *American Political Science Review*, Vol. 87, No. 2, pp. 334–47.

Scott, W. R. and Meyer, J. W. (1991) 'the organization of societal sectors: propositions and early evidence', in W. W. Powell and P. J. DiMaggio (eds) *The New Institutionalism in Organizational Analysis*, Chicago, IL: University of Chicago Press, pp. 108–40.

Simons, H., Kushner, S. and James, D. (2003) 'From evidence-based practice to practice-based evidence: the idea of situated generalization', *Research Papers in Education Policy and Practice*, Vol. 8, No. 4, December, pp. 347–64.

Spillane, J. P., Reiser, B. J. and Reimer, T. (2002) 'Policy implementation and cognition: Reframing and refocusing implementation research', *Review of Educational Research*, Vol. 72, No. 3, pp. 387–431.

Van Meter, D. and Van Horn, C. E. (1975) 'The policy implementation process: a conceptual framework', *Administration and Society*, Vol. 6, No. 4, pp. 443–88.

Weatherley, R. and Lipsky, M. (1977) 'Street-level bureaucrats and institutional innovation: implementing special education reform', *Harvard Educational Review*, Vol. 47, pp. 171–97.

Weick, K. E. and Roberts, K. H. (1993) 'Collective mind in organizations: heedful interrelating on flight decks', *Administrative Science Quarterly*, Vol. 38, No. 3, September, pp. 357–81.

Young, V. M. (2005) 'Teachers' use of data: embedded contexts and institutional logics', unpublished doctoral dissertation, Stanford, CA: Stanford University.

11 The knowledge society as a trigger for contemporary change in education policy and practice

Judyth Sachs

Introduction

> In every intellectual age some one style of reflection tends to become a common denominator of cultural life. Nowadays, it is true, many intellectual fads are widely taken up before they are dropped for new ones in the course of a year or two. Such enthusiasm may add spice to cultural play, but leave little or no intellectual trace.
>
> (Wright-Mills, 2000: 13)

Wright-Mills originally made this observation in 1959 at the beginning of his influential book *The Sociological Imagination* in which he defined the parameters of social science and how best it could contribute to our understanding of the factors that shape social, political and economic life. Nearly fifty years later this observation is equally apposite. For my purposes here I would like to include policy among the constellation of fads. Over the years we have seen many intellectual fads taken up, others rejected and new ones – some theories/policies will have ascendency while others are rejected for scholarly, political or ideological reasons. In this chapter I argue that the *Zeitgeist* at the beginning of the twenty-first century circulates around debates and practices of the 'information society' (Castells, 1996; Webster, 2006), 'knowledge society' (Leadbeater, 1999), 'audit society' (Power, 1999) or 'network society' (Barney, 2004; Day and Schuler, 2004). Common to all of these debates is their attempt to understand the complexity and the implications of living in a society characterised by increasingly rapid technological change, and how this challenges our assumptions about political, economic and social activity as evidenced in the practices of institutions and people. Variously these ideas grapple with issues of power as expressed through regimes of accountability and surveillance (audit society), they focus on flows of information/knowledge and how that knowledge/information is distributed, consumed and applied.

I organise the chapter in two parts. Part one contextualises the knowledge society and identifies a set of practices emerging from it that can shape and constrain education policy and practice. I argue that the erosion of trust and the development of risk anxiety, the domination of audit and accountability, the focus on performativity and performance regimes, and the rise of standards are all responses to the conditions created by the knowledge society. Part two presents some ideas on the implications of the knowledge society for education research and teacher practice. My focus is on the generative and innovative possibilities of the knowledge society. The position I take is that the information/knowledge society creates a particular set of conditions which have consequences for education policy and teacher practice. There are two options which can emerge: first is a focus on control, regulation and surveillance, which is the focus of the audit society. In many cases this leads to standardisation of practice and ideas and, in the end, mediocrity. An alternative is to have standards of performance which have the development and growth of people at the centre and hence focus on relationships between teachers and teachers, teachers and students and schools and their communities. These relationships encourage and support risk taking and hence there is potential for innovation through which new kinds of knowledge and new forms of engagement and practice will emerge.

Information, society, knowledge society or network society?

The terms information age, information economy, knowledge society and knowledge economy are often used interchangeably but for different ends. Cammaerts (2005: 73), for example, argues that 'the information society is foremost a normative concept and thus entails making choices: about what kind of society we want in the future; about how inclusive that society has to be; about the balance of power between state, civil society and market – choices concerning the scope and meaning of public interest and goods'. The same point could be particularised to education by asking what sort of education system, schools, teachers and pupils do we want in a context characterised by flows of information and the proliferation of technologies that enable widespread communication of large volumes of information across vast territories instantaneously (Barney, 2004: 29).

Informational labour (Castells, 1997) is the key category for the new age. This is the group in the information age whose membership 'manages, initiates and shapes affairs, by being well educated, having initiative, welcoming the frenetic pace of change which typifies the current epoch, and having the capacity to self program itself'. Informational labour jobs 'embody information and knowledge' (Webster, 2006: 447). In many respects teachers can be included in this category as the mediators and implementers of what counts as important knowledge.

My intention here is not to engage in great detail over issues of nomenclature, but rather for consistency to refer to the knowledge society which is a progression from the information society to the extent that 'the use of information and communication technologies must be linked to the recognition that knowledge is the principal force of the social, political, cultural and institutional dimensions of development, founded on human rights' (UNESCO, 2003: 2). Hargreaves (2003: 17) captures the dimensions of the knowledge society as follows:

- expanded scientific, technical and educational spheres;
- complex ways of processing and circulating knowledge in a service-based economy;
- basic changes to organisational functions for the continuing enhancement of products and services by creating systems, teams and cultures that maximise opportunities for mutual and spontaneous learning.

The knowledge society could be seen as deterministic with economic imperatives shaping social and education policy and practice through its sophisticated use of technology for purposes of surveillance and accountability. Knowledge becomes a major commodity and a force to exert power and influence.

Network societies reflect opportunities where the interface between information and information communication technologies can be utilised as a social tool to build capacity and empower communities, groups and individuals (Day and Schuler, 2004: 349). They support Leadbeater's (1999) claim of the emancipatory potential rather than deterministic imposition of knowledge-driven society. In such societies democratic values (and the social values and virtues which are associated with them) drive and support practice. However, as Pring (2003: 66) notes they are difficult to sustain where policy and practice are increasingly controlled by government whereby these controls become embodied in policies and everyday practices.

Factors at play in shaping education policy

If the knowledge society is about power, control and the distribution of knowledge, then it will have a significant impact on education policy and teacher practice. The discourses and practices of performativity, audit, accountability, and standards can be seen as policy technologies informing and shaping current education policy. They will have different degrees of emphasis depending on particular political and economic contexts, and provide the basis for judging how effective and economic educational provision is and will provide the justification for state intervention.

Risk and trust

In climates of rapid change, uncertainty and ambiguity and where performativity is a dominating discourse, the erosion of trust in people and institutions are one of the first casualties. Risk, danger and blame characterise institutional responses to uncertainty and ambiguity. As Morley (2003: 69) argues 'Accountability, audit and the relentless pursuit of evidence of professional competence are challenges to relationships of trust'. Checking only becomes required in a climate of distrust (Douglas, 1992). Audit cultures and standards regimes are indicators of that distrust and have become technologies of control to reduce autonomy and influence of the teaching profession. Importantly, accountability itself isn't the enemy – teachers need to be accountable to their students, their colleagues and their school communities – but rather that this accountability to narrow sets of 'performance' standards and to the whims of the government of the day is antithetical to any kind of transformative vision of the profession or of education.

For teachers working in a climate of increasing distrust, risk awareness and risk consciousness are now part of an everyday lexicon that prescribe and proscribe their activities. As Douglas (1992: 14) argues, the language of danger has turned to the language of risk, moreover risk now means danger; high risk means a lot of danger (p. 24). Classrooms and playgrounds are now dangerous places for both children and teachers.

The development of increased risk consciousness by teachers across both public and private spheres needs to be understood in the light of the erosion of trust. As Caplan (2000: 23) observes 'one aspect of risk management is that, in its name, control can be asserted by governments and other bodies over populations'. By its very nature risk is about power and control – who has the power to make decisions about what constitutes risk and what kind of strategies or regulatory frameworks are to be put in place to ensure compliance? The strong and sustained push for accountability required by governments, and various risk management and quality assurance methods to ensure that this is done, has to be seen in this light.

For teachers, risk is present in their taken-for-granted practices in classrooms, and expressed in terms of how they interact with their students, both verbally and in a behavioural sense – through encouragement or nurturing through touch. At the very core of teachers' practice is how they enact their duty of care both in terms of taking reasonable care to ensure a child's physical and, more recently, emotional safety. Not surprisingly, risk is synonymous with danger for both students and teachers. The prevailing logic is that children are seen as being an 'at risk group', vulnerable to harmful risks and in need of protection.

Inside and outside of schools, concerns are also being expressed that new 'safer' practices (e.g. distancing, 'no touch', new forms of teacher and student surveillance) are reducing teachers' capacities to foster child development (e.g. motor skills, perceptual skills, interpersonal skills (McWilliam and Sachs, 2005)). Here lies the major paradox of the interpretation and application of current policies in general and child protection in particular. On the one hand, teachers are modifying their classroom behaviour as a risk minimisation response to new child protection policies, while on the other they are going against the axiom that risk taking is required for child learning to occur.

Audit and accountability

In a context where the enactment of power is taken for granted, audit and accountability become powerful technologies of control. As Morley (2003) observes, accountability is a common sense term that over-simplifies power relations. Significantly however, 'it is value laden in so far as it privileges certain types of knowledge, pedagogies, outcomes and management processes over others' (Morley, 2003: 53). It values technical over theoretical knowledge, instrumental and highly visible and measurable pedagogies over creative and innovative ones and is concerned with outcomes that can be measured according to various prescribed metrics. It sees the spectre of danger and harm in any interaction and in its purest form actively works against innovative practice in that it aims to minimise risk-taking in all contexts. It embodies contractual forms of accountability which are concerned with the degree to which educators are fulfilling the expectations of particular audiences in terms of standards, outcomes and results (Mulford, 2005: 283).

The processes of audit and the emergent audit society motif symbolises what Power (1999: 14) sees as 'a collection of systematic tendencies and dramatises the extreme case of checking gone wild, of ritualised practices of verification whose technical efficacy is less significant than their role in the production of organisational efficiency'.

Inherent in this is a discourse about accountability which signals a lack of trust in the professions at the same time that it also provided a way for organisations and the state to manage professionals that were seen to be unable to self-regulate. Indeed, 'the more intense the gaze of the audit, the less the trust invested in the moral competence of the practitioners to respond to the needs of those they serve' (Groundwater-Smith and Sachs, 2002: 341). This lack of trust in teachers and the focus on standardised testing and benchmarks is counterproductive as it is more likely to lead to a 'trained incapacity' rather than to critical thinking or academic excellence.

Performativity

The knowledge society engenders what Lyotard (1984) refers to as the terrors of performativity. For Ball (2000: 1) this is 'a technology, a culture and mode of regulation ... that employs judgements, comparisons and displays as a means of control, attrition and change'. It is a central aspect of the quality and standards agenda as it works as a disciplinary system of judgements, classifications and targets towards which teachers and others engaged in information labour must strive and against which they are judged and evaluated. It is as much about being seen to perform, as actually engaging in the performance. The performances (of individual subjects or organisations) serve as measures of productivity or output, or displays of 'quality', or 'moments' of promotion or inspection. As such they stand for, encapsulate or represent the worth, 'quality or value of an individual or organisation within a field of judgement' (Ball, 2003: 26).

The audit process provides the vehicle for this to happen as it offers both transparency and accountability while promising quality under conditions of scarcity and unpredictable consumer demand. Accordingly, it promotes a view where excellence is the norm to which individuals and institutions aspire.

For Elliott (1996: 16) the emphasis on 'performativity' as a policy device is not simply or even mainly about raising standards, but rather plays a central role in *changing the rules which shape educational thought and practice ... part of a language game which serves the interests of power and legitimates those interests in terms of performative criterion* (cited in Osborne and McNess, 2005).

Not surprisingly, 'it is not that performativity gets in the way of real 'work' or 'proper' learning, it is the vehicle for changing what work and learning are (Ball, 2003: 6)! Accordingly, performativity is a trigger for the development of particular performance measures which are circulated and implemented, and set the bar for what is to be achieved.

Standards and standardisation

Standards regimes are about accountability and represent a dimension of the audit society (Power, 1999) and through their processes create and sustain audit cultures which currently characterise public institutions (Strathern, 2000). Regulation, enforcement and sanctions are required to ensure its compliance. Standards as a technology to control the teaching profession are being developed by education bureaucracies in Australia, UK and elsewhere.

While debates about standards focus on either *teaching* standards or *teacher* standards they are not necessarily that clear cut. Sometimes teacher standards masquerade as teaching standards. This is at least in part about how they are applied and used at a local level, regardless of whether their primary focus is on the process or on the teacher. Nevertheless, these terms are often used interchangeably but have quite clear political implications. Teaching standards treat teaching as a process that can be improved. They seek to build and hone teacher creativity and professional judgement at the local and individual level to help teachers understand their practice and improve it. Teacher standards, on the other hand, are concerned with measuring teacher performance, placing teachers as objects for measurement. In their most extreme form, they become a form of regulation, dictating and standardising professional practice, removing the ability of teachers to be creative, innovative, and use their professional judgement.

In some instances teacher standards have been developed to improve performance, support the performativity agenda and used as a basis for reforming the teaching profession. Elsewhere these standards have been imposed and used by governments as regulatory frameworks and bureaucratic controls over teachers, particularly as they relate to licensing and certification procedures. In other instances they are used as an initiative for teachers to gain professional control over what constitutes professional work. Its most positive reading is that 'Recently developed professional standards for teaching hold promise for mobilising reforms of the teaching career and helping to structure the learning opportunities that reflect the complex, reciprocal nature of teaching work' (Darling-Hammond, 1999: 39).

Alternatively, Andy Hargreaves (2003: 61) suggests that

> the rightful pursuit of higher standards has degenerated into a counter-productive obsession with soulless standardization … . Downsizing and standardization have corroded collaboration, depleted teacher leadership and reduced teachers' investment in their own professional learning – destroying the collective investment that is vital for knowledge-based organizations.

Standardisation comes with its own particular problems at both the school and the individual level. For Bottery (2004: 91)

> Excessive standards through externally-imposed targets can negatively affect the aims and objectives of a school, reduce trust in policy makers, and depress educators' self concepts ... . Not only can targets deflect attention from the prime concern of an educational organisation, but because of their ever changing nature, they can prevent people from being satisfied with their efforts.

Absent from much of the standards debate is any mention of the impact of these controlling devices on teacher professional judgement – the presence of which is a cornerstone for calls of teacher professionalism. Standards whose intentions are regulatory, seek, in their most extreme form, to spell out and standardise professional practice in ways which eliminate the legitimacy of professional judgement as well as the need to use it as part of their everyday classroom practice. Regulatory approaches may, at their worst, be seen to deny the creative, intellectual and relational work implicit in good teaching, reducing it to a set of measurable attributes or behaviours. Everything about good teaching – from curriculum design, the adoption and application of innovative pedagogies, the development of appropriate authentic assessment strategies to devising methods of effectively differentiating curriculum, to name a few, is creative and intellectual work. Importantly, learning is about the development of relationships, and an authentic and effective learning relationship is one which is reflexive and responsive on the part of both teacher and learner. A learning environment which is transformative in its intent is therefore highly creative and relational and thus difficult to reduce to specific numeric targets as is implicit in some regulatory standards. Perhaps this is why professional judgements are absent from much of the debate – they are too difficult to measure.

Developmental standards, which seek, on the other hand, to build and hone teacher professional judgement can effectively do so if they are used at the local and individual level to help teachers understand their practice and improve it. When this is the focus, conversations about pedagogy, classroom practice and so on become a professional norm. In such a regulatory environment where the achievement of constantly changing external targets is made the over-riding objective, morale can be dramatically lowered. Teacher professional judgement has always been fragile, but in this age we run the risk of it disappearing altogether.

Clearly then two sets of tensions are present. On the one hand, developmental standards give promise to a revitalised and dynamic teaching profession; on the other hand, regulatory standards regimes can remove professional autonomy and expertise away from teachers, reduce diversity of practice and opinion and promote 'safe' practice. At a time when governments are attempting to reduce the power and control of professions, it is clear which type of standards would be most attractive to them in the achievement of this aim.

Having laid out my ideas about how the knowledge society is influencing and shaping education policy and teachers' practices, I now turn to identifying some opportunities for research and teaching and the development of 'radical' and emancipatory practice that a knowledge driven society can provide.

Teachers and the knowledge society

Social networks harness information and knowledge as key resources of communicative action, through which social goals can be achieved (Day and Schuler, 2004: 354). These social networks provide the basis for collective action (Sachs, 2003) which acts as a strategy to take stock of what is happening in communities, schools and classrooms. People working collectively in such ways are able to motivate and sustain each other, test ideas, debate strategies and negotiate shared meaning about how best to improve the status and practice of teachers. This type of work has previously been undertaken by subject or professional associations. However, to be more effective a broader constituency needs to be mobilised. One in which teachers, community members and other interested parties debate and negotiate what are the purposes of standards and how can they be used to develop and improve teachers' practice and students' learning.

Lieberman and Miller (1999) identify the new social realities of teaching, in particular the shift from the individualism of previous times to the development of a professional community; the significant shift in practice from teaching at the centre to learning at the centre; from the focus on technical work to a focus on inquiry into practice; and finally from a view that teaching has a weak knowledge base to one that acknowledges a broad knowledge base.

In times characterised by an erosion of trust, in an expositional increase in information and knowledge, teachers need to develop new skills and capabilities. First and foremost they need to be technologically literate – they will need to know how to access information but more importantly have the skills to decode what is ideological from that which is supposedly value neutral. Second, they need to find new ways of working, both individually and collectively, to be more productive in terms of the time and energy they invest in their teaching but also in exchanging ideas and testing theories about practice. Their pedagogies will need to change to take advantage of the opportunities afforded by ICT, in particular in relation to how and when learning is organised, and how learning management systems can facilitate certain kinds of learning. Finally, there is a need to develop professional learning communities. Hargreaves (2003: 134) argues that 'these bring together the knowledge, skills and dispositions in a school or across schools to promote shared learning and improvement'. Such learning communities, through their reliance on social relations and processes, foster the shift from information into knowledge and create the conditions for the creation and dissemination of new knowledge. Importantly, as a strategy to enact change and improve practice, these learning communities 'promote and presume key knowledge society attributes such as team work, inquiry and continuous learning' (Hargreaves 2003: 134).

Having made some comments about teacher professional learning communities, I now focus my attention on teachers individually.

Teacher learning

If teacher learning is the desired outcome of the knowledge society, what kind of learning is possible? The learning that I envisage would have many of the characteristics of constructivist learning – that is it is contextual, active and social. By being contextual it takes into account teachers' understanding of curriculum, pedagogy and the cultural and social background of their students. Being active it encourages teachers in professional learning experiences that use analysis, criticism and reflection to test their ideas and practices inside and outside classrooms. Finally, it is social because it involves interaction with colleagues in an environment in which respect and trust are clearly evident. In such an environment teachers can test ideas in a setting where risk taking is accepted and valued as part of the 'way we do things around here'. Unfortunately many schools are devoid of trust and this is a problem for sustained professional learning.

Given that I have pointed here to the importance of constructivist learning being at the heart of professional discourse and professional learning communities, we need to ask what kind of knowledge stands at the core of teachers' professional deliberations and learning. For Cochran-Smith and Lytle (1999) three conceptions of knowledge are associated with teachers' learning:

> *Knowledge-for-practice:* knowledge generated by researchers outside the school (for example research-based programmes, new theories of teaching, learning and assessment).
>
> *Knowledge-of-practice:* generated by teachers critically examining their own classroom and schools, alone or with others, in terms of broader issues of social justice, equity and student achievement.
>
> *Knowledge-in-practice:* teachers' practical knowledge generated through their own systematic inquiry, stimulated by questions raised concerning their own classroom effectiveness.

To this triad, Day and Sachs (2004) added a fourth:

> *Knowledge of self:* generated by teachers engaging regularly in reflection in, on and about values, purposes, emotions and relationships.

Knowledge of self provides the necessary social glue for collaborative learning to take place. It links personal and professional relationships with aspirations that legitimate teachers' ongoing learning as a fundamental part of their practice in classrooms and outside of them. These four kinds of knowledge form the fabric of a richly textured professional experience. When teachers talk about their knowledge these kinds of knowledge may stand alone or intersect, each enhancing the other to give greater insights into classroom or professional practice.

Critical practice

For Barnett (1997: 48) 'The expression of critical thought calls for emotion, (if only emotional control), commitment and courage. Criticality therefore embraces action and the self, just as much as it embraces thinking'. It gets beyond the notion of the reflective practitioner which is often reduced to the therapeutic, knowing oneself better, labelling leadership styles through superficial psychological tests, and 'feel good, do nothing' professional development. Critical professionalism is more than the instrumental approach of evidence-based policy and practice, in that it recognises the underpinning political and ethical assumptions informing and shaping policy and practice. Critical professionalism goes hand in hand with activist professionalism, it is about examining one's privilege, breaking 'inscribed habits of (in)attention', moving beyond passive empathy as a means to develop the social imagination that rids us of fear of 'the other', while 'questioning cherished beliefs and assumptions' and 'learning to see differently' (Boler, 1999: 176). The removal of fear during periods of rapid change and uncertainty, provides opportunities for risk taking both in terms of classroom practice and professional relationships. It provides opportunities for the engagement of individuals to contribute to the collective action of groups.

To be effective, engagement requires reciprocal forms of association, which I suggest have three purposes. First, teachers work towards building joint endeavours that are themselves concerned with promoting further collaborative development. Through joint endeavours, teachers begin to understand and extend how they work in their various contexts, and how they experience opportunities to exchange expertise. Second, by promoting collaborative development, teachers are given the opportunity to elaborate practical theories. This enables and encourages them to examine the relationship between their espoused theories and their theories-in-use as they define and direct their separate and shared improvement efforts. In so doing, teachers generate and sustain the energy for change and become mutually engaged towards common goals. Finally, such practices enhance professional dialogue, generating analytical insights into and improvements of classroom practices in a variety of settings. They enable teachers to move away from the isolation engendered through individualism and move towards the creation of professional learning communities and networks.

These new kinds of affiliation and collaboration move all parties beyond traditional technical notions of professional development and create spaces for new kinds of conversations to emerge. They provide opportunities for teachers to be engaged in public critical dialogues and debates about the nature of practice, how it can be communicated with others and how it can be continually improved. All parties move from peripheral involvements in individual and collective projects to full participation. Dialogue is initiated about education in all of its contexts and dimensions, and about how people can learn from the experiences and the collective wisdom of each other. It supports and sustains efforts to achieve social justice and equity agendas. Dialogue becomes an integral part of the strategy for activating a community of critical and activist professionals. It is on-going, and while there are interruptions when the exigencies and pressures of life and work get in the way, the learning emerging from the dialogue can be returned to, reflected upon and provide the basis for new dialogues, positions and strategies.

Collective action

Collective action is rooted in the processes and procedures of democratic participation. It is a complex choreography of relationships between individuals and groups and involves navigating the uncertainties of institutional structures, policies and processes. In its most robust forms it breaks down isolation within diverse constituencies. It acts as a strategy to 'take stock' of what is happening in communities, schools, and classrooms. People working collaboratively in a shared enterprise of improving the status of teaching and having students benefiting from this are able to sustain their interest and energy with other group members. They are able to motivate and inspire each other, test ideas, debate strategies and negotiate shared meanings about the various activist projects in which they are involved.

Creating political and institutional spaces in which rigorous public debate can take place is an outcome of collective action. In so doing, educating and improving the relationships between diverse stakeholders and interest groups can take place. To bring parents, for example, into the debate on children's learning, we need to ask them what they want. We may be surprised to find out that they are more interested in promoting the idea of children learning how to learn rather than being interested only in the results of testing as some are leading us to believe.

Conclusion

The knowledge society has become a common denominator of cultural life in the twenty-first century. The increasing pace of knowledge production and circulation through the use of ICT means that it will leave considerable intellectual trace. Knowledge can be both a social tool and a political and economic resource, and those who have access to knowledge also have access to power. Knowledge is our most precious resource: we should organise society to maximise its creation and use. It has far-reaching implications for how companies are owned, organised and managed; the ways in which rewards are distributed to match talent, creativity and contribution; how education, learning and research is organised.

Education has a significant role to play in realising the potential of the knowledge society. Its role is not only of developing knowledge workers who have the requisite skills, training and understanding to apprehend the potential of ICT, but also to create a society in which democratic values are communicated and enacted through the social networks afforded by the knowledge society.

While the performative and surveillance dimensions of the knowledge society represent the darker side of new political and social arrangements, a knowledge driven society as conceived by Leadbeater (1999) presents opportunities for new forms of professional engagement and affiliation to emerge. For teachers the creation of learning communities can provide legitimate opportunities for practice to be systematically investigated and for robust discussions about education policy and practice to occur. Moreover, these communities contribute to new forms of teacher professionalism – critical and activist – to emerge and be taken up. Fundamental to these new types of professionalism is a commitment to learning and improving practice. It brings the teaching profession back to the centre of social and cultural change initiatives. Teachers become the architects of their own future by creating the possibilities for radical and emancipatory action. The teaching profession must have a major role to play in contributing to debates which shape education policy and research agendas. They cannot be silent or complacent observers watching from the sidelines to see what will be imposed on them next. The legacy of the knowledge society can be a significant paradigm shift which permeates all aspects of social life or it could sink without leaving an intellectual trace. This challenge will be addressed somewhat through various policy initiatives and new developments in ICT. However, there are significant choices to be made and teachers have an essential role to play in those choices.

References

Ball, S. (2000) 'Performativities and fabrications in the education economy: towards the performative society', *Australian Education Researcher*, Vol. 27, No. 2, pp. 1–24.

Ball, S. (2003) 'The teacher's soul and the terrors of performativity', *Journal of Education Policy*, Vol. 18, No. 2, pp. 215–18.

Barnett, R. (1997) *Higher Education: A Critical Business*, Buckingham: Open University Press.

Barney, D. (2004) *The Network Society*, Cambridge: Polity Press.

Boler, M. (1999) *Feeling Power: Emotions and Education*, London and New York: Routledge.

Bottery, M. (2004) *The Challenges of Educational Leadership*, London: Paul Chapman.

Bullen, E., Fahey, J. and Kenway, J. (2006) 'The knowledge economy and innovation: certain uncertainty and the risk economy', *Discourse*, Vol. 27, No. 1, pp. 53–68.

Cammaerts, B. (2005) 'Review essay: critical European perspectives on the information society', *The Information Society*, Vol. 21, pp. 73–5.

Caplan, P. (2000) *Risk Revisited*, London: Pluto Press.

Castells, M. (1996) *The Rise of the Network Society*, Oxford: Blackwell.

Cochran-Smith, M. and Lytle, S. (1999) 'Relationships of knowledge and practice: teacher learning in communities', in A. Iran Nejad and C. Pearson (eds) *Review of Research in Education*, Vol. 24, No. 2, pp. 251–307.

Darling-Hammond, L. (1999) *Reshaping Teaching Policy, Preparation and Practice: Influences on the National Board for Teaching Professional Standards*, Washington: AACTE Publications.

Day, C. and Sachs, J. (2004) 'Professionalism, performativity and empowerment discourses in the politics, policies and purposes of continuing professional development', in C. Day and J. Sachs (eds) *International Handbook on the Continuing Professional Development of Teachers*, Maidenhead: Open University Press.

Day, P. and Schuler, D. (2004) 'Prospects for a new public sphere', in D. Schuler and P. Day (eds) *Shaping the Network Society*, Cambridge, MA: MIT Press.

Douglas, M. (1992) *Risk and Blame: Essays in Cultural Theory*, London: Routledge.

Elliott, J. (1996) 'Quality assurance: the educational standards debate, and the commodi-fication of educational research', *Curriculum Journal*, Vol. 8, No. 6, pp. 63–83.

Groundwater Smith, S. and Sachs, J. (2002) 'The activist professional and the re-instatement of trust', *Cambridge Journal of Education*, Vol. 32, No. 3, pp. 341–56.

Hargreaves, A. (2003) *Teaching in the Knowledge Society: Education in the Age of Insecurity*, Maidenhead: Open University Press.

Leadbeater, C. (1999) *Living on Thin Air*, London: Viking.

Lieberman, A. and Miller, J. (1999) *Teachers: Transforming Their World and Their Work*, New York: Teachers College Press.

Lyotard, J. (1984) *The Post Modern Condition: A Report on Knowledge*, Manchester: Manchester University Press.

McWilliam, E. and Sachs, J. (2004) 'Towards the victimless school: power, professionalism and proberty in teaching', *Educational Research for Policy and Practice*, Vol. 3, No. 1, pp. 17–30.

Morley, L. (2003) *Quality and Power in Higher Education*, Maidenhead and New York: Open University Press.

Mulford, B. (2005) 'Accountability policies and their effects', in N. Bascia, A. Cumming, A. Datnow, K. Leithwood and D. Livingston (eds) *International Handbook of Educational Policy*, Dordrecht: Springer.

Osborne, M. and McNess, E. (2005) 'The cultural context of teachers' work: policy, practice and performance', in N. Bascia, A. Cumming, A. Datnow, K. Leithwood and D. Livingston (eds) *International Handbook of Educational Policy*, Dordrecht: Springer.

Power, M. (1999) *The Audit Society: Rituals of Verification*, Oxford: Oxford University Press.

Pring, R. (2003) 'The virtues and vices of the educational researcher', in P. Sikes, J. Nixon and W. Carr (eds) *The Moral Foundations of Education Research*, Maidenhead and New York: Open University.

Sachs, J. (2003) 'Teacher activism: mobilising the profession', Keynote Address, British Education Research Association Conference, Heriot-Watt University, Edinburgh, September.

Strathern, M. (ed.) (2000) *Audit Cultures*, London: Routledge.

UNESCO (2003) 'Towards knowledge societies, background paper: from information society to knowledge societies', UNESCO at the World Summit on the Information Society, Geneva.

Webster, F (2006) 'Making sense of the information age: sociology and cultural studies', *Information, Communication and Society*, Vol. 8, No. 4, pp. 439–58.

Wright-Mills, C (2000) *The Sociological Imagination*, New York: Oxford University Press.

12 How do teachers learn to lead?

Ann Lieberman

Although teacher leadership has been a serious area of study for several decades few have had the opportunity to study, observe or work closely with teachers as they *learn* the variety of organizational skills, abilities and dispositions that are necessary to take on leadership responsibilities in their schools and beyond (Smylie, 1997; Wasley, 1991; Miles *et al.*, 1988; Lieberman and Miller, 2004; Lambert, 2003; Little, 1995). In this era with its press for 'high quality teachers for all students' in the United States and elsewhere, it seems almost impossible that we could work for that ideal without the assistance of teachers who play leadership roles with both experienced and novice colleagues. Interestingly enough, these roles are proliferating alongside prescriptions for change, pacing guides and other strong mandates for change in the US and elsewhere. Contrary to conventional wisdom, perhaps this is an especially good time to understand how teachers really learn to lead in different contexts despite the inevitable tensions that come with leading their peers in an essentially egalitarian culture (Lortie, 1975) while negotiating an increasingly prescriptive curriculum.

Expanding our understanding of leadership

In recent years researchers have begun to talk about 'distributed leadership' (Spillane *et al.*, 2003) and a redefinition of leadership for teachers and principals (Fullan, 1995; Lambert, 2003; Sergiovanni, 2006; Leithwood, 1992). These researchers have added immeasurably to our understanding of leadership development and its possibilities in this era. We are learning that good principals share leadership responsibilities as they build a team; that teachers take on a lot of responsibility for instructional improvement; and that for improvement to be sustained a professional learning community needs to be developed and supported. What is still an area in need of greater understanding and conceptualization is how teachers learn to lead in a variety of contexts; what experiences and practices seem seminal to their development; and what supports appear to make a difference in the various roles and responsibilities they take on. The focus for this chapter is understanding what we can learn from studying and analyzing several projects that have focused on teachers' conceptions of their work and the subsequent leadership learning that appears to have resulted as a consequence.

Learning in practice

The concept of learning-in-practice is viewed as foundational to an understanding of teacher leadership. It is now recognized that teachers as leaders are more collaborative and social and often learn skills that are context-dependent. These ways of thinking about learning in practice took hold in education with the work of Schon (1983) when he began to write about how professionals learn in the practice of their work. He argued that professionals don't apply theory – they often create it when they reflect on their practice – hence the term 'reflective practice'. Learning by professionals involves one in making the *private* – what you do on the job – *public*, and making what is *implicit, explicit*. This shift in focus is a dramatic change from the traditional views of leadership particularly for teachers and those who describe them. For researchers this kind of thinking meant that one could begin to document what teachers in leadership positions do in different contexts and situations and learn more about organizational change and new roles for teachers by studying the realities of their practice. Wenger (1998) broadened our knowledge and understanding by explaining through his studies that 'practice' could best be understood by looking at 'what people say as well as what they don't say; their sensitivities, shared world views, their subtle cues as well as their abilities to share their work publicly' (p. 47). Wenger introduced the idea that people learned by belonging to 'communities of practice', that is, people sharing commonalities who do the same work. In these 'communities of practice', Wenger noted, learning rests on three processes – learning, meaning and identity. Learning comes about through social participation, by experience and practice. In short, people learn through practice (learning by doing); through discovering meaning (learning as intentionality) and through identity (learning as changing who we are). In Wenger's terms 'Such participation in communities of practice shapes not only what we do, but also who we are, and how we interpret what we do' (p. 4).

To both build an argument and accrue some evidence, this chapter describes three different projects where teachers provide leadership to their peers in different roles and in different ways, but as important, the paper describes the contexts within which the teachers learn and practice the skills, abilities and dispositions they need to work with their colleagues. The three projects to be described were very different in purpose, context and continuity, yet they share some common themes that begin to teach us what the learning conditions can be for teachers and how different groups support these conditions and provide the foundation for teachers assuming both formal and informal leadership roles.

Learning from a national network: the development of teacher consultants

The National Writing Project (NWP), now thirty years old, offers us an extraordinary opportunity to understand teacher learning and leading in a network context. The NWP began in 1974 in Northern California at the University of California at

Berkeley. Jim Gray, its founder, had been a secondary English teacher who had for many years been disappointed with the standard 'three-poems-per-poet' approach to the teaching of literature. In his own classroom he began to build a library, encourage 'book talks', and provide students with a greater freedom to talk with their peers about the books they were reading. This participatory approach sowed the seeds of what was to become 'the Writing Project'.

Gray and his fellow teacher colleagues began to rebel against the standard professional development practices which was to bring in an expert to create a new English curriculum. As an antidote, Gray and his peers began to ask why teachers' knowledge and experience wasn't another way to improve the English curriculum and its pedagogy. If teachers had invented a way of working with their students that was producing good results, it seemed reasonable that this could be shared among colleagues. What was needed was a way of developing opportunities for teachers to teach teachers and become the recipients of the 'wisdom of practice' (Shulman, 1987). Teachers had to become readers and writers themselves, experience what students experience in order to become sensitive to their own teaching and by so doing, improve it.[1]

The Bay Area Writing Project (BAWP) was born, when Gray who had become a supervisor of student teachers at the University of California at Berkeley, proposed and received funding to call together 29 teachers to enact these simple propositions:

- A 'site' would be a group of local teachers in partnership with a university or college.
- Teachers would teach one another their best practices.
- Teachers would write, get critiqued and present their writing to their peers.
- Teachers would read, discuss and analyze research, reforms and other literature.

Shaped and nuanced over the years, these principles have become the 'core' of the National Writing Project which now has 189 sites in the United States and other international partners as well.

A number of studies have already found that students who are in writing project teachers' classrooms learn more about writing than non-writing project classrooms (Fancsali and Nelsestuen, 2001; St John, M. 1999) and that teachers who attend summer institutes are very satisfied with what they learn and they use what they learn in their classrooms (St John *et al.*, 2001; Lieberman and Wood, 2003). The NWP is well known for its ability to engage teachers in thinking about writing and learning how to enhance their repertoire as teachers. But it is less well known for its explicit development of teachers who leave the summer institute and become consultants in professional development in their school, district or state. How does this happen? What is it that teachers learn? What supports do they have after leaving the five week institute? Two studies illuminate some of the answers to these questions: one a two year study by Lieberman and Wood (2003), and a second study done by the NWP research team on the work of the teacher consultants (in progress, 2006).

Learning in the summer institute: opportunities to lead

During our two year study we were told repeatedly that if we wanted to understand the writing project, we needed to study the summer institute. So we did. We studied an urban site (Los Angeles/University of California at Los Angeles (UCLA) and a rural site (Stillwater/Oklahoma State University). From the beginning we found something very different from the usual professional development offerings.

Teachers who are accepted into the summer invitational are given a small stipend for their attendance and they are expected to bring a teaching practice with them that they will demonstrate for their peers. The experience of the institute is so powerful that strangers from different schools, and often without shared backgrounds or beliefs, come together as a group, share their practices with one another, write, and present something themselves, critique one another's work, give constructive feedback to their peers on their writing, read and discuss research and contemporary literature, and become part of a professional learning community. When they leave the institute they have accepted and embraced the idea that improving one's practice is part of what it means to be a teacher. Teachers find that in making their practice public, they become more aware of their intentions, their knowledge of their subject matter, and the influence of context on their students and themselves.

As the summer goes on, leadership opportunities arise. Some teachers find it rewarding to teach adults, to share their dilemmas and engage them in efforts at alternative solutions. The site directors are always looking for teachers who have developed effective strategies that they have nuanced over the years and who show their talents during the institute. Although theoretically everyone becomes a *teacher consultant* after taking the summer institute, some become active in teaching other teachers and discover the power of teaching adults as well as students. Besides their teaching of other adults, it is the social practices of the summer institute that are internalized as, in its way, the institute models a way of engaging learners of all ages in a learning community.[2] Slowly and powerfully teachers learn to make their practice public; discuss educational ideas; write and revise a piece of writing; and give and receive feedback from one another. They become intellectually and emotionally connected to their peers and to their profession. For many it is a transformative experience being in an authentic learning community sustained by a local and national network. What we learned was that the social practices were both an approach to learning, but also sowed the transformative seeds for how one approaches their colleagues in an improvement effort. Without using the L word, teacher consultants were learning to lead!

Teacher consultants: developing a leadership cadre in the NWP

Becoming a teacher consultant is recognized as both an opportunity for growth and as a way of making a professional contribution to teaching. Teachers who do this get paid for after-school workshops, becoming coaches, leading special interest groups, and more. These teacher consultants become the backbone of the NWP as the more of them who take on responsibility for leadership, the more teachers who get served and the more influence teacher leaders have in a given local community. There are currently over 4,500 teachers playing these roles while most of them stay in teaching, others go on to accept leadership roles in their school, district, state and the NWP itself. The conditions for learning to practice what it means to lead are of great interest here as teachers learn in the summer institute to focus on practice and a number of engaging strategies, but they also learn how to create the conditions for a continuous learning community for their students. Many learn in the process that what is good for their students is also good for their fellow teachers. It is this idea that is being followed by a current study of teacher leaders in the NWP.[3] We are attempting to find out what the work of teacher consultants is; what contexts they work in; and how they learn to enact their leadership roles.

Learning from teacher consultants: vignettes on leadership

As part of a larger study of teacher consultants in the NWP, a small team has mounted a vignette study with the idea of getting from TCs themselves narratives of their leadership learning in a variety of roles and settings.[4] The theory and practice of using vignettes was first reported by Miles (1990) and Lieberman (1987).

> Vignettes provide a snapshot, or perhaps a mini-movie of a practitioner at work. They engage the professional directly in reflecting on a recent episode of practice, first describing it, and then producing thoughtful explanations. They combine a systematic, structured approach with an expression of personal meanings.
>
> (Miles, 1990: 38)

In our study we provided an explanation of prompts that related to the writing project. (See Appendix for vignette prompts.) In 2005, we did a pilot study of ten TCs to test out the use of the vignette as a viable way to gain information on teachers who have assumed a variety of leadership roles in and out of their school. We found that the vignette prompts were very useful and decided that we needed a larger sample and a way of organizing a group of TCs where we could get at the variety of roles TCs play and the numerous contexts within which they work.

The larger study engaged 33 TCs who were chosen by site directors all over the country to insure geographic, racial, ethnic and gender differences as well as differences in experience and role. These TCs were brought together in two writing retreats.[5] TCs were introduced to the idea of writing a vignette which got at a slice of their leadership life at the first retreat. TCs were put in groups with a facilitator. We asked people to talk about a leadership story that got at what they were learning. Initially almost all of the group denied that they were leaders. Their view of leadership was colored by the expectation that leaders tell people what to do and are not sensitive to the complexities of teaching. These ideas were in keeping with the norms of egalitarianism that many teachers hold, making it difficult for teachers to admit publicly that they are in a leadership position and in some ways different from their peers. The conversation about leadership changed by the time the retreat was over (two days later). TCs tried out their ideas with their group getting at details and a focus for their vignette. They then went home and wrote a first draft of their vignettes over a two month period of time. Each facilitator provided feedback to their group of writers. The last retreat will be an occasion to get more feedback and write a final draft. The 'finished' vignettes are yet to be completed but there is already abundant evidence that the strategy for writing vignettes in a group, with feedback, discussion and support yields some important understandings about leadership when written by the participants themselves. A few examples of the descriptions and insights of several of the TCs show us, from an insider's perspective, how these TCs think about their leadership learning.

Three leadership vignettes: *the director, the thinker* and *leadership in three voices*

These three vignettes were chosen as their contexts and roles differ widely as well as the way they describe their learning about how to lead. All of them note the powerful norms of the writing project on their subsequent leadership experiences.

Back seat driver: in this vignette we learn about the early journey of Ben Bates who never wanted to direct, but just to act. In fact before he was a teacher, Ben was an actor. Years later finding himself at an historically black college in Oklahoma and reading about the success of 'A Raisin in the Sun' during its fortieth anniversary on the Broadway stage, Ben decided that he should put on plays at his college and be a director. Although this production reminded him of all the headaches that directors suffer (people miss rehearsals; don't study their lines; sets are often poor …), Ben got his head turned around when he went to the summer institute of the writing project where he joined a group of people all 'striving to create learning environments in which everyone, including the instructor, participates.' When he went home he began to build his classes around the theatrical process developing the idea that a 'director' succeeds when he is least noticed. Ben goes on to describe his leadership as being more about 'the student's effort rather than the instructor's endorsement.' As a director Ben talks about building a shared goal and getting students to contribute. His leadership all happens *before* the production – selecting plays; creating writing assignments that get at the guts of the plays; assigning parts; having rehearsals; building sets; encouraging students to stick with it from the beginning to opening night. Thirteen productions later Ben has helped students contribute to the vitality of this small, under-funded black college and to the community who lovingly attend all the plays. The vignette shows how Ben came to direct; his experiences in doing so, and his ultimate understanding that this kind of leadership seems almost invisible, yet is full of a number of principles that guide his work.

In *thinker seeks doer*, Kathleen O'Shaughnessy writes about how she became co-director of her writing project site in Louisiana and then later *de facto* director when no one filled the university-based position. Having heard other site directors talk about how they loved to make opportunities for other teachers, Kathleen figured that 'if you build it, they will come.' Being a 'good Southern girl', she took the job of director. But she soon found out that she was *not* a builder or a doer, but a thinker who falls in love with ideas, visions and theories. In short, she found that she lacked practical skills in translating visions into action. Because people saw her as efficient and effective she remained the director of her site and soon realized that she was actually too shy to ask for help and that it was easier to do all the work herself. This finally led her to quit her position and really learn about what kind of leader she was and what it can look like 'when you are not the know-it-all, do-it-all dynamo that teacher leaders appear to be'. She is now working with a group of teachers on an *idea* which she created – an inquiry group. In this group she asks questions, encourages others, gently nudges and helps people nuance and shape their ideas. Her leadership is quiet, strong and steady and she has learned to work with 'doers'. Together they have built a learning community that has room for both thinkers and doers. And Kathleen has found her strength and regained her confidence as a 'different kind of leader', one who is respected for her insights and her persistence and hard work as a teacher.

In *leadership in three voices*, Ronni Michelin describes the three voices that form the basis of her leadership as an Assistant Principal in a New York City high school. She has been at this position for four years after being a teacher for many years. She finds that there are several voices that make up her persona as a VP.

One voice is that of the Assistant Principal, one is the teacher voice and lastly her writing project voice. The conversations between these three voices which come replete with knowledge, skills, dispositions and expectations frame her stresses and struggles as well as her excitement and success in moving the work forward. The writing project has taught her about facilitating, mentoring, celebrating, and learning from mistakes, sharing practice and seeing teachers as professionals. How she works with teachers is the way teachers can work with students, engaging them in both intellectual and socio/emotional work. This culture of respect, care and competence she brings to her weekly faculty meetings. Ronni describes how the teachers sit in a circle and share writing and reading together. In this high school where the population is primarily Dominican, students will be the first to graduate from high school in their family.

As an Assistant Principal, Ronni describes how there are times when being a coach and friend is inappropriate as when she was going to share her office and the space outside it with teachers. When the outside space became noisy and gossipy rather than a collaboration between 'administration and teachers', and when her office became a lunch room for some teachers, she realized that she must uphold the expectations of 'the administration'. In this case the boundaries were crossed and she learned that there needed to be some physical space between her and the teachers. The vignette goes on to describe other incidents that teach Ronni (and us) how to hold onto both vision and values and at the same time conduct (or lead) the various parts of the orchestra in her school. In leading and conducting, each 'musician plays his or her part, allowing solos, encouraging individuals to shine, of practicing and rehearsing and revisiting and revising until we get it right.' With these voices always there, Ronni is learning that she must deal with the teachers' expectations as well as her own and that shifting when appropriate has expanded her leadership repertoire. Sometimes the voices are in tension and she struggles hard to learn to negotiate both the voices and her actions in the school.

Several themes are already apparent in these narratives. There are teachers who learn to negotiate their teacher learnings with their newfound positions of authority. There are those who learn to facilitate new structures and engage people in experiencing a new way to do things, rather than using their authority to prescribe. There are still others who learn to be change agents by taking risks that new structures and new opportunities to learn for teachers will help them engage in new practices. Behind them all is *their* community, the writing project, that has taught them the excitement of learning and the expectation that they are always involved in their own improvement as well as that of others.

Learning from developing teachers as scholars

From 1999 to the present time, the Carnegie Foundation for the Advancement of Teaching (CFAT) has been developing a program investigating how teachers could develop a 'scholarship of teaching'. The program is entitled: The Carnegie Academy for the Scholarship of Teaching and Learning (CASTL). We began with the idea that scholarship was made up of three defining characteristics: scholars make their work public; open to critique; and presented in some form where it can be passed on and built upon by others. The idea of the program was for teachers to study their own work and make it public and available to others, thus elevating teaching and at the same time providing an opportunity for this teacher scholarship to go public. Its intent was to somehow begin to codify 'the wisdom of practice' (Shulman, 1987). We have collected data from the participants since the beginning of the program and have done several small studies on the participants (Hatch, 2006). A serendipitous finding from the work has been that in the act of producing some piece of their own work and making it public, teachers have not only become more articulate about their practice, but they have also become more confident about and more conscious of what they value, what they know and how they relate to their peers.

From the beginning we worked in groups helping teachers define some aspect of their teaching practice that they thought could be described in all its complexity

– yet simple enough for others to understand. The project has had three cohorts of teachers. The teachers would come to Carnegie which is in Northern California for ten days during the summer and three days in January. The cohorts had two years to finish their work. At the end of the first cohort, a colleague well versed in multi-media introduced the idea that teachers could show their work better if they could describe it in the non-linear fashion of a website instead of with paper and pencil. Our understanding grew when we observed teachers thinking openly about their practice; how their practices are connected to their values and commitments; and how layered even a small bite of teaching is when you try to display it publicly. All of us, teachers and staff alike, realized that we were involved in not only learning about technology with all its attractiveness and quirkiness, but how to help teachers conceptualize a piece of their practice that could be meaningful to them and to an eventual audience for their work. (See: www.carnegiefoundation.org for examples of the k-12 websites and Hatch *et al.*, 2005.)[6] We describe two teacher sites as examples of how studying and displaying their work publicly helped teachers to become more articulate about what they knew, what their commitments were and how going public with their teaching practice gave them additional credibility with their peers.

Yvonne Divans-Hutchinson

Yvonne is a National Board Certified teacher who has been teaching for over 35 years. She is also a long term member of the National Writing Project and has been a teacher consultant for many years. She has been a literacy coach, a curriculum coordinator and resource teacher. She's also been an instructor at the University of California in Los Angeles and a professional developer for Los Angeles Unified School District.

In all of these roles, Yvonne holds fast to a set of principles learned in her youth growing up in the segregated South in the 1940s. As a young child, she was encouraged by her mother and other African American women to love reading and to care passionately about humanity. It is precisely these two ideas that permeate her classroom at King-Drew Magnet School for Medicine and Science in Compton, California. Before that she had taught for many years in a middle school. The school serves a largely minority population that is 72 percent African American and 22 percent Latino. Her major goals are that her students learn to become good readers and writers; that they become good human beings; and that they care about the diversity in their classroom and the world.

When Yvonne came to Carnegie as a scholar, she decided to do her website on teaching her students how to participate in a small group discussion about a literary text.[7] Her website draws on her oral and literate discourse strategies as these are the centerpiece of her high school English curriculum.

> I draw from the rich oral traditions of my African-American and Latino students and encourage them to use their oral skills to investigate rigorous

literary texts to engage them-selves and each other in substantive discussions about controversial issues.

(Hutchinson, 2004)

Her website shows the numerous strategies she uses to involve her students in both learning to read, discuss and critique literary texts and learning about racial diversity. When students first enter her classroom, many are reticent to speak in a group. For those students, Hutchinson has a set of 'stock responses' that ensures that everyone will learn to participate (e.g. 'I regret to say I am not prepared; or I don't know, but I will try to find out, etc.). After Yvonne calls on the first person, students manage the participation by each person calling on another one. You get the idea pretty quickly that the entire classroom is set up for group participation and that students are provided with many opportunities to learn how to become a good group member having many opportunities to use their oral expression. Many other strategies are used to build up and build upon students growing confidence in their abilities to critique, apply, understand and connect their world to the literature that is the content for the course.

Yvonne's leadership is tightly connected to her commitments to her students. Having thought about, written about, and nuanced her practice, she never leaves the role of teacher behind; she takes it with her when she mentors new teachers or when she is a leader among her peers. She views leadership in the same way she views teaching; not as handing down information, but rather as 'creating a circle of friends' who come together to share and learn from one another. She does this by demonstration rather than remonstration. She engages teachers in conversations about their practice. She redirects complaints about students by asking: 'What would you like to see?' They, like her students, find their own voice. She uses her site to show possibilities rooted in real practice, while she encourages teachers to build new strategies that enlarge and deepen their repertoire. She leads as she teaches by modeling how to place student work at the center. She has learned to vary her approach depending on whether she is teaching new or veteran teachers. With new teachers who are more deferent, she models her own inquiries into her practice avoiding the 'sage on the stage' which is so prevalent. With veteran teachers she starts with their questions (What else can I do? I have already tried many things which haven't worked.) Here she states that she doesn't have the answers, but has tried some things with her students. The website shows her students having a sophisticated conversation about text (after she has scaffolded a number of activities first).

Yvonne's website of her teaching work has given her a complicated, yet readily accessible picture of what her approach to students looks like in practice, but it has also provided an anatomy of a teaching life for others to peruse. Her site teaches us how to create community; how to engage reluctant learners; how to motivate students to participate; how to involve *all* students in reading and discussing a classroom text; how to handle controversial subjects, as well as how to love literature (http://gallery.carnegiefoundation.org/yhutchinson). Valuing community building, Hutchinson finds ways for teachers to learn more about their own work and improve it – the same values that drive her classroom instruction.

Sarah Capitelli

Sarah came to Carnegie after four years of teaching in a bi-lingual school in Oakland, California. She began research in her own classroom as a second year teacher. Her interests were in understanding why some students did not improve in their ability to speak English. She began collecting data in the form of notes to herself.

When she came to Carnegie she was still puzzling over why the students who were poor in English in kindergarten were still struggling by the time they were in fourth grade. She had been assigned to teach the lowest performing group and for most of the time had been troubled by her lack of success. At Carnegie she wanted to use her data to make a case for fundamental change in the structure and form of bilingual instruction and to dismantle the practice of ability grouping for language learning.

After much discussion she convinced her colleagues to let her try a pilot project of a heterogeneously grouped class where she would collect data and present it to them. She got their approval and structured a new program where students had multiple opportunities to talk with one another in English; where better English speakers would work with less able students; where the students would interview their parents and grandparents (and videotape the process) and where students would learn to manage a video camera and describe the pictures they were taking (see: http://kml.carnegiefoundation.org/gallery/scapitelli/index.html).

Sarah, like Yvonne, has a website that contains a series of video clips that demonstrate her classroom strategies and the impact of those strategies on her students. She shows video clips to other teachers in her presentations and engages them in the problems of teaching bilingual classrooms, questions of pedagogy, and strategies for student learning. With no formal role in her school, Sarah leads as a colleague struggling with many of the same problems as her peers. She is willing to go public with her practice, her questions, her data and her strategies for inquiring into what is going on in her classroom. Teachers find such openness and authenticity attractive and inspiring. Leading for Sarah is informal, collegial, and focused on inquiry. She demonstrates to others what inquiry can yield when teachers make it a part of their teaching and continued professional learning (Eiler-White, 2004). Word got around in her district and she has been asked to provide professional development for others. With her own inquiries into the practices of bi-lingual classrooms she leads with a focus on inquiry – a sure-fire winner with her peers.

Learning to lead

Observing these three studies of teachers, it is becoming evident that we can describe how teachers learn and the conditions that appear to support them. Teachers who lead:

- Develop strong commitments to their students through their life experiences and their own teaching.
- Become inquirers into their own practice, helping them to become more articulate about learning and teaching.
- Provide leadership through their example of becoming lifelong learners themselves.
- Take risks by expanding their own comfort zones and modeling experimentation.
- Inspire their peers through their commitment to the continual struggle to improve their practice.
- Work hard at expanding their circle of friends and their own knowledge base.
- Organize novice and veteran teachers into communities of support.
- Care about the content and character of colleagueship as well as the content of subject matter.
- Understand that sensitivity to context and culture is a critical part of leadership.
- Go public with their understandings about students, strategies for student learning, and the organization of the curriculum.
- Pursue improvement with their peers despite sometimes negative responses to change. (Lieberman and Miller, 2004)

Whether large scale networks or small scale development projects, the supportive conditions for teachers turns out to be similar. Teachers who are learning to lead participate in becoming learners themselves in a group of their peers. They engage in reflection on practice, intellectual discourse about teaching and learning, and they go public with their teaching. In the process, teachers find that they are engaged with a professional community of peers that expects, encourages and supports continuous learning about teaching practice. In the best of circumstances they find a connection between the intellectual and emotional parts of teaching and help others learn the same.

Any real transformation of schooling and teaching demands just these conditions and the teachers who will organize them, but they must be afforded opportunities to learn both from their own and others' practice as well as to learn from the accumulation of knowledge by others. But which comes first is critical. Teachers appear to need an opportunity to generate knowledge about their own practice *first*, then they become excited about and motivated to consume knowledge from others. These research and development projects begin to build an evidence base for the importance of providing conditions for learning to lead for teachers. Without them, we will be setting teachers up for failure. With them we can build a cadre of teachers who can help transform teaching and learning in the twenty-first century.

Notes

1   For a fascinating description of the origins of the Bay Area Writing Project, see: Gray, Jim, *Teachers at the Center: A Memoir of the Early Years of the National Writing Project*, Berkeley, CA: The National Writing Project.
2   The social practices include: approaching each colleague as a potentially valuable contributor; honoring teacher knowledge; creating public forums for sharing, dialog and critique; turning ownership over to learners; situating learning in practice and relationships; providing multiple entry points into the community; guiding reflection on teaching through reflection on learning; sharing leadership; promoting an inquiry stance; and encouraging a reconceptualization of professional identity and linking it to professional community.
3   The NWP research team is engaged in a program of research related to the work, knowledge, development and contributions of teachers who engage in leadership. One part of the study is engaging 33 NWP teacher consultants who are writing about one slice of their leadership life. There are also case studies, interviews and a lengthy survey study of the Legacy of the National Writing Project.
4   The idea of a vignette is that it is a short narrative that provides a flow of events that show how (in this case) leadership evolves. Vignettes provide a snapshot of a professional practitioner engaging in an episode of practice.
5   As of this writing, one retreat has already been held. A second retreat is also planned.
6   The project is now about teacher educators using the teacher web sites in their classes for both new teachers and for novice teachers. The sites are also used for professional development purposes.
7   To see how Yvonne teaches and to hear her students have an actual discussion and to view a videotape of the class see: http://goingpublicwithteaching.org/yhutchinson/.

References

Eiler-White, M. (2004) 'Going public: the representation and travel of teacher research', unpublished doctoral dissertation, Stanford University.

Fancsali, C. and Nelsestuen, K. (2001) *Evaluation of the National Writing Project, Overview of Year 2 Results*, Presentation to the NWP TaskForce, New York: Academy for Educational Development.

Fullan, M. (1995) 'Broadening the concept of teacher leadership', paper presented at the National Staff Development Council: New Directions Conference, Chicago, IL.

Hatch, T. (2006) *Into the Classroom: Developing the Scholarship of Teaching and Learning*, San Francisco, CA: Jossey-Bass Inc.

Hatch, T., Ahmed, D., Lieberman, A., Faigenbaum, D., Whilte, M. E. and Pointer-Mace, D. H. (eds) (2005) *Going Public with our Teaching: An Anthology of Practice*, New York: Teachers College Press.

Hutchinson, Y. D. (2003) 'A friend of their minds: capitalizing on the oral tradition of my African American students', available online at http://gallery.carnegiefoundation.org/hutchinson, retrieved 5 April 2004.

Lambert, L. (2003) 'Shifting conceptions of leadership: towards a redefinition of leadership for the twenty-first century', in B. Davies and J. West Burnham (eds) *Handbook of Educational Leadership and Management*, London: Pearson Education, pp. 5–15.

Leithwood, K. (1992) 'The move toward transformational leadership', *Educational Leadership*, Vol. 49, No. 5, February, pp. 8–12.

Lieberman, A. (1987) 'Documenting professional practice: the vignette as a qualitative tool', paper read at Symposium on Examining New Professional Roles: Innovative Methods for Collecting and Analyzing Qualitative Data, American Educational Research Association, Annual Meeting, Washington, DC.

Lieberman, A. and Miller, L. (2004) *Teacher Leadership*, San Francisco, CA: Jossey-Bass, pp. 90–1.

Lieberman, A. and Wood, D. (2003) *Inside the National Writing Project: Connecting Network Learning and Classroom Teaching*, New York: Teachers College Press.

Little, J. W. (1995) 'Contested ground: the basis of teacher leadership in two restructuring high schools', *Elementary School Journal*, Vol. 96, No. 1, pp. 47–63.

Lortie, D. (1975) *Schoolteacher*, Chicago, IL: University of Chicago Press.

Miles, M. B. (1990) 'New methods for qualitative data collection and analysis: vignettes and pre-structured cases', *Qualitative Studies in Education*, Vol. 3, No. 1, pp. 37–51.

Miles, M., Saxl, E. and Lieberman, A. (1988) 'What skills do educational "change agents" need? An empirical view', *Curriculum Inquiry*, Vol. 18, No. 2, pp. 157–93.

Schon, D. (1983) *The Reflective Practitioner: How Professionals Think in Action*, New York: Basic Books.

Sergiovanni, T. (2006) *Strengthening the Heartbeat*, San Francisco, CA: Jossey-Bass.

Shulman, L. (1987) 'The wisdom of practice: managing complexity in medicine and teaching', in D. Berliner and B. Rosenshine (eds) *Talks to Teachers: A Festschrift for N. L. Gage*, New York: Random House, pp. 370–86.

Shulman, L. (2000) 'Teacher development: roles of domain expertise and pedagogical knowledge', *Journal of Applied Developmental Psychology*, Vol. 21, No. 1, pp. 129–35.

Smylie, M. A. (1997) 'Research on teacher leadership: assessing the state of the art', in B. J. Biddle, T. L. Good and I. F. Goodson (eds) *International Handbook of Teachers and Teaching*, Dordrecht: Kluwer Academic Publishers, pp. 521–92.

Spillane, J. P., Hallett, T. and Diamond, J. B. (2003) 'Forms of capital and the construction of leadership: Leadership in elementary schools', *Sociology of Education*, Vol. 76, No. 1, pp. 1–17.

St John, M. (1999) 'A national writing project model: a five-year retrospective on findings from the annual site survey', a talk given in November at the Annual Meeting of the National Writing Project. Inverness: CA: Inverness Research Associates.

St John, M., Dickey, K., Hirabayashi, J. and Stokes, L., with assistance from Murray, A. (2001) 'The National Writing Project: client satisfaction and program impact', Results from a follow-up survey of participants of summer 2000 invitational institutes. Inverness, CA: Inverness Research Associates.

Wasley, P. (1991) *Teachers who Lead: The Rhetoric of Reform and the Realities of Practice*, New York: Teachers College Press.

Wenger, E. (1998) *Communities of Practice: Learning, Meaning, and Identity*, Cambridge: Cambridge University Press.

Appendix: the work of the teacher consultant: a vignette

We are doing a study of the work of writing project teacher-consultants. We are looking at what TCs do, the content of their work, how TCs develop and get supported in their work with colleagues, their systems and their students.

In no more than five pages tell us about a concrete example of your work with colleagues, your school, your writing project site or your school district, that has occurred recently or in the past year. It may be a situation that includes a set of activities that took time to unfold.

Tell us a story of this situation framing it by using the guiding questions below:

DESCRIBE:
- what you were hoping would happen or be accomplished;
- the context within which this work occurred;
- what was involved;
- the impact of the work;
- why you think it happened;
- the role you played;
- what feels most important about this work for you and why.

Epilogue

The future of educational change?

Ciaran Sugrue

The word change itself is rather small, perhaps even insignificant, and most likely quite inadequate to capture its Hydra-like meanings and mutations. For example, Roget's Thesaurus provides a total of forty-seven alternative words or phrases including – alteration, variation, divergence, modulation, renewal, adaptation, improvement and continuity (Chapman, 1989: 139), and these are just the positives! It goes on to include more negative or disruptive alternatives such as – deterioration, radical, violent or revolutionary change and discontinuity. In between these polarities are included – innovation, transformation, reform and revive. It is obvious, therefore, that it is possible to have 'change for the better' or 'change for the worse'; to have gentle, incremental change, or radical, revolutionary and/or violent disjunctures, and ruptures with past and present. Nevertheless, implicit in all of these diverse continuities and discontinuities is the influence or actual presence of 'the hand of history', in the sense that seeking either to build on past accomplishments or to depart from them, there is always a degree of continuity and discontinuity involved in paving the way to the future. Even the paradoxical statement 'continuous change', consistent with the conceptual 'revolution' enunciated by Heraclitus, is Janus-faced, since if change is ongoing, this in itself is a continuity. It is very evident therefore that in the field of educational change, options for the future are many and varied, while some alternatives are more likely than others. What of the future of educational change then?

In that wonderfully evocative anthem recorded by Fleetwood Mac, and adopted by Bill Clinton as a rallying cry for his 1992 election campaign, we are repeatedly urged: 'Don't stop thinking about tomorrow', and this chorus line appears to have been translated by politicians, commentators and media experts into the mantra – 'going forward'! Similarly, those on Wall Street and elsewhere who trade in 'futures' are speculating on the future direction of the market, with an eye on maximising profits. Such 'high stakes' testing of the market, even with others' money, comes with risks attached, with considerable potential for careers to end in tears or incarceration, and financial ruin for individuals and institutions, while it is also possible – no pun intended – to make a fortune, for 'fortune(s)' favour the brave' risk takers, often labelled the 'high rollers'. Of course, traders are likely to respond to those of us who continue to work in what some regard disparagingly as the cosseted public sector, that the key to dealing in futures is risk assessment and management. In order to do this successfully, it is necessary to pay attention to previous trends, both long and short term, to develop a comprehensive understanding of how the system works – to identify lessons from past and present in an attempt to predict, shape, influence if not control future trends. In many respects, educational change is no different, save for the crucially important caveat that public schooling is concerned with the common good, the public sphere, and not individual or private gain. As Stiglitz asserts:

> While ... there is vigorous debate ... about what the precise role of government should be, there is broad agreement that government has a role in making any society, any economy, function efficiently – and humanely.
>
> (Stiglitz, 2002: 218)

To continue the market trading metaphor, in a globalised world, seeking to reduce risk to manageable proportions is an important consideration in building bridges to the future. What the chapters of this book have done in various ways is to distil lessons that have some generative potential in constructing the future. Nevertheless, it is important to acknowledge the cautionary advice provided by Stone as characteristic of the field of education when she states:

> There is an 'uneasy relationship between social scientists and public officials', because one group provides 'disciplined research' while the other has 'undisciplined problems'. Policy is potentially a sphere of rational analysis, objectivity, allegiance to truth, and pursuit of the well-being of society as a whole. Politics is the sphere of emotion and passion, irrationality, self-interest, shortsightedness, and raw power.
>
> (Stone, 2002: 377)

The future of educational change is dependent on the dynamics of the field of education generally, while readily acknowledging also that due to the moral and ethical dimensions of provision, there is likely to be less rather than more agreement about a desired future. Thus risk and uncertainty are a persistent presence, all the more real in a globalised world that hurtles headlong into the future at increasing velocity so that 'going forward' can rapidly become a blind leap of faith that jettisons past and present, ignoring the 'lessons' they proffer. On the cusp of the twenty-first century, Fullan predicted with a degree of optimism and confidence an increasing realisation that regardless of location in the world, 'all now appear to agree that transformation of societies – individually and interdependently – is essential, and that educational reform is the critical strategic intervention that will achieve these goals' (Fullan, 1998: 672).

In this epilogue therefore, it is necessary and appropriate to identify 'lessons learned' and to discuss then in a generative but open-ended manner as important 'food for the journey' into, as well as giving direction to, the future of educational change.

Dis-order is the order of the day

The paradox of the iron cage of 'the market' of a neo-liberal economic hegemony is its imposed order, the only game in town, that also creates a disorder of – downsizing, relocation, uncertainty, insecurity, loss of trust, of loyalty and a consequent fracturing of social bonds. These ingredients become more volatile when fuelled by rapidly changing technological innovation, and enable individuals to retreat further into virtual realities that frequently also undermine real relationships and communities. It is not, therefore, only 'the economy stupid', it is stupid not to recognise society as the habitus of educational change, now and in the future. While as evidenced in several of the foregoing chapters, identity politics of the postmodern points to the erosion of the solidity of the public sphere, the future of education in particular depends crucially upon it. The current dysfunctional disorder–order relationship requires serious amelioration, for as Kingswell suggests:

> We are … happier not with more stuff but with more meaning: more creative leisure time, stronger connections to groups of friends, deeper commitment to common social projects, and a greater opportunity to reflect. In short, the life of the well-rounded person, including crucially the orienting aspect of life associated with virtuous citizenship.
>
> (Kingswell, 2000: 218)

The emergent lessons from this manuscript, though partial only, become important ingredients of a policy rhetoric, where the future is not just about the market, but rather a 'struggle over ideas' (Stone, 2002: 11). The ideas that have emerged from the preceding chapters are the 'ground truth' distilled from prominent actors in the field of educational change (Putnam *et al.*, 2004: 6). The remaining challenge is to reconfigure these ideas in a generative manner, while avoiding over-abstraction and descent into shibboleths.

Agency, capacity, density

Archer asserts:

> … authentic ethical behaviour can only work if persons are not ultimately motivated by personal gain, but by something other than the satisfaction of their own preferences.
>
> (Archer, 2000: 79)

This assertion resonates with the analysis provided in several chapters. When freed from the iron cage of rigid accountability systems or the climate induced by a relentless effort to undermine the public sector, actors gain the confidence, creativity and commitment to work towards common goals beyond private gain. Time and again, when institutional climate, external environment and policy contexts are rendered more conducive to positive rather than defensive behaviour and self-preserving actions, more generous, spirited and engaged activity and common purposes emerge; *'collective accountability'* begins to take hold (Hargreaves and Fink, 2006: 157). Without doubt therefore, there is greater need than ever to find common cause in ways that identity politics moves from a more exclusive inward-looking self-serving motivational mindset, to recognising that there is more to be gained for all by meaningful and prolonged engagement. This requires recognition that such engagement needs to be patient, tolerant, resolute and generous, and runs counter to the time-poor work lives that many endure.

This individual agency, working in consort, has potential to build sustainable and self-sustaining capacity, such as the Writers' Workshop, while the learning conditions created in such communities, release, support and develop the leadership potential of individuals and groups also. Elmore advocates a more systematic approach to building capacity through the principle or reciprocity, which he describes in the following terms:

> For each unit of performance I demand of you, I have an equal and reciprocal responsibility to provide you with a unit of capacity to produce that performance, if you do not already have that capacity.
>
> (Elmore, 2004: 245)

While this may be appropriate from a systemic, planned change perspective, it needs to be surrounded by more informal networks of professional learning and support that complement and enhance more formal endeavours. Without this, specific capacities may be enhanced, but may not create sufficient capacity density with appropriate creativity and leadership to bring matters to the next phase or stage of development. Building capacity must be understood as a dynamic, ongoing process where capacity density is sufficient to be sustainable, and the source of subsequent capacity building. Clearly, also, various approaches to research have a major contribution to make in this regard.

Research contribution and transformation

Decades of 'misery research' indicate unerringly that underestimation of the complexity of change processes, as well as the limitations of research designs, and the consequent partial and sometimes misleading accounts of previous change efforts, call for renewed efforts to conduct more sophisticated, robust, longitudinal research. There needs to be commitment to the research enterprise, as well as recommitment to public debate concerning rigour, while this volume also provides evidence that educational research has often focused too narrowly on schools to the relative exclusion of communities. Research, therefore, is not simply the preserve of social science and policy elites. Rather, broadening what counts as legitimate research is vital to include – connecting with communities, building the capacity of communities to generate their own knowledge and understanding of educational issues of direct concern to themselves and their families; whether this is 'grassroots' organising, participatory social inquiry or greater recognition of the necessity to use the wider lens of a social sector framework, it is operating out of a mindset that seeks to re-create more vibrant communities through knowledge generation. In a climate where identity politics has come to colonise the public sphere, such agency and knowledge generating activities re-create new social bonds and collective agenda. Such reconfiguring of the habitus of policy-making has potential also to give shape to the future of educational change. Simultaneously, the narrative capital of individual actors is enhanced and this too has transformative potential. These are lessons that require re-configuration also by the education community, by individual teachers in collaboration with colleagues; silent or silenced voices of learners within and beyond the school precincts develop the knowledge and confidence to articulate their views and concerns, where everyone becomes a champion thus shedding dependence, while developing more democratic, inclusive and worthwhile educational experiences for all. Nevertheless, teachers are likely to remain at the centre.

A generative politics of teacher professionalism

Teachers are critical to the future of educational change. In large measure, it is in their hands. However, if those hands are tied by regimes of accountability that ignore 'many critically important aspects of educational quality that cannot be captured by standardized tests', then teacher attrition numbers are likely to rise, and recruitment and retention will not only be a problem in relation to principalship but in the profession as a whole (Koretz, 2005: 117). Loosed from the dominant cage of accountability, there is potential for transformative engagement. In this context also, moving beyond survival, self-interest, beyond narcissistic reflections to more public encounters becomes a necessity as a means of creating an emergent professionalism. As Sachs asserts:

> A politics of transformation requires various strategies to engage with and to change the taken-for-granted assumptions about the role of education in society and the place of teachers within current and future education policy and practices. It requires new forms of collective identity, ... [and engagement] with discursive practices that construct new political subjects and create new political spaces in which to act.
>
> (Sachs, 2004: 146)

The thread of continuity woven through the emergent fabric of educational change is the necessity for new forms of engagement that are populated by 'coalitions of the willing' rather than the serried phalanx of the coerced. Instead, individual agency that is readily reciprocated becomes the senate for new beginnings, new forms of leadership and collective agency. This will also necessitate new and emergent partnerships, networks that harness the potential of new technologies. Some pioneering individuals have already pointed the way where they have learned that it is more productive and more sustainable to pool resources and expertise for the benefit of all rather than deploy scarce resources in competition with others, that predictably results in 'gain' at the expense of others. Hargreaves and Fink describe the collective accountability of Australian high school principals who determined to collaborate rather than compete:

> ... they exercised their courage and creativity to work together as a federation of schools dedicated to shared improvement for the whole community instead of frittering their resources on enhancing their individual images.
>
> (Hargreaves and Fink, 2006: 157)

As part of individual and collective agency it is evident also that re-working much older concepts such as equity and justice into the fabric of education as its mosaic changes hue, lends qualities to teaching and learning that are often invisible, yet tangible, marginalised, yet present, and much less often taken into account when seeking to establish what matters.

Sustainability: equity and justice

While the issues discussed above are very likely to feature prominently in the fabric of educational change as its weave extends into the future, long term sustainability of change will depend on more enduring concerns. Although there is neither time nor space to engage in a discourse on such important concepts as equity and justice, it is important to recognise that in many respects they have been marginalised by the dominance of neo-liberal economic priorities; when this is sustained with little or no restraint, inequities and injustices are exacerbated, and become taken for granted by many as endemic, part of the way we are. In a globalised world, interdependence becomes daily more evident, even if we choose to be blind to these realities. Another paradox of globalising tendencies is the emergence of new networks and communities, a re-invention of the local and its relation to the wider world in a variety of ways. This generative politics of transformation 'is not self-interested; its concern is with wider issues of equity and social justice' (Sachs, 2003: 146). Additionally, 'its focus is on long rather than the short term' while readily recognising that 'short-term gains are important in sustaining the energy and interest of participants.' As 'peak oil' encroaches on the consciousness of individuals, the necessity to act, to engage with what Sachs describes as 'discursive practices that construct new political subjects and create new political spaces in which to act' (p. 146) will become an urgent necessity rather than an option. While never unimportant, it is at such a crucial tipping point that the re-inscribing of the values that under-write concern for equity and social justice will be at their most potent and vulnerable. In some respects, the stakes have never been higher, but, as the chapters of this text have sought to illustrate in various ways, getting the road to the future reasonably right, just and equitable, has many intrinsic as well as more tangible rewards, not least of which is a better educational future for all. It is my sincere hope that this book will encourage you to play your part; 'making a difference' requires you at act now, for the future of educational change depends on you; bring a friend. The good news is you are not alone.

References

Archer, M. S. (2000) *Being Human: the Problem of Agency*, Cambridge: Cambridge University Press.

Chapman, R. L. (1989) *Roget's International Thesaurus*, 4th edn, London, Glasgow and New York: Collins Publishers and Harper Row Publishers.

Elmore, R. (2004) *School Reform from the Inside Out: Policy, Practice and Performance*, Cambridge, MA: Harvard University Press.

Fullan, M. (1998) 'Scaling up the educational change process', in A. Hargreaves, A. Lieberman, M. Fullan and D. Hopkins (eds) *International Handbook of Educational Change*, part two, Dordrecht, Boston, MA and London: Kluwer, pp. 671–2.

Hargreaves, A. and Fink, D. (2006) *Sustainable leadership*, San Francisco: Jossey Bass.

Kingwell, M. (2000) *The World We Want: Virtue, Vice and the Good Citizen*, Toronto: Penguin.

Kotrez, D. (2005) 'Alignment, high stakes, and the inflation of test scores', in J. Herman, and E. Haertel (eds) *Uses and Misuses of Data for Educational Accountability and Improvement*, London and New York: Blackwell Publishing, pp. 99–118.

Putnam, R. and Feldstein, L. M., with Cohen, D. (2004) *Better Together: Restoring the American Community*, New York, London, Toronto and Sydney: Simon and Schuster Paperbacks.

Sachs, J. (2004) *The Activist Teaching Profession*, Buckingham and Philadelphia, PA: Open University Press.

Stiglitz, J. (2003) *The Roaring Nineties Seeds of Destruction*, London: Allen Lane.

Stone, D. (2002) *Policy Paradox. The Art of Political Decision Making*, rev. edn, New York and London: W. W. Norton and Company.

Index